My China Experience

Living, Working, Studying, Teaching and Marrying in China

Alex Rooth

My China Experience: Living, Working, Studying, Teaching and Marrying in China

Copyright © 2017 Alex Rooth

First published as "A Lack of Lingerie: A Graduate in the Garment Industry, China 1992" © 2014 Alex Rooth

Cover photo and design copyright © 2017 Alex Rooth

ISBN: 1502464268
ISBN-13: 978-1502464262

For Min
Mum and Dad and
My children

CONTENTS

Preface

1	Blowing up a cow skin	1
2	Cleaning light fittings	14
3	Famous flower has master	22
4	Work study doesn't work	38
5	The place called Pan Mountain	54
6	Not accustomed to the water and earth	64
7	Dey got more mah lee dan you!	76
8	Try and see	89
9	Of the 36 strategies the best is to run away	97
10	Rating	109
11	Quality number one	128
12	The ghost boy is coming	139
13	Where is that fellow Alfred?	153
14	You speak Chinese no?	165

15	Do you mind sharing?	177
16	New spring sweep the dust	190
17	Wunday, Tooday, Feeday, Forday, Fiday	206
18	Lotus Flower Mountain	219
19	Warp and weft	228
20	Steve told me to sit around and do nothing like	240
21	Treated like a dog	247
22	When the city gate catches fire the fish in the moat suffer	258
23	The gruel is meagre and the monks are many	272
24	Shrinking the dragon to an inch in length	286
25	Roll up the sleeping mat and fry some squid	302
	Afterword	

Preface

I first wrote this book around 20 years ago based on letters written from Panyu County, China, to my family back in England. After completion the manuscript took up residence in my parents' attic, only to move a decade or so later to what I believed to be its final resting place in another roof space, this time that of my own house.

But the world has changed in two decades and in the era of the internet and digital publishing no book need moulder away in anyone's attic. In any case I felt the content was still relevant, in terms of human interest, the story of our employment and the fortunes of our employer, and also as a historical glimpse of life in China during the late eighties and early nineties.

China has changed greatly since then and not just in terms of the obvious major developments in construction, infrastructure, wealth and technology. In 1987 when I first met my Chinese wife-to-be Min in Leeds I was surprised to discover our relationship was being closely observed by two political instructors and details reported back to Min's university in China. A few months ago when narrating these circumstances to a young Chinese woman from Shanghai she said "political instructor, what's that?", an exact echo of my first reaction at the time.

To protect identities I have changed the names of everyone in the book, even Office Head Wang. My comments on the hotels we stayed in are historical and in no way supposed to reflect the current state of those establishments.

Translations from Chinese texts are my own.

Alex Rooth
January 2014

1 Blowing up a cow skin

I was no frequent flyer and felt uneasy as the Boeing 747 banked sharply, the pilot lining up for his descent to Hong Kong Kai Tak International Airport.

We came level with tower blocks and glimpsed choppy green sea, white spray and the decks of fishing boats below. The runway appeared, engines roared and we decelerated to a rapid halt. With a clunk and hiss the doors opened and the methane odour of Victoria Harbour suffused the cabin. Stepping outside we were enveloped by the weighty, humid air of Hong Kong.

A chauffeur in an air-conditioned BMW waited at the airport to take us to the Sheraton Hotel. We felt like VIPs as we floated off on a ring road that detoured away from the busy streets of Kowloon.

Along the side of the bay we saw the dramatic descent of a plane as it approached the runway we had just left. High-rise buildings towered beside the road. Clothes drying on bamboo poles hung limp in the heavy air. Banana trees and palms thrived among the roads and overpasses, despite having leaves bedraggled and dusty from passing traffic. Pale tower blocks stretched into the distance and the flat green fields around Heathrow already seemed a distant memory. Our vehicle slowed and we were back on shopping streets dense with people and fleets of red and white taxis.

The hotel bedroom had a panoramic view of Victoria Bay and the Bank of China Tower, famous at the time for being the tallest building in Asia. Kicking off our shoes we flopped down on the bed and watched a bird of prey wheeling like a kite between the skyscrapers. But we were not here on holiday; we had come to work. I sat up and pulled my crumpled M&S suit from the case.

Months previously my eye had been caught by a notice that appeared in the Chinese department at Leeds University. I was about to graduate from a four year course in Modern Chinese Studies.

"We are a rapidly expanding international garment company seeking ambitious university graduates fluent in Cantonese for a number of positions in our world-wide operations. We offer an excellent compensation package which reflects the calibre of individual sought. No specific degree concentration is required but demonstrated numeracy is an advantage. This position will not suit the parochial, timid or lazy."

I had already been offered an editorial job on a Chinese-English translation publication at the Chinese University of Hong Kong but I thought of my wife Min, who spoke Cantonese as well as Mandarin and Shanghai dialect. Min contacted the company and they promptly invited her for an interview at their London office. After an uneventful journey by coach we found the building in good time and while Min went upstairs for her interview, I sat down with a book and made myself comfortable. I had barely read a page when I heard a noise, looked up and saw Min coming back down the stairs.

"They want to interview you for a job too," she said.

I followed her up and was greeted by a woman who introduced herself as Clara. Slender, in her forties and wearing loose flowing garments in black and charcoal grey, she had a loud throaty voice and a welcoming smile.

"Come in, come in, and take a pew!"

Pink, crimson and other brightly coloured garments lay on every surface, bursting free from clothing racks and trailing from conference table to chair, and back again. A folder of garment patterns balanced precariously on a stack of boxes on the one free seat unadorned with clothing.

Clara made space for us by sweeping aside the garments and draping them over a filing cabinet. She seated herself on the table. Its surface was a light grey that matched her clothes perfectly, as did the chairs and carpet.

"We'll be joined shortly by Rod Highbury, the owner of the company and Chris Twist, CEO. They're both visiting from Hong Kong," she said.

Clara told us that the company made garments in China and other countries in the Far East and sold them in the United States.

"This is a style we're working on at the moment," she said, opening a filing cabinet and placing some design sheets in front of us.

I hadn't given much thought as to what sort of garments the company made. T-shirts and jeans or maybe coats would be good, I thought, as I could consider myself reasonably up-to-speed in those areas.

The design we were looking at, however, could in no way be mistaken for a coat. It was considerably less substantial. Clara rifled through a stack of papers on her desk and passed across a glossy catalogue. A tanned and sleek-limbed woman wearing high heels and little else gazed from the cover with half-closed eyes.

"We make lingerie," said Clara by way of explanation.

"Lingerie?" I thought with sudden unease, a loud parochial "no" forming in the back of my mind. I like lingerie as much as the next man but had seen myself more in the role of appreciative observer rather than industry connoisseur. I imagined meeting new people at parties or other social occasions.

"So what d'you do then?"

"I'm a doctor."

"Me, I'm an engineer."

"I work on the oil rigs."

"I'm a rugby player and he's a builder. What d'you do, mate?"

"Women's underwear."

No, that wouldn't do at all. My musings were interrupted by Clara handing me the catalogue. Had she sensed my misgivings?

"This catalogue belongs to our largest customer. Have a look."

I opened it and saw more beautiful women sitting,

standing, reclining and arching gracefully in their underwear, fixing me with limpid beckoning eyes. On the other hand maybe a career in the garment industry wouldn't be that bad.

Thumbing through the pages, educating myself rapidly and musing as to how an item with less material than that of a handkerchief could qualify as a garment, I was distracted by a cough from Clara. Had I spent too long looking at the catalogue? There was a fine line to tread here. If I wanted the job I must show just the right amount of professional interest. I shouldn't appear too engrossed yet on the other hand didn't want to look bored and put it down too soon. A fine line indeed, I thought, as I continued to peruse the catalogue until I felt Min pulling it from my hands. I looked up.

"Our customer has been in the news lately," said Clara producing a newspaper clipping from a folder and summarizing the story for us. It concerned a woman who had been assaulted while wearing the company's underwear.

"The panties will be used as evidence at trial. They didn't break and it shows how well our products are made," added Clara.

My first thought was that no matter how long I worked in the garment industry I would never be able to utter the word "panties". How could a grown man say a word like that? For me it would have to be "underpants", y-fronts or some other equivalent, such as "the p-word". Then it occurred to me that perhaps the company's marketing department should get a kick in the p-word for the dubious strategy of creating an association between lingerie and sexual assault.

Clara looked at her watch and commented that Rod and Chris must be running a few minutes late. Min asked about the company's operations in China. Clara said they had a factory in a place called Panyu County in Guangdong Province, two hours' ferry ride from Hong Kong.

"It's quite scenic," she continued and in my mind's eye I saw peasants planting rice seedlings in lush and watery paddy fields. Two years previously I was a student in Beijing and I liked the idea of spending some time in a small village, remote and unknown, perhaps untouched by the West.

During my Beijing year I had also spent a lot of time visiting Min in Shanghai. I was first prompted into action by a remark of hers during one of the rather public phone calls I used to make from the reception area of the Beijing Foreign Languages Institute.

In the late eighties Westerners were a rare sight in China and the chance to hear them speak English more unusual still. I was often aware of an audience of surreptitious listeners during these conversations. They perched casually within earshot, testing their levels of English comprehension. (I've done the same with my Chinese studies many a time.) Standing there contemplating this phenomenon, some sixth sense had detected a change of tone at the end of the telephone.

"Shen told me that if I was his girlfriend, and we were in the same country, he would already have visited me," Min had said.

"Really? But it's quite far isn't it, Beijing to Shanghai?" I had replied. "The term hasn't ended yet you know. Min? Hello? Are you still there? Min?"

An earnest Chinese student in thick black glasses raised an eyebrow questioningly, and then averted his gaze. It was alright for the noble Shen, I thought, talking so casually about a journey of a thousand miles across China when he'd only had to potter from one street to another in Leeds to visit his girlfriend.

A day later I had set out for Beijing Railway Station to buy a ticket and book my seat for the 17 hour train journey to Shanghai.

The station was a roiling scrum of people from all over China and it was an epic journey in itself to find the ticket office for "Foreign Guests". On top of that I had food-poisoning from eating soup from a roadside stall the night before. The smell of coriander still makes me nauseous to this day. I threw up on the way there and on the way back but was now the proud owner of one hard seat ticket to Shanghai.

My reverie was interrupted by the sound of loud voices and the door being pushed open.

"Ah. That must be Rod and Chris," said Clara.

Rod was an avuncular figure in his late fifties, ruddy-faced, wide-of-girth and wearing a fancy embroidered waistcoat of floral design, displayed to good effect as he slung his jacket over a chair before putting forward a hand to shake.

He didn't look like a businessman but reminded me of one of my old school teachers, a baggy man who wore tweed and smoked a pipe. You would get a strong whiff of old tobacco as he (the teacher I mean, not Rod) dandled you on his knee in a way perfectly acceptable for the times. The teacher was usually good-natured and bantering but also prone to fits of rage, not that any negative emotion clouded Rod's face on this occasion. He sat back in his chair and smiled expansively as Chris took over, the latter introducing himself as the CEO of the company.

"Look," he said. "We have a presentation we're going to give to a major retailer here in London tomorrow. We have to run through it anyway and it would be helpful if we have some people to listen to it. Also it'll give you an idea of what we do."

The first slide was a caption outlining the company's "mission statement". The term was not widely used in England at the time and I found it amusing, seeming to suggest involvement in a high and lofty calling. In any event the company's mission statement was basically to be better than everyone else at everything in the garment industry. And to do it faster too.

"Speed, speed and more speed," said Rod. "That's what we're all about."

"Of course quality is an important issue as well. Speed and quality, the two things we're all about," added Chris. "We specialize in speed sourcing, a systematic procedure for reducing the time period between the making of an order and delivery to the customer. We can do this because we have our own manufacturing as well as trading capabilities."

The next slide was a cluster of charts illustrating recent profits. Colourful bars climbed upwards like a staircase.

"Haven't you been hit by the recession?" I asked, surprised by how well the company appeared to be doing despite the economic downtown affecting much of the world at that time.

"No. Not at all," said Rod with a quick frown and

shake of his head. "If anything we're doing better than ever before. We're expanding rapidly."

The slides continued with photos of smiling employees in company premises around the world.

"We own all these buildings," said Rod. He gestured round the room. "This office we're sitting in is owned by us. We don't rent property and so have more security and freedom. We have factories in the Philippines, South Korea, China and Taiwan."

Chris moved on to a picture of bales of blue cloth.

"We buy silk in Suzhou in China and then transport it to Korea which has the highest quality fabric dying facilities. From Korea the dyed fabric is shipped to Hong Kong and then on to the Panyu factory in China where the garments are made."

The next slide was of a man cutting a stack of cloth with a band saw.

"You'll see that the operator is wearing steel gloves. In all our factories safety comes first. That's top priority for us. It's what we're all about. We don't run a sweat shop. When we bought the Panyu factory we installed air conditioning. Locally we have an excellent reputation and every day turn away people queuing up outside the gates."

The final slides were of parties and team games with employees wearing yellow and red sweat shirts. The last was a picture of a monkey. "That's Rod the chairman," said Chris. "Ha, ha, ha."

"Did you pull out of China after Tiananmen?" I asked after they had stopped laughing at Chris's joke. Many companies left China during this period and there had been a huge drop of confidence in the country. A senior lecturer in the Chinese department at

Leeds University had been quite despondent on the subject and felt that the country had done itself irreversible damage in terms of business and future foreign investment. With hindsight this did not turn out to be an accurate forecasting of events, but was typical of a mood of pessimism at the time, Rod being the exception.

"No way did we pull out," said Rod firmly. "We're in China to stay. They respect that and because we didn't take away our business they let us buy the Panyu factory. We're the only foreign company in China to completely own a Chinese factory."

"Was the business affected at all?" I asked.

"Absolutely not. It's different down there in the South of China. In Guangdong the Cantonese don't give a bugger about politics. All they care about is making money."

There was a pause and Rod asked what sort of work the two of us expected to find in China.

"I've been offered a job in Hong Kong as an editor," I replied. "My interest is in the Chinese language, particularly Cantonese. I did a year's basic Cantonese-"

"You want to learn Cantonese?" interrupted Rod. "Oh well that's no problem. If you worked for us you'd be in the perfect Cantonese speaking environment. You could work all over the factory where you wouldn't hear a word of English all day long. We'd get you a VCR and you could immerse yourself in Chinese television in the evenings. It would be brilliant! Fantastic! You could start off helping in the canteen. The guys in the factory would love you. A *gwailo* that can speak Chinese. They'd be amazed."

A job as editor of a translation journal began to sound a little dry in comparison. "It might take me a while to become fully proficient in Cantonese," I said. Rod was nodding with satisfaction and did not appear to hear my comment.

"You speak Mandarin don't you?" joined in Chris. "We need someone like you we could train up to represent us in transactions with the Chinese Government."

Even better, I thought, as my future position progressed to corporate negotiator in the space of an instant. What a role that would be! I imagined myself seated at a conference table negotiating hard for the company and clinching that previously elusive deal. Rod turned to Min.

"As for you Min, we need someone with your language skills in our Panyu factory. We've invested a great deal of money in it but we're having communication problems. We could really use you to help liaise between British management and the local Chinese people. We need someone in a senior management position who understands both cultures."

"You're just the sort of people we're looking for," Chris concluded. "We have an ongoing plan to take in between six and twelve high calibre graduates for top management posts. As part of our management training package you would spend a few months in each major department of the company and at the end of the training would assume a full management role. If you come in at the beginning you'll be in a very strong position."

"I really envy you guys," said Rod. "There's so much opportunity out there for people like you who speak the language. It would be amazing! Of course we have excellent fully furnished accommodation for foreign staff based in the area. Are you interested?"

How could we say no? It seemed to be the perfect graduate job with the chance to use our language skills and at the same time join a management training programme that led straight to the top. In addition to that we would have the best of accommodation.

"So when can you start?" asked Rod. "We need you out there right away."

"It might be a couple of months," replied Min. She explained that she needed to obtain permanent residence status from the Home Office before going back abroad. Rod looked concerned and asked Chris if this delay would be manageable. Chris replied that it should be possible to work within this timeframe.

"Okay. No problem then," said Rod, his smile returning.

Min explained that without permanent residence status, also known as ILR or indefinite leave to remain in the UK (equivalent to having a US green card), she would not be able to leave China again.

"No problem," said Rod, looking at his watch. "Let us know if you need any help with the application."

I was mystified as to what clout Rod thought he or his company might have with the Home Office. Was there some sort of clandestine arrangement involving lingerie? As it turned out, obtaining Min's ILR status involved several months of frustrating bureaucratic procedures, but once we had it were ready to travel at a moment's notice.

While we were waiting for the visa we received formal job offers and signed contracts with the company. We were also sent a thick manual with office policies concerning compensation, holidays, travel expenses and the other usual items. The requirement that differed from the average company manual was the stricture that employees do not leave toilet paper on their desks. This was ominous. I recalled some bad toilet experiences while in Beijing and when travelling by train to Shanghai.

A sudden phone call from Clara announced that we were urgently needed in China to attend a training course starting within the next few days. Our jet-setting life in the fast lane of management, manufacturing, language studies and cross-cultural negotiation had begun. And sexy underwear too.

2 Cleaning light fittings

Our first task after arriving in Hong Kong was to report to the company office. Clara had warned us that it was difficult to find and she had given us a piece of paper with the address written in Chinese characters. It also had the Romanized version which sounded like the words "Wank Street". Perhaps when I was more established in the company I could have a quiet word with someone about that.

The address proved problematic for our taxi driver and he looked vacant when we gave him the street name. But he set off with a shrug and after leaving the busy streets behind we were soon driving through a deserted industrial area past gas tanks and fenced-off patches of wasteland. Following one or two U-turns at the bottom of dead end roads he announced that we had arrived. Then he speedily exited.

"Is this really it, d'you think?" I asked Min, looking round at nondescript warehouse entrances where lorries and trucks unloaded goods, and a man with rolled-up trousers shouted noisy instructions at labourers. "It doesn't look like an office."

When lost in a strange place, as does sometimes happen to me, I simply follow my instincts and walk in one direction expecting it to be the right one; if it isn't I turn round and try again. This system works fine unless you're under any form of time pressure, or you're with a wife with better navigational instincts than a homing pigeon but limited tolerance for following behind a man doubling back and forth like a bloodhound.

"This way," said Min indicating the required direction. After a few minutes we spotted the company logo in Chinese characters above a loading bay. We entered a large industrial lift.

Due to limited land and the tendency to build upwards, lifts are a daily phenomenon for people in Hong Kong, particularly in the busy central areas. For office commuters they enforce a static calm and brief opportunity for reflection in an otherwise noisy, hectic world. It was cool and quiet in the lift after the bright sunlight of the streets outside and we stood there waiting, not certain what to expect or even entirely sure we had come to the correct building.

But as the doors opened we were reassured. On the wall opposite was a large photograph of a woman languishing in company lingerie. Was she a future colleague perhaps? I recognized her from Clara's catalogue. I had done my homework in that respect and this time I was able to lead as we followed a trail of lingerie photographs along the corridor and to reception.

The receptionist scanned the list of names and

appointments in front of her but ours were not included. We seemed to have dropped out of the system somewhere between London and Hong Kong.

"We're expected," I said hurriedly. "We've just got in from London. We're the new trainee managers."

"Huh?"

If it weren't for yet another photo of a woman in a black lace babydoll smiling at me over the receptionist's shoulder, I would have been assailed by doubts again. I suggested the receptionist announce our arrival to Bart Ryder, the General Manager. We had been in contact with him while waiting in England.

"Bart is expecting us here this morning," I said.

"He's gone out."

"Oh. When will he be back?"

"Don't know."

In a strange sort of way I could see we had come to the right place. This was a company sorely in need of help with communication. Clara had previously mentioned Joan Wong, the Hong Kong office personnel manager, and I asked if she was in the building. The receptionist leant into a microphone and announced her name across a public address system. We stood waiting but no one appeared and after a while the receptionist called Joan's name again. Once more there was no response. We sat down on a sofa and watched people bustling past.

Eventually I became aware of footsteps and saw a woman approaching. Chinese people generally don't shake hands or perform other greeting rituals such as hugging and kissing. There was no danger of the latter from Joan Wong. She came to a halt at a safe distance and managed somehow to display no expression at all. Describing her manner as reserved would have implied emotion that was not there and the faltering smile on my face seemed wildly over-exuberant. Perhaps we had summoned her from a poker game in the bowels of the building and she was still in role. That would explain the long wait anyway.

As we stood there awkwardly it dawned on me that she didn't know who we were and had no idea what to do with us. I had lately been a student and could not claim to be a veteran of corporate life or the business world, but it did strike me as odd that the personnel manager knew nothing about the arrival of new employees.

"Will you be staying in China long?" she asked.

"We're going to be working there," I replied. "We're the new trainee managers."

Joan turned abruptly. She beckoned minutely with the tip of her index finger and we followed her through a noisy open plan area to her office. She pulled up two chairs and said she had some work to be getting on with. I could see the main office through her window. It was a hive of activity with people working at desks or carrying garments to and fro. By the time her phone rang with the news that Bart had returned to the office, Joan must have been wondering if she would have to put us up for the night.

Bart arrived a minute or two later and shook us by the hand. As he was introducing himself, Rod put his head round the door. He had put on a lot of weight since we had last seen him in England.

"Pleased to have you on board. How are you?" he said.

"Not too bad." I replied, but the long wait in Joan's office had made me sleepy. "Still a bit jet-lagged," I added and saw a frown appear on Rod's ruddy forehead. A buzzer seemed to go off. Eeeeuuh! Wrong answer. Rod withdrew his head from Joan's office saying he was terribly busy and had to go.

Bart took us to a conference room with a large white oval table and padded black office chairs. Transparent items of pink and black lingerie were clipped with pegs to metal frames on the wall.

He offered us a mug of coffee and said he would give us a presentation on the company. The first slide came up with the company's mission statement. It hadn't changed since we'd last seen it but I did learn a new word for underwear which was "intimate apparel". Bart had no problem with the p-word and referred more than once to the company's "panty production potential".

As the slide show was finishing Chris Twist came in and sat down. He had just flown in from Taiwan and like Rod had put on some serious weight since we saw him last. If I had been an older Chinese person on reasonably familiar terms with him I might have said, "*ni pang le*" which literally means "you've got fatter" or "you are pudgier". Chinese people have explained to me that this is a compliment meaning something like "you've put on weight in a healthy chubby appealing way". I doubt Chris would have seen it like that. In any case he did just look fatter. But some old people do seem pleased when they greet each other with mutual cries of "*ni pang le*", presumably because the opposite might suggest some kind of wasting disease.

Young Chinese women should not be greeted in

this way. The use of the word *pang* can result in a cross-cultural misunderstanding that casts a long shadow in a relationship.

"This is what we visualise for you guys," said Bart as he came to the end of his presentation. He looked up enthusiastically. "We envisage the Panyu factory as a training centre for our entire organisation. It's the company university and we've invested millions of dollars in it. We're running a work study course there for the next couple of months that we think it would be helpful for you to take. It's gonna be fantastic."

"Oh great."

This was the last thing I wanted to do. The company had sent us on a work study course at a business college near Nottingham a couple of months previously. I did not cover myself in glory on that occasion, managing to fail the exam at the end of the fortnight. Min flew through with a distinction and I heard Bart commending her for the fantastic mark. He looked at me and politely refrained from making any comment.

We learned enough work study in Nottingham to last a lifetime; well one of us did anyway. In fact the course hadn't been a complete waste of time for me as I now had a good idea of the concepts involved. The basic idea is to time someone performing a repetitive menial task and work out how long you think it should take. You have to break the task down into separate elements and measure them with a stopwatch. So, for example, if the task involves some type of assembly, the first element might involve laying out all the materials on the work surface, the second taking up the first two pieces to be assembled, and the third applying glue. Once you know how long the process takes you should in theory be in a better position to plan your business.

I think I failed the course because my mind began to wander during the video known as "assembling beehive frames" but that was a jolt of neuron-frying stimulation compared to the second video "cleaning light fittings". It featured a man with a rag who had to climb up a ladder and clean the cover of a fluorescent light.

"The work study instructor is called Michael and his course is phenomenal," continued Bart. "We would really like everyone in the company to go on the course because work study is central to what we do. It is absolutely fundamental to our business. I'd really like to go on it myself but I just don't have the time."

Despite Bart's endorsement of Michael's course the prospect of two or three months did not fill me with joy. Bart talked further about the fantastic setup in Panyu. Min asked Bart about the location of the company accommodation that Rod had described in such appealing terms back in London.

"We've booked you guys into the Panyu Hotel for now. The accommodation will be ready in a couple of weeks."

Not quite what we were expecting but a fortnight in a hotel would be no great hardship. The conference room was about to be used for a management meeting Bart wanted us to attend. The main presentation concerned some computer software the company was installing.

"The new system will enable us to transmit more data instantaneously and efficiently. It will also enable us to plan and predict things way in advance."

He said it was going to be very expensive but I thought it money well spent if it helped predict the arrival of new colleagues or employees. At the end Chris leaned over and fixed us with his eye.

"In a few months you might wonder what you've let yourselves in for, but stick with it and I guarantee it'll be worth it."

I was already wondering just that but I had learned from Joan and adopted a poker-faced expression.

3 Famous flower has master

We enjoyed our brief stay in the Sheraton Hong Kong Hotel. The atmosphere was very different from my last visit to Hong Kong two years previously when I and other Leeds students were evacuated from Beijing during the bloody climax to the 1989 Tiananmen Square demonstrations. On that occasion the British government put us up in the Hong Kong Police Training College. Arriving had been a culture shock, from the chaos of Beijing to the bright lights of Kowloon and Scots policemen wearing long olive green shorts.

There was little time to reminisce as next morning we were up at 5.45 a.m. to catch the Star Ferry to Lianhuashan Port in Panyu County. The name Lianhuashan (Lotus Flower Mountain) was promising. It sounded like the location of a Chinese fairy tale or one of the Liao Zhai ghost stories, the sort of place where a man would have an afternoon nap and wake to a romantic encounter with a snake goddess or female fox spirit.

"We're travelling light," I had told Min optimistically before leaving England, but having no idea what to expect in Panyu we kept adding things until we ended up with the maximum weight allowed. At Heathrow one of our larger suitcases burst open in the departure lounge and it was now strapped shut with brightly coloured belts.

Arriving at the Star Ferry taxi disembarkation area we hauled our luggage to a lengthy escalator, ascended slowly to the main terminal above, located the ferry to Lianhuashan on one of the many airport-style departure boards and finally checked in two of the larger cases. We were relieved to be rid of them if only for a couple of hours.

Our ferry was announced shortly afterwards and we joined a crowd of fellow passengers stampeding towards the boat. There was little in the way of "after you, no I insist after you" and I found myself out of practice at this unexpected rough and tumble. In Beijing and Shanghai I had got quite used to hurling myself bodily into the mass of humanity waiting to board approaching buses. But now a scrum of elderly shoppers returning to China rushed to be first on board and I was knocked aside by a group of old ladies wheeling huge rectangular packs of red, blue and white chequered material.

Bringing up the rear we felt fresh sea air in our faces as we descended the ramp to the boat below. The water was choppy and surged below the gang-plank, slapping and splashing between the waiting ferries.

We seemed to be the only people to have checked

in luggage, and bales of goods and other items blocked the passageways. The old ladies had settled down but two middle-aged men were fighting over a seat, shouting insults in Cantonese at each other. Next to us a young man in a suit was reading the instructions for a new pocket computer. He was fully absorbed, undisturbed by the clanging as the doors were locked and the engines roared into action.

We churned away from Hong Kong into the South China Sea and shortly after entered the mouth of the Pearl River. Lianhuashan Port was around 60 nautical miles from Hong Kong and en route I tried unsuccessfully to pick out Humen (literally "Tiger Gate"), also known by the Portuguese name Bocca Tigris. I had read about it during my degree. This was where the Treaty of the Bogue was signed between the British and the Chinese in 1843. It was a supplementary agreement to the Treaty of Nanking which concluded the First Opium War. Though the British referred to the latter as a "Treaty of Perpetual Peace and Friendship", presumably without irony, the Chinese have never viewed it other than as a humiliation.

The combined treaties granted extraterritorial rights and Most Favoured Nation status to Britain, opened up five ports including Shanghai and Guangzhou to foreign merchants for trade and residence, ceded Hong Kong to Britain in perpetuity, imposed a fine on China of 21 million dollars (of which 12 million were war costs indemnity), all so British merchants could ply their trade in opium.

It all happened a long time ago but in my recent visits to China I saw parallels in the way tobacco was being pushed by foreign companies. Cigarettes were so in demand they had almost become a kind of currency; cartons and packs were constantly being passed around or changing hands. I attended a large event in a Shanghai hotel at which smiling women in miniskirts mingled with the crowd handing out handfuls of free cigarettes.

My musings were interrupted by the sound of the boat reducing speed. It swung round slowly with a roaring of engines and reversed into the landing stage, coming to a halt with a bump.

The last to disembark, we followed stragglers into a large arrivals hall and discovered why other passengers had not checked in their luggage; after paying to check it in at the Hong Kong ferry terminal you had to pay to get it back in Panyu. It was an enviable scam for the diminutive but voluble old lady, who blocked me with a determined finger in my navel and demanded payment with an interesting variation on the principle of "speak loudly and clearly".

The queue moved slowly in the arrivals area and there was plenty of time to take in the dreary bare hall with flaps of paint bubbling away from the walls.

We had to fill out forms declaring we were not suffering a variety of conditions ranging from eczema to AIDS. At least it was just a declaration this time. Before studying in China in 1988 all Leeds students had to have an HIV test, though a university spokesperson gave us prior warning that having the test might attach a certain stigma to our persons, and could create issues when looking for work in the future. But it was have the test or don't go to China so there wasn't a huge choice in the matter. I became an old hand at HIV tests as later I had another one when returning to get married in Shanghai.

Through an open window we had our first view of Panyu countryside and a leisurely pace of life unfolded before our eyes. It was late morning and looked very hot outside. Banana trees with wavy corrugated leaves browning at the edges stretched into the distance beyond a dusty road. Peasants chewing sugarcane squatted in the shade and a blue-jacketed figure cycled slowly past leaving a dusty wake.

I couldn't wait to get out there but we were delayed by more administrative procedures and the requirement to fill out forms specifying the electrical devices we were carrying. It was a feeble attempt to combat smuggling in the area where large scale operations included towing huge items into China underwater. The customs official insisted I produce my Walkman from the bottom of the strapped-up case.

The queue moved forward slowly. Min was anxious to confirm that there wouldn't be any problems with her leaving China again and asked an official about the procedure. The woman took her passport and flicked through it.

"Where's your green card?" she asked.

Min explained that permanent residents in the UK are not issued with a green card. She pointed to the Home Office stamp in her passport indicating indefinite leave to remain (ILR). The woman shook her head doubtfully so Min explained again in more detail that green cards are part of the US system and have nothing to do with permanent residence in England. Chinese law is clear on the subject and states that a person with permanent residence in another country may leave China without restriction.

"But where's your green card?" the official asked again. "You can't leave without a green card."

The crowd of travellers from the ferry thinned to a trickle with the final few collecting their cases from the X-ray machines and disappearing out of sight. The hall was suddenly empty apart from Min and me, and two more border officials came over to see what was happening. When it comes to border officials it is not a case of the more the merrier and as their numbers increased the more entrenched they became in the idea that Min could only leave China again if she had a green card. I began to regret coming back.

"Have a look," said Min pointing at the ILR stamp in her passport. It was in English and I thought they probably couldn't read it as they just repeated the phrase, "*bu xing, bu xing*" ("no good, no good").

Often accompanied by a frown and an index finger rotated to and fro at arm's length like a little windscreen wiper, it was a phrase I had often encountered in Beijing, a favourite of the official or bureaucrat. The unspoken meaning of *bu xing* is "whatever you want and I don't care what it is, you can't have it. You don't need to know why you can't and I'm not going to tell you why you can't, but I rather like saying you can't, so I'm going to keep saying it, *bu xing*. And while you're at it, go away too".

Customs consisted of an X-ray machine watched by a sleepy young man in a green jacket. I was struggling to pick up our other hippo of a case when I heard an angry shout, the tone of voice reserved for some low unfortunate caught urinating in a public place. I looked round but there was no one there. The customs officer was looking less sleepily at someone directly behind me. I turned round again. He pointed an angry finger at me and stabbed it emphatically in the air. Was the horrid man talking to me? Surely not.

"Baaaaaaai!" he shouted in Chinese, having pegged me for an old China hand.

"Uh?" I replied.

"Baaaaaaaiii!" he shouted, more loudly this time, climbing to his feet. This was worrying. I had spent the last four years learning Chinese but he might as well have been speaking Glaswegian for all I could understand him. I pointed at my nose in the Chinese "who me?" gesture (perfected from years of watching Jackie Chan films) and he waved his arms angrily, indicating the case.

That monstrous piece of luggage would nowadays be banned on the grounds of health and safety, a hernia-inducing risk to anyone in its vicinity. Initial attempts at scientific packing had given way to first standing on it while Min attempted zipping it up, then jumping up and down and wrestling it closed. The case, bulging fit to burst like its unfortunate sibling back in Heathrow, was designed to be opened once only during the course of the journey, that being at its final destination.

But the official was now alarmingly alert, unsympathetic and then unamused as the case opened like an exploding air bag, sending trousers, T-shirts and underpants onto the table, followed by a large Dr Martens boot rolling onto the floor.

He plunged his hands into our clothes up to his elbows and ploughed his way round the inside of the case. Then uttering the Chinese equivalent of "hah!" he pulled out a VHS video tape and held it high.

"Confiscated," he said and tossed the tape to one side. I had read about Chinese "sweep up the yellow" or anti-pornography campaigns and assumed this was the motivation for the official's search. For some reason pornography is considered "yellow" in China rather than "blue" as people say in England. Such campaigns are also a handy justification for keeping a watch on any unauthorized printed or audio-visual material coming into China.

I thought it ironic that in my twenty something years of life the only pornographic film I had ever seen was as a student two years before while studying Mandarin in Beijing, though admittedly it wasn't a Chinese production. At that time the foreign students dormitory (architecturally a sort of red brick barracks) at the Beijing Foreign Languages Institute, later renamed the Beijing Foreign Studies University, was home to an interesting mix of students from all over the world. As well as 25 individuals from Leeds University there were Germans, French, Poles, Russians, Americans, Japanese and North Koreans, all living in close proximity in rooms situated on two long, dark corridors, one on the ground floor and the other on the first.

The rooms were basic but reasonably clean with a radiator below the window. The heating was a significant luxury during cold winters that few local students in China would have had at the time. One of my neighbours was French and the other was North Korean. I saw little of the French neighbour but spoke to the North Korean occasionally. He was friendly and lent me a Chinese textbook on socialism and the Four Modernizations but his conversation often tended towards politics and his favourite topic, Problems With the West. The Korean students had a large portrait of Kim Il Sung above their beds and wore a small badge with his face in miniature. Needless to say no Leeds students had a picture of Margaret Thatcher on the wall.

The one nationality conspicuously absent from our dormitory was the Chinese and this was a problem if you had come to China to learn Mandarin. The campus grounds were split down the middle by a multi-lane ring road and it was beyond this that the Chinese students lived and studied. The general idea seemed to be to keep foreign and Chinese students separate and it worked pretty well. As there were no social events, no sports clubs (no clubs of any kind for that matter), no common rooms, no restaurants or any other areas to socialize in across the road, the best we could do, and I tried it a few times, was to wander around the other campus hoping to meet Chinese people with whom I could speak Mandarin.

Help arrived in the form of a loose band of individuals who referred to themselves as *getihu*, a term meaning a small business operator or private entrepreneur.

Behind our dormitory and a short walk along a winding semi-ornamental path was an unlikely building which, like an oasis in a desert, contained a small bar. The beer cost the equivalent of 10p for a very large bottle and I and a number of others spent many a happy evening there. No Chinese students frequented the bar, the patrons mainly being a handful of Leeds students and one or two Russians, but it was a favourite meeting place for the *getihu*.

The exact business of the *getihu* was unclear but part of it seemed to involve the resale of garments and to be a very successful operation judging from the carrier bags of cash they sometimes had with them. The brick-like wads stacked casually on the table in front of us were more than the average person in China would earn in many lifetimes. Whether their business was legitimate I never knew but after a while one of their number disappeared and in response to my enquiry as to his whereabouts the others said he was in prison. This may have been a joke to test my credulity but I never saw him again.

Anaesthetized with vast quantities of beer they were happy to put up with my Mandarin, halting at the beginning of the evening yet fluent by the end. But it was like a spell that could only work its magic on my Chinese when in the vicinity of the bar; by classes the next morning I was back to my old standard.

Though many of the topics covered in that oasis of drink were already hazy by the time my head hit the pillow, years later I still remember discussing subjects as diverse as the handing back of Hong Kong to the Chinese, the difference between northern and southern styles of kung fu and who among their female acquaintances would be a suitable girlfriend for me.

The last matter required delicate handling as unknown to the *getihu*, "famous flower has master" or mistress in my case, i.e. Min, and I must regretfully decline meeting Beijing women in any context other than as "Little Sister", "Big Sister" or maybe "Aunt" if she was a lot older.

"Already got one, Chinese woman," I replied in my basic Mandarin when the topic of finding me a girlfriend was brought up again. As I had only been in Beijing for a short period (and spent much of it in the bar with them) this was greeted with claps on the back and howls of disbelieving laughter but general approval of my attitude.

It was over an afternoon drink some time later that the subject of kung fu came up again and one of the *getihu*, Xiao Wang, said he had a new Jackie Chan film that I might like to watch.

I, a friend from Leeds and some of the others followed him back to his flat and he took us through a small kitchen into a back room with a television, VCR and double bed. The bed was covered with a pile of blankets and Xiao Wang indicated that we should sit at its foot.

The film involved lots of guns and explosions and some kung fu but it wasn't Jackie Chan. After I pointed this out, Xiao Wang rummaged through a stack of videos and put on another film, this one involving no more war and not exactly love either, though amorous relations were the main theme.

The protagonists were all Westerners (the men with 1970s beards) speaking a European tongue reminiscent of the eccentric homicidal cook on the Muppets. I couldn't understand what they were saying but it didn't seem terribly important to the plot; in any case the language of the action was universal. It took place in a stable generously fitted out with bales of hay and straw on the ground but empty of four-footed occupants and anything they might have left behind.

Thankfully the film did not venture into territory boldly explored in the Chinese classic short story "The Adulterous Dog" by Pu Songling, author of "Strange Tales from a Chinese Studio" published early in the Qing Dynasty (1644-1912). Many of Mr Pu's tales fully deserve the title "strange" with the most mainstream among them exploring intimate relations between men and female fox spirits. Nor did the characters in the film demonstrate the variety of practices undertaken by protagonist Ximen Qing in the earlier Ming Dynasty (1368-1644) explicit novel "The Golden Lotus"; which was why I found it odd that pornography seemed to be viewed so much as a thing of the West and having little to do with China or Chinese people. Perhaps this vanguard of European filmmakers had something to do with it.

I asked Xiao Wang why we had moved from kung fu to porn and he replied that this is what he thought foreigners liked to watch. It reminded me of another stereotype that we Westerners walked around with pockets stuffed full of marijuana (though to be fair some students did just that having found what they believed to be wild cannabis growing by the roadside near the Summer Palace outside Beijing).

I don't know if the action in Xiao Wang's film ever moved beyond the immaculate stable because a few minutes after it started the blankets behind me were suddenly thrown off and a young woman sat up in bed and began shouting abuse at our host.

What we had taken for an old pile of blankets was Xiao Wang's concealed wife. He had never mentioned a spouse and realizing we were in her bedroom and on her bed while she had been trying to take an afternoon nap, we hastily apologized and exited the flat, almost bumping into a neat and tidy old lady in a blue smock (Xiao Wang's mother?) chopping up vegetables in the kitchen.

The Panyu customs officer looked pleased with himself for confiscating the video but if he was looking for porn he would be in for a disappointment. The film was the science fiction adventure "Back to the Future", deliberately chosen by Min and me as apolitical, asexual and unlikely to cause offence.

Finally we were out of the building and standing in a vast empty car-park. It was brilliantly white after the gloom of the customs hall. Waves of dusty heat radiated from the ground and a circular stone fountain in the middle stood still and dry.

From the outside the customs building looked impressive. It was grand in scale with a series of flat roofs decorated with sparkling orange tiles. Above a row of brightly coloured flags large red characters said *Lian Hua Shan Gang* (Lotus Flower Mountain Port). The heat was staggering for December.

"Do you work for us?" a friendly voice asked in English. Looking round we saw a large chubby man. He had come across the car park from a minibus with the word "lingerie" on the front in large letters. Introducing himself as Johnson, he turned and we followed him across the parking area to the vehicle.

The bus pulled slowly away from the car-park and bumped along an empty road with small grey flat-roofed buildings and lean-to stalls on either side.

Clara had said Panyu was quite scenic but after the stretch of banana trees visible from the window of the arrivals hall the environment changed rapidly. The earth, if you could call it that, was dusty and drought-ridden, the paddy fields pale grey with dead stalks sticking into the air. We drove past rocks being quarried and smashed. They popped and cracked as they were fed through makeshift stone crushing machinery. Small hills were being dismantled piece-by-piece and levelled to the ground by bulldozers and excavators. Raw gravel pits and slag heaps gaped like wounds in the land. Beside the road were the remains of cars, trucks and the hulks of great lorries. They were all rusting, iron oxide reds and oranges stark against the grey-white dust.

The destruction of the countryside added to the gloom I was feeling at being told Min would not be able to leave China again, and for the rest of the journey my imagination worked on increasingly desperate and unlikely scenarios of escape. Freedom of travel took on a meaning I had been unaware of before.

After about forty minutes we reached a more populated area and drove past shops, buildings and roadside stalls. A sliding metal gate that opened like a concertina was pulled aside by a security guard and we drove up a ramp into a courtyard. Johnson said he would announce our arrival at the factory office. Disembarking with the others we hastily retreated out of the dazzling rays of the noon-day sun to the cool shadow of the minibus and looked at our new surroundings.

Several storeys high, in pink, white and green, the main building did not resemble my idea of what a factory should look like at all. I had expected something gloomy and industrial but this was light and spotlessly clean, like a school or hospital.

We saw Johnson climbing an external spiral stairway that wound around a single pillar and on each floor opened onto long walkways running the length of the building. These were ornamented with built-in overhanging baskets decorated with green and white tiles. Hedges of greenery grew from them and trailed towards the ground. A mosaic flooring of shiny stone in the courtyard stretched beyond the factory gate to the edge of the dusty road. Our driver had parked the minibus next to a gleaming red Volvo. It was still dripping after a recent cleaning by a man in Wellington boots. He stood with a hose in one hand and a cigarette in the other.

"Caw, caw, whoop, whoop, whoop," came a noise from somewhere close by. It sounded like a screeching parrot followed by a pack of howler monkeys. Maybe I was suffering from the midday heat.

Johnson came back down the spiral staircase followed by a thin, nervous man with a moustache. The new arrival had an awkward shifty manner that immediately brought to mind the stereotypical bad guy in old nationalistic Chinese movies. Such characters were usually denounced at the end as "running dog" or worse.

"This is Lenny Long the factory manager," said Johnson.

Lenny did not look pleased to see us. In fact he looked as if our arrival had just made a bad day worse. Avoiding eye contact, one hand drumming nervously on his leg near his groin he asked, "so will you be staying here long?"

He was as surprised by my answer, that we had

arrived to take up positions as trainee managers in his factory, as I was by his question. I had the feeling he was thinking in terms of a couple of days' stay at the very most. Lenny's eyes widened and his hand twitched noticeably at the mention of the term work study.

"Where will you be staying?" asked Lenny.

"We were told the Panyu Hotel."

"Has a room been booked?"

Nonplussed, Lenny stood looking at us for a moment. He laughed suddenly, muttered in Cantonese and suggested we unload our suitcases and leave them temporarily in the factory.

He led the way across the courtyard and through some glass doors into a large open area clattering with the buzz and hum of countless sewing machines. Young women were operating the machines and those nearby stopped what they were doing to watch us. Many of them were in their late teens or early twenties.

Pointing to some racks of shirt-like garments, Lenny raised his voice and said we could leave our cases behind them. It was hot on the factory floor and as I hauled our cases out of the bus and placed them behind the racks I felt a film of sweat starting to my forehead. I was relieved to finally be rid of our luggage and resolved that next time we really would travel light.

Lenny disappeared but came back a few minutes later and said, "I think, maybe, we go to the hotel first. Shall we put the cases back in the bus?"

4 Work study doesn't work

After the dusty streets around the factory and the port at Lianhuashan, the Panyu Hotel was an oasis of greenery. We swept into its forecourt under a traditional Chinese archway decorated with bright orange roof tiles. Three palm trees with trunks like smooth plastic stood in the middle of an immaculate lawn watered by sprinklers. Black and white autographed footballs were exhibited in a glass cabinet in the reception area. A notice nearby said that a stadium in Panyu had been used for the first FIFA Women's World Cup football championships held that same year in 1991.

At reception Lenny announced us as company employees and said that the factory would be paying for the room. In marked contrast to the officers at Lianhuashan Port the staff at the Panyu Hotel were cheerful and welcoming. One of them looked embarrassed at having to request our marriage certificate in addition to our passports.

China has numerous laws, regulations and legal interpretations, all of which are readily available for perusal. It also has many unpublished rules intended for internal consumption only. There is little recourse against an official, government employee or even hotel owner who prohibits you from doing something due to the invisible barrier of the "internal regulation". Foreign students would often encounter this grey area of law while travelling and trying to stay in guest houses or hostels. Seemingly arbitrarily they would be refused admittance and often redirected to the biggest (and most expensive) hotel in town.

Luckily Min was aware of the rule stating that a couple intending to share a room in a Chinese hotel must produce a valid marriage certificate. It was good planning on her part as we had not expected to stay in a hotel at all during our time in Panyu, believing we would move straight into company accommodation.

Whether forcing guests to produce a marriage certificate would have any effect in restricting prostitution, solicitation or "lascivious and lewd behaviour" I did not know, but on this occasion it served as a good ice-breaker with the staff at the Panyu Hotel. They crowded round to have a look at the certificate. It was an impressive looking document in red and gold, with black and white photographs of Min and me on the inside.

We had been married in Shanghai while still students. I had a month's holiday to come out to Shanghai to complete the formalities after which I was to return to Leeds to finish my degree. Prior to this I had to obtain a "single status certificate" and numerous other documents.

The single status certificate was known by various names including "certificate of non-impediment", "marital status certificate", and "certificate of marriageability". But not one of these names was familiar to the first lawyer I saw who offered the opinion that there was no such document in English law.

After informing the lawyer, with all due and sincere respect regarding said learned opinion, that the client would still like to get married if at all possible, he drafted a one line affidavit, only to have it rejected by counsel Min as not looking official enough. Somehow it was required to pad out the phrase "I promise I'm not married already" and turn it into a thick document covered with stamps, seals and official-looking writing.

A second lawyer had a good attempt at this and I succeeded in having it verified and notified by the Chinese and British authorities. In pre-internet days (and pre-telephone days for most houses in China) this was a long process.

The other requirement, carried out in a local hospital shortly after my arrival in Shanghai, was to undergo a pre-marital medical examination, compulsory at the time for anyone getting married in China (I read later that this requirement was rescinded as an infringement on the right to privacy of the individual). Min, usually a detail-oriented person, had been vague about this part of the marriage proceedings.

The examination took place in a large but poorly lit room with a strong chemical smell of disinfectant. The door stood wide open and as I waited I watched the bustle and commotion of a busy hospital corridor.

Chinese hospitals are easy to spot as the roads in the immediate vicinity often have streams of people wandering about in their pyjamas. On this occasion, however, the majority had congregated outside the examination room and there they were chatting, stretching and generally passing the time of day.

A small middle aged woman wearing a white lab coat approached me, frowning sternly as she squeezed her hands into a pair of rubber gloves. Without so much as a "*ni hao ma?*" or "how d'you do?" she commanded:

"Drop trouser floor!"

We were well off the pages of the "Practical Chinese Reader" textbook now. I'd had some odd greetings in China but this took the biscuit. A group of people looked in our direction from the corridor, curiosity aroused by the sudden sound of English, and shuffled forward as one. An old man in his pyjamas came to the threshold of the room. He made eye contact with me and half raised his hand in greeting. I knew that look; it was of someone keen to practice English.

I looked back at the doctor who was frowning at me crossly. Had I done something wrong or been uncooperative in some way? I thought I had done as commanded.

"Drop udderpan!"

"What the..?"

Did she really expect me to stand there, an attentive group of pyjama-clad onlookers surveying me amiably, as if standing around a bar for evening drinks, but me with my trousers and underpants round my ankles? The door was still wide open, a permanent state of

41

affairs judging from the dusty items stacked around it.

"Drop udderpan floor."

Someone else came into the room apparently looking for a stethoscope. There was nothing for it. I remembered a school medical; a little embarrassing but a quick cough and it was over, all present and correct. Turning to expose my rear to the well-wishers outside I waited for the command to cough but it never came. More than a quarter of a century later and I remember it as if it were yesterday, the smell of disinfectant, the gaping door, the audience, the long and thorough examination as if I were the Emperor of China himself, or parts of me were anyway. In short no stone was unturned and long were the shadows by the time I was able to move on to the next hurdle, the hospital X-ray machine.

Normally I never have an X-ray if I can help it and this machine did not inspire confidence. It had a rough and ready look as if it had been stolen from the airport and I should be putting my suitcases through it, not my flesh and bone self. Medical staff scrambled for safety and told me not to move. I tried not to think of the dose I was getting as I held my breath, imagining my lungs disintegrating on the TV screen they were watching.

Min had already been pronounced "normal" and it was just a question of waiting for me to get the same result, though my time in Shanghai was running out. When the result finally came I was suddenly nervous and wondered about the consequences of failing the medical. Would we really be prevented from marrying? But it didn't come to that and soon after we were able to go to one of the special registry offices in Shanghai for Chinese individuals marrying foreigners. No one had told us that the fees had to be paid in Foreign Exchange Certificates (FEC) instead of RMB and the first time we tried to get married we were turned away. It was one of my last few days in Shanghai and we had a desperate final run to a nearby bank and back for FEC before the registry office closed.

Shortly after, I was back in England, married but without Min. She remained in China for more than eight months due to British bureaucratic procedures.

"We go eat," said Lenny, interrupting my reminiscence. He led us away from the Panyu Hotel reception, past a goldfish pond, across an expanse of green water and into a large empty restaurant.

The ambience was quite different from that of the establishment where we had our last meal in England a couple of days previously. That had been the Langham Hilton, a grand 5-star hotel in the West End of London. It had been our last stop before going on to Heathrow and flying to Hong Kong. Built in 1865 it was apparently the favourite choice of well-known playwrights and authors, politicians, prominent members of the royal family much pursued by the media, and also trainee managers in the garment industry.

The Langham Hilton was proud of its Victorian origins and boasted a restaurant called "Memories of the Empire". According to a booklet lying open on the bedroom table, the restaurant aimed to provide a service reminiscent of a "bygone era" by serving exotic dishes from remote corners of former British territories.

This was a new kind of retro. I couldn't see the

concept catching on in Beijing or anywhere else in China for that matter where Britain's imperial past is not viewed with a rosy glow of nostalgia, afternoon tea or not. What could possibly be on the menu in such a place? Opium Den Dumplings? Colonial Crackers? Gunboat Garoupa? And for dessert perhaps a Slice of China Cake? I recalled the late 19th century French cartoon showing China as a cake before which sits a knife-wielding Queen Victoria and other European leaders. It was often used as an illustration in history textbooks to show the carving up of China by imperial powers.

It had been late by the time we were ready to experience Memories of the Empire and the opulent room was already crowded, mainly with foreign tourists and business people. The restaurant had a pale ceiling with delicately painted swallows swooping and diving against a leafy background. Several tables away a harpist in a flowing diaphanous dress plucked at popular classics.

The waiter, a nimble man despite considerable bulk, danced across the floor with two large wicker baskets that he placed in front of us with a flourish. He seemed to have jumped from the pages of a comic book, a caricature with his comfortable paunch, hook nose and slicked-back hair.

"Compliments of ze chef," he said.

Ignoring the atrocious fake French accent I opened the wicker basket and saw that it contained a small dish with a smaller square of salad on it. Next to the salad was a coiled object that looked like a compliment from one of the swallows on the ceiling.

"Ze spinach and salmon sir."

I had no wish to be a party pooper (I'd leave that to the swallows) but clearly the chef had not been expecting any vegetarian guests. The waiter's genial manner faltered at my reference to vegetarianism as if I had come in off-cue but he gathered himself, sprang forward and removed the wicker basket to return in a few minutes with a vegetarian version. As if I had metamorphosed into a guinea pig in his absence I was presented with a piece of lettuce artfully cut into four tiny rectangular strips.

This was vegetarian cooking made easy; simply remove the meat dish and re-serve. My chosen line of work was the garment industry (lingerie specialist) but previously I had also forayed into the world of catering with various pot washing jobs. With virtually no effort I could upgrade myself to becoming a gourmet vegetarian chef. I could feed a whole room full of people with a lettuce and a pair of scissors.

By the next morning the rest of the meal was fast becoming a memory itself and we prepared to check out of the hotel. The company had done us proud with the Langham Hilton but it wasn't the type of place you tried to pay with a photocopy of someone else's credit card, no matter that Clara had assured us there would be no problem with this novel mode of payment. The member of staff didn't so much start as become extraordinarily still as I handed over a piece of A4 paper with a credit card photocopy in the middle of it and some scribbled writing of Clara's to the effect that it was all okay, just run it through the system my good man.

"Could you bear with me one moment, sir," he said after a long pause and disappeared, leaving us standing looking at each other. Were we being checked against a database of young con artists? Did Scotland Yard have a search warrant out for the alluring and mysterious Miss Min from Shanghai? Apparently not because several phone calls and a relatively short wait later we were out of the hotel and heading towards Heathrow.

The restaurant in the Panyu Hotel was a lot more informal than the Langham Hilton. The waitress stood relaxed as she took Lenny's order, occasionally inspecting her nails or loudly greeting colleagues. She was wearing a crumpled lilac suit and every now and then ran her hand through a wavy perm.

Another waitress brought across a plate of nuts and some crunchy pickled onions known locally as *kiutao*. Quite a challenge to pick up with chopsticks but I was able to demonstrate the easy facility of the old China hand, having learned previously that if peanuts or *kiutao* are catapulting off across the table or onto your neighbour's lap, all you have to do is ease up on the pressure. While I brushed up on my chopsticks kung fu I tried to pick out some of Lenny's Cantonese and speculated as to what he was talking about to the driver. It was an animated discussion in low voices that went on for some time and I could only make out a few words between the occasional belch. I presumed it to be something about work.

During one of the few pauses in their conversation, Min asked Lenny about the use of work study in the factory.

"Work study doesn't work," he blurted with a strained laugh. I looked at him in surprise and like a foolish chopsticks newbie dropped a peanut back into the communal bowl. Bad form and a violation of the basic chopsticks etiquette that you take what you have touched. I located and extracted my peanut as Min attempted further clarification from Lenny, but he just shook his head and laughed awkwardly.

Bart the general manager had said work study was key to the company's business yet here was the factory manager dismissing it with a shake of his head. There must be an interesting dynamic between Lenny and the work study instructor.

On the way back to the factory I asked Min what Lenny and the driver had been talking about. "Food and horse racing," she replied.

A solitary figure was standing immobile in the centre of the factory courtyard. There was something listless about his posture, as if he had been waiting there for a long time; yet he stepped out of the way smartly as the bus rolled up the ramp towards him.

"Now where have you all been?" he asked Lenny as we descended. "I have been waiting all this time." The man had a pleasant mild face, a Pinocchio nose, black curly hair and a slow careful way of talking, managing to sound aggrieved, sad and accusatory all at once. He smiled at us unhappily. Lenny mumbled a reply about the Panyu Hotel and introduced the man as Michael, the work study instructor. He would be in charge of us from now on.

"Oh no!" said Michael to the fast retreating Lenny. "I already am booking them in the Hotel Miramar." He added with a sigh, "Now I am having to ring and cancel."

"Caw! Caw! Whoop! Whoop! Whoop!"

The unmistakeable sound of a parrot and monkeys carried across the air. Michael did not react to the noise and told us to wait while he made his telephone call. We stood in the heat on the staircase and exchanged glances.

After a few minutes he reappeared looking more relaxed and led us with a calm and deliberate tread, arms hanging limply down by his sides, round the corner of the factory. The speed or rather lack of speed of Michael's locomotion was that of someone who had grown up in a very hot place.

Hearing beast-like noises again I looked round and this time saw a cage full of monkeys. Several large animals were leaping wildly from the sides to ceiling and back, gibbering and screaming and making agitated faces. One smaller but more demonstrative than the rest urinated in our direction through the bars of the cage. I had a sudden flashback to Chris's presentation in London with his joke about a monkey being the chairman of the company. Next to them was another cage with large parrots screaming and cawing. Above the noise I said to Michael that I hadn't expected to find zoo animals in a factory.

"Oh yes. Once we are having a factory dog," he replied.

I could understand how the factory might acquire a dog as I had seen numerous strays sniffing alertly around the streets, but a cage full of monkeys was surely a different matter. Michael offered no further comment and leaving the cage and the noise behind we followed a path that skirted a small garden. A green lawn, interspersed with clusters of bamboo and miniature palm trees, extended to the base of the factory wall.

"This is the factory garden," said Michael pointing

at a pond with a cement bridge, a pavilion of traditional design (decorated with yellow-orange roof tiles) and an ornamental boat. Intermittent beeping and shouts in Cantonese came across the wall from the main street beyond.

Michael unlocked a door and took us into a large building. A narrow staircase led up to a second floor. "Probably just one person at a time is best," he said, looking back over his shoulder as he ascended. It seemed good advice as the flimsy staircase had a lot more ladder than stair in its makeup and appeared to have been knocked together the day before, giving the impression it was a temporary stand-in for the real thing.

At the top we found ourselves in a classroom with whitewashed walls, thin curtains covering cracked windows and a blackboard at one end. A strong sickly-sweet chemical smell hung in the air. Michael gestured at two desks and sat back in a large broken office chair. It was so battered it appeared to have been hauled from a skip.

A faint crunching came from beneath my feet and looking down I saw that the floor was covered with a layer of dead mosquitos. "We are having to spray against them," said Michael, following my gaze. Whatever he was spraying was doing the job alright. The dead covered the floor like a carpet, two or three bodies thick in places, as if a mighty war of miniature flying machines had been waged in the room among the desk and chair legs. The casualties still gave off an air of menace with their angular splayed legs and deadly spike in front.

"Well this is the company university," said Michael,

looking round the room. "I am your work study instructor. We will be starting the course as soon as more colleagues arrive from Sri Lanka. They will be here soon. For now you should become familiar with how garments are made. Come with me."

We had only just sat down but Michael was already rising. He pulled open a desk drawer, removed two aerosol cans and sprayed under the tables and chairs in a crouching retreat while we descended the stairs one person at a time, followed by waves of the sweet smell I had noticed when we entered.

Back at the main courtyard Michael led us up the external staircase and as we climbed we looked through windows to see more lines of sewing machines, the noise and bustle temporarily silenced by glass. We paused at the third floor as Michael caught his breath. Beyond the green lawn of the factory garden and its abrupt termination in a red brick perimeter wall we saw a dense jumble of grey factory-like structures several storeys high, below which people wandered among stalls and shop-fronts. The buildings were pale and colourless, the ultimate in utilitarian construction.

Along the main road approaching the factory, slow-motion cyclists made lazy detours round a pile of bricks that had fallen from a building site into their path. Labourers in bamboo hard hats were setting in place the concrete foundations of a new construction five times the size of its nearest neighbour. The muted sound of thrumming machinery and shouts in Cantonese floated upwards.

One or two cyclists and pedestrians followed the road onwards as it narrowed and continued past the factory. It wound past large pools of still water on one side, and more grey buildings, these small and blocky with balconies and flat roofs, on the other. Our view into the distance was finally obscured by haze and the occasional small hill rising like an abrupt bump in a landscape otherwise flat as a table top.

There was a cough and I turned to see Michael holding a door open, waiting for us patiently.

"Now this is the cutting room," he announced, entering a large open space with great rolls of brightly coloured material at one end and a stack of cardboard boxes at the other. A man was face down on a long table, dead to the world but presumably otherwise alive and enjoying an afternoon siesta. Nearby a small but voluble group of women were chatting among themselves, occasionally pausing to make measurements on a roll of cloth.

"The fabric is being stored in this room and is then cut according to requirements," said Michael. "It is the job of the line supervisors from each floor to collect the cut fabric so it can then be sewn together by the operators. Follow me."

Pushing through the glass doors we were enveloped once more by the clatter of sewing machines, the noise loud but with a lively broken rhythm and hum. The activity was a welcome contrast to the torpor of the cutting room and the early afternoon heat outside. Machine operators, almost all young women in t-shirts and jeans, were working on a rich purple garment and partially assembled pieces streamed between them. A purple haze floated in the air and coloured the shadows at the bottom of the whitewashed walls, tinting the bare arms of the operators a violet blue.

Many of them turned to look with curiosity at us, some stopping work completely.

"Assembly of the garment is starting here," said Michael, pointing to the machines near the door by which we had entered. "It will be completed at the far end. You should look closely and find out how is it made."

He bent forward and picked up two pieces of fabric that an operator was sewing together. Her eyes flicked towards him but she continued working, selecting two pieces of material from a bundle on her lap, sewing them together and then letting them trail into a basket in front of her sewing machine for the next person in front.

"This is called the facing," said Michael, pointing at one of the pieces. "And this is the front panel. She is sewing the facing to the front panel using overlock stitch."

Some specialist Cantonese vocabulary was going to be required in this job; and English too for that matter, as I had no idea what was meant by "facing" or "overlock" in either language.

We followed the line of sewing machines and saw the garment taking shape as we approached the end of the shop floor. When it was finished it was inspected by several older women against white boards, and then finally hung from racks and placed ready for packing. The whole process was like a conveyor belt with each operator endlessly repeating the same task, the pieces finally coming together to form the finished product. It didn't look like lingerie to me though, more like a shapeless baggy shirt, and I was pretty sure I hadn't seen it in Clara's catalogue.

"Okay. You can continue familiarising yourselves with the process. Now I have some work to do."

Our arrival had apparently taken a few people in the company by surprise, namely Bart Ryder general manager, Joan Wong personnel manager and Lenny Long factory manager, but at least Michael had been expecting us and we spent the rest of our first day in Panyu carrying out his assigned task, looking round the factory and trying to get a basic understanding of how garments were made.

As well as the cutting room, several shop floors with many lines of sewing machines between them, classroom area (or "university"), garden and monkey cages, there were also two modern offices with rows of desks, whiteboards on the walls and a computer in the corner for electronic mail.

The second floor office was to be our new home. We spent what little remained of the day chatting to our colleagues till it was time to assemble in the courtyard below for the company bus ride back to the Panyu Hotel.

5 The place called Pan Mountain

Shortly after our arrival we asked at the hotel reception for some information about the area. They gave us a tourist map and local investment guide. According to a brief introduction to the map, the county was named after two legendary mountains, one called "Pan" and the other "Yu". The origins of this story were lost in the mists of time but the map was specific as to the establishment of Panyu as a city in 214 B.C. during the Qin Dynasty (221-207 B.C.).

Shiqiao, location of the hotel, was also the seat of the county government and the administrative capital of Panyu. It was classified as a *zhen* or small town. There were another 20 or so of these in the county as well as over 300 villages, between them supporting a population of 768,000 over a total land area of around 1,314 square kilometres.

The map showed Panyu's borders naturally defined by the Pearl River with tributaries crisscrossing the county like arteries and veins. All this water together with fertile soil and a balmy average annual temperature of 22 °C provided ideal conditions for crops such as rice, sugarcane, peanuts and bananas. Historically Panyu had been known as a "land of rice and fish" due to its rich productive countryside. According to the investment guide, land in Panyu County comprised 59.5% alluvial plain, 5.4% hilly mesa and also vast tracts of reclaimed marshland.

Though the wider Panyu area was largely rural, it was not the sleepy place I had imagined. Instead it was a thriving area in rapid transition, developing fast and taking advantage of China's economic reforms introduced in the 1980s.

The investment guide, written entirely in long-form Chinese characters, presumably to attract overseas Chinese investors, referred to tax breaks and other incentives and preferential policies for foreign companies investing in the area. The garment business was just one aspect of diverse local industry that included paper making, food products, building materials, footwear, toys, ship building, agricultural machinery, automobile assembly and electrical components. The chemical, plastic and rubber industries were well represented in Panyu too.

The Panyu Hotel itself was an example of new construction in the area and a pleasant surprise. Clara had warned us that it would be basic but since her visit a whole new wing had been built for the women's world football championships. This was immaculately clean and the cool air-conditioned lobby was filled with a strong smell of new furnishings and polish. The floor gleamed, wall fittings and light switches sparkled and the wall was decorated with sensuous wooden carvings of ethnic minority women.

At the end of a long day during our first week in Panyu the hotel was welcoming with its friendly staff and peaceful atmosphere. The layout was similar to a traditional Chinese house with a main entrance at the front and living quarters tucked away at the back.

The noise of beeping and bicycle bells gradually receded as we entered the grounds. We passed through several sets of doors into an air-conditioned lobby and glided upwards in a spotless lift to emerge into the quiet of the corridor leading to our room. There the furnishings looked untouched by human hand and a window the length of one wall had a view over the hotel grounds and buildings that lined the streets of Shiqiao. The television could receive local and Hong Kong Cantonese programmes and central Beijing television channels in Mandarin. Disconcertingly, Hong Kong TV would sometimes suddenly cut out and be replaced by local news.

In the evenings we wandered round the darkening streets of Shiqiao with other people out shopping or strolling, enjoying the warmth and prosperous atmosphere. The archway in front of the Panyu Hotel was decorated with neon and Christmas tree lights and there was a holiday feeling in the air. Unlike the sprawling impersonal vastness of other Chinese cities, Shiqiao was compact with small streets lined with shops. Together with large department stores these sold everything from Colgate toothpaste and Ferrero Rocher chocolate to widescreen televisions.

Two years previously in Beijing and Shanghai I had only ever seen one design of table lamp wherever I went, whether in shops, flats, offices or hotels. I had found it surprising to visit Min's family in Shanghai and to see the identical make of table lamp that I had bought for myself in Beijing, a robust functional model with a yellow shade. I thought it an incredible coincidence at the time, only later realizing that this was one of the few lamps available throughout the length and breadth of China. Here in Panyu two years later the choice was endless. We could have bought everything locally and needn't have come loaded with so much luggage.

Along the street at ground level were also office entrances, tourist centres and restaurants. Above were balconies with trailing plants and vertical signs with bright red neon characters advertising products and businesses. There were sea-food restaurants, bars and a new shopping centre where brick dust and wood shavings littered the floor. A night-club inside had already opened and music thumped noisily into the street. A couple of doors down, a man crooned into a karaoke set, seemingly unselfconscious and oblivious to passers-by. I imagined the outcry this behaviour would cause in a high street in England.

Local people were friendly and generally didn't stare. On one occasion when a child was looking at me balefully his mother reprimanded him. Frequent staring was something I had found difficult to get used to in Beijing and Shanghai. There was no hostility but being subject to so much scrutiny made it difficult to relax when out on the streets or in public places. Sometimes it could lead to a feeling of alienation though some foreigners seemed to enjoy the attention. It was like being a minor celebrity with people following you around wherever you went. If you stopped to look at something or buy anything a crowd would gather. No matter the time of day there would always be plenty of people who apparently had no need to be anywhere else and could stand there surveying you leisurely from top to bottom, speculating loudly about your appearance, age and nationality, and occasionally sex too.

Shaggy perms were the latest fashion in Panyu and the task of curling straight Chinese hair was providing a lot of work. There were hairdressers on every corner. Local people had attractive lively faces and Panyu women wore colourful tops and tight black mini-skirts. "Stop staring," said Min, but I was merely noting the contrast with my last visit to Shanghai. I vividly recalled walking on an overpass to avoid the roaring non-stop traffic below and seeing that in the thronging crowd around me, every single person, man and woman alike, was wearing a black coat or jacket in a complete absence of colour like a frame from a de-saturated film.

Most nights after work we stopped off at a cake and bread shop next to the hotel where there was a self-service system with trays and plastic tongs. The bread resembled cake but it was still fresh by next morning and together with coffee made a good breakfast to start the working day. On television each morning for at least a week was a music video called "Xiao Beijing" ("Little Beijing") featuring three teenage girls skipping round Beijing and smiling sweetly at the camera.

Beijing looked cold and bleak, a city far away with little relevance to life in the south. My student days there seemed to belong to a different world and time.

The video had karaoke subtitles with a ball that bounced along the Chinese characters but I was not tempted to join in first thing in the morning; the factory hours were taking time to get used to, 8.30 a.m. to 6.00 p.m. six days a week.

Each morning we were picked up by the company minibus at the gates of the hotel and jolted along a length of road that already looked familiar. As we approached the factory the modern buildings of Shiqiao were left behind. On one side of the road stood ancient dwellings that backed on to small hills. On the other was a pool that was almost a lake. Its distant banks were lost in greenery and morning mist.

Well established trees grew along the side of the road and people walked and cycled to work at a leisurely pace, or sat astride motorbikes chatting. Dogs roamed along the pavement keeping a safe distance from the company driver and other vehicles. CEO Chris Twist had said that job hunters queuing up outside the factory were turned away each day, but the only queue I could see every morning, and it was a long one, was for people buying their breakfast at a roadside stall.

Following a series of loud beeps from the driver, the factory gates were opened by a serious young guard in a blue uniform. The morning shift of machine operators usually arrived at the same time as us and they milled round a clocking-in machine, chatting and laughing. Others had just had breakfast and washed their food bowls at some outside taps, the water splashing and pooling on the shiny stone of the courtyard.

Michael was relaxed about the pace of work and

though we had left England in an urgent rush to start his course he kept saying that we couldn't begin till the Sri Lankans arrived. He spent his time sitting in the company university inhaling too much of the sickly-sweet mosquito spray, and when we asked him for something to do he said we should go and "familiarise" ourselves with the factory. There's only so much time you want to spend wandering about a factory with such a loosely defined objective and we set to work on a more pressing issue, that of whether Min would be able to leave China again. Our tourist map of Panyu showed that three ferries a day travelled from Lianhuashan to Hong Kong. Min telephoned the border control office at Lianhuashan Port and was put through to the person in charge, Office Head Wang.

"Do you have a foreign permanent residence visa?" asked Wang.

"Yes," replied Min.

"Do you have a Hong Kong visa?"

"Yes."

"Then there should be no problem," he concluded, and added as if by afterthought, "but maybe I should come and check your passport. I'll come over now."

How extraordinarily helpful, I said to Min, at this unprecedented behaviour from a government official. But when an hour later the message reached the second floor office that Office Head Wang had arrived, we went down to meet a man practically stamping his feet with anger.

"Hello," said Min, putting out a hand for Mr Wang to shake. He looked at it for a moment as if not quite sure what to do with it. "We've put you to great inconvenience, making you come all this way."

The expression she used, *mafan ni*, literally "inconvenience you" is another concise Chinese phrase with many uses. It can be an apology for something that has already happened, "sorry to have inconvenienced you", or for events still unfolding, "sorry to trouble you but…" or for an anticipated favour or help in the future, "could I trouble you to..?" On the other hand once in a Beijing hotel close to Tiananmen Square when asking for a glass of water the waiter replied *tai mafan* "too much bother". This was not unusual at the time. During my stay in Beijing, whether it was buying a pencil, train ticket, bicycle, beer or a meal, with each fresh encounter staff seemed to attain greater heights of surliness.

Office Head Wang was proving to be a hot new contender in this category and when Min introduced me he said, "I've never met such a rude person before", turning to face her as I shook him by the hand. After a moment I realized he wasn't referring to me but to the security guard who opened the gate every morning for the company minibus. The man in question looked sulky and was pointedly ignoring our visitor. Perhaps the guard didn't like the look of Office Head Wang and so had initially refused to let him in, but then adding insult to injury had been leisurely about announcing his arrival.

Maybe it wasn't entirely the guard's fault. He was a guard after all and here was a chance to do some guarding. As for the delay in announcing Mr Wang, things did happen slowly in the factory and on reflection I found it impressive that we had got the message at all. I kept my observations to myself however, as Office Head Wang was continuing to harangue Min as she led him towards the office.

Out of breath from the climb to the second floor, Office Head Wang quietened down and I had a chance to look at him more closely. A middle-aged man with a round face (still scowling) he plumped down into a seat unasked, loosened a gold button at his neck, pulled out a packet of cigarettes and threw them onto the table. He wore an olive green trouser and jacket combination with gold braid at the shoulders.

Another man was with him though I barely noticed him at first as he was as discreet as Wang was loud. A silent angular man with high cheekbones, he said nothing throughout the visit but sat and smoked, unmoving like a terracotta figure, miles away, in a world of his own. Wang lapsed into a moody silence. He took out a cigarette and joined his smoking colleague. He appeared to have forgotten why he had come to the factory and his eyes flicked gloomily round the office and at the other people working away in the room. Eventually he focused back on Min.

"Don't you have a conference room?" he asked. The nearest thing to such a place in the factory was the classroom, or the company university as it was called. But when Michael wasn't in it the door was locked and he jealously guarded the key as if at any moment someone was going to make off with a bag of dead mosquitoes.

Min delicately steered Wang back to the matter in hand and showed him her passport and the permanent residence visa stamp. Office Head Wang looked at it uncomprehendingly and passed it to his subordinate, who weighed it in his hands and rotated it to the right and then to the left as if by holding it at the correct angle all would line up and the meaning become clear.

"What about your green card?" asked Wang. He didn't respond to Min's explanation but sat and smoked, seemingly unaware of the falling ash as it formed delicate grey cones on the desk. After smoking some more and conferring with his companion, who acknowledged his comments with the tiniest movement of his head and the words "uh", "uh", Wang finally told us that he couldn't make a decision. He would take a copy of Min's passport to his superior in Guangzhou and let us know what the man said.

He stood up suddenly and the precise mountains of ash broke apart, drifting among the papers and pens on the desk. We thanked Mr Wang and escorted the two of them out. Office Head Wang started moaning about the guard again and pointed an angry finger at him as he approached the gate.

We were mystified by Wang's trip to the factory. His offer to show the passport to a senior official in Guangzhou seemed helpful, yet his visit bore a striking resemblance to the frustrating negotiating strategy whereby following discussions between two sides and an apparent deal, one party unexpectedly claims not to have the authority to reach an agreement in the first place.

On the other hand maybe I was reading too much into the matter and Office Head Wang just couldn't understand the English writing on Min's permanent residence visa.

6 Not accustomed to the water and earth

While the shop floor was staffed entirely by mainland Chinese people, the second floor office was an international community with Filipinos, Sri Lankans and Hong Kong Chinese, as well as seven or eight local clerks in charge of payroll and accounts. The Filipino work study engineers were the most numerous, speaking no Chinese but fluent English and Tagalog among themselves. Until recently they had been supervised and supported by an English boss but she had moved to one of the company's other factories outside China.

There were also two local work study engineers, one from Panyu called Charlotte and the other John from Hunan Province. Two production managers also worked in the office, Ah Ban from Hong Kong and Anne, another mainland Chinese employee. In our interview Rod and Chris had spoken of a plan to train from six to a dozen trainee managers, but so far, in the Panyu factory at least, it was just Min and me.

Our new colleagues had a well-established timetable for the working week. After disembarking from the company minibus and trooping into the office each morning they sat down to work at several rows of desks facing the front like a classroom. At half past twelve, not a minute before or after, they jumped up and congregated round a glass cupboard at the back of the office and took out plastic bowls and spoons in preparation for lunch. Next was a brief walk across the factory courtyard and down a short flight of concrete steps into the company canteen, a dark hall with foldup tables and chairs placed at intervals on a paved stone floor. There was no artificial light but the walls were whitewashed and reflected some of the natural light entering by windows at the far end or trickling in through gaps in the overlapping tiles of the roof, which together with supporting beams, were visible from below. It was like eating in a cave.

Time spent in Chinese restaurants in the UK is no preparation for the canteen food served up in mainland Chinese institutions as I had discovered as a student in Beijing. The basic living conditions, dusty coal-flavoured phlegm-inducing air, desperately overcrowded buses and public transport were all part of the experience of living in China but the food in the canteen at the Beijing Foreign Languages Institute was a pass I could not cross. Part of the problem was my vegetarian diet as most of the pre-prepared dishes contained meat. The options remaining were so alien and unpleasant to my sense of taste that I never returned to the building.

There was a small shop on the campus that sold yoghurt (the Chinese *suannai* literally meaning sour milk) in little glass bottles and other cake-like snacks, but the former wasn't filling and the latter dry and tasteless.

Street food was my saviour and for the first couple of weeks I survived on *jianbing*, a delicious savoury Chinese crepe made with batter, egg, spring onions, red bean paste and chili sauce. Usually I would get two from an old street vendor who did brisk business outside the Institute each morning. Before frying the *jianbing*, the old man would quickly rub a grimy block of well-worn fat around the griddle, whether animal or vegetable I never knew. In any case my years of vegetarian purity were soon challenged by the *getihu*, who on one occasion were most pressing I try out a local vegetable. I did so to be obliging. After I had swallowed it I was told it was fish, much to everyone's amusement.

The humorous fish incident had occurred in another establishment a few minutes' walk from our dormitory, though like the nearby bar frequented by the *getihu*, I was never quite sure if it was part of the university or not. With its concrete floor, stained windowless walls, dark interior and earthy clientele who got drunk, swore and spat loudly (sometimes against the wall), "restaurant" seemed the wrong word for it but it wasn't quite a canteen either. Despite appearances the large plates of food were appetizing and we washed them down with bottles of Qingdao beer.

Dishes were ordered from an impassive but not unfriendly young woman in a big chef's hat who sat at a table near the kitchen and calculated the bill on a large abacus, fingers flying. Towards the end of our time in Beijing she disappeared from her post and we heard a rumour that she had been removed due to becoming too friendly with some foreign students. I know it wasn't me as she had been quite unmoved by the old English charm and would barely respond to a greeting. Once she surprised me by predicting my order but this wasn't a huge feat of memory as for months I had only eaten one dish, *jidan xihongshi*, egg-fried tomato. For variety I would occasionally have *jidan huanggua*, egg-fried cucumber.

It wasn't the only time we heard a story like this. I was told that a North Korean was repatriated because he was spending too much time with some of the Leeds students. I never found out whether this was true due to the increasing amount of time I was spending in Shanghai, and the sudden, unexpected exit from Beijing that brought my year in China to its premature close. But it was true that some North Koreans got on very well with students from Britain, an affirmation that basic human friendship can overcome vast differences in culture, political systems and upbringing.

No one was spitting on the walls in the Panyu factory canteen though it was quite similar to the Beijing eating place in terms of general décor. For our food we climbed onto a wooden stage and passed our bowls through a hatch to one of the cooks in a kitchen at the back. This area was basic with a concrete floor, concrete shelves running round the walls at waist height and a final slab of concrete that served as a food preparation table in the middle of the room. The cook filled the bowl with the day's meal and a ladle or two of rice from a tub that stood nearby.

The first time we went for lunch I didn't immediately see that we were actually standing on a stage in the literal sense of the word, but waiting in line behind Charlotte as she asked for more food, I glanced up and saw spider webs trailing in sheets from suspended ladders, platforms and ropes and other backstage paraphernalia. It was like peering into an old junk room filled with remnants of the past, all intact but seemingly abandoned one night in the middle of a performance and since then touched only by dust.

The true shape of the stage below had been concealed by stacks of cardboard boxes and packed garments waiting for transport, but once revealed the main hall also took form before my eyes as the audience seating area of an old theatre. The company manual had mentioned "training facilities in a reconstructed opera house" and this was presumably where we were standing.

After being given our food we would continue across the stage, descend at the other side and find a clean spot at which to eat our lunch. On each table was a brightly coloured plastic bowl into which people were supposed to scrape the leftovers of their meal before leaving the eating area. The bowls were large but previous diners often ignored them and dumped rice and a selection of chewed up bones on the table and floor.

Min thought the factory lunch was good and said that she had been brought up on similar food while at school and university. For her it was the equivalent of beans on toast or sausage and mash and though I didn't find it as bad as the canteen food at the Beijing Foreign Languages Institute, I still found it unappetizing.

I toyed with my rice and tried one of the two hardboiled eggs nestling amongst my greens but it was almost neat salt and I found it inedible. Charlotte, the local Panyu work study engineer, asked if she could have the other. "Aiyah, you're really greedy," said Anne, the production manager, as Charlotte helped herself.

One of the older cooks was hovering round our table and had watched the hardboiled egg passing from my bowl to Charlotte's, my lack of enthusiasm for the food apparent. She edged a little closer and looking at me wisely said in a deep, hoarse voice, "*soy toe bat fook*" ("water, earth not accustomed").

Four-character phrases pervade the Chinese language and all aspects of life in China, whether politics, art, food, literature, history or martial arts. Thousands are in everyday use, many derived from classical Chinese, others from the vernacular and common wisdom. Some are obvious: "blue sky thunder bolt", a bolt from the blue; some vivid: "open door see mountain", direct and to the point; some philosophical: "extreme joy begets sorrow"; some crude: "the farts roll and the piss flows", very scared (or to quote my Chinese-English dictionary, "wet one's pants in terror"); and some are incomprehensible without a knowledge of the story behind them: "Lord Ye's love of dragons", liking the idea of something but not the reality.

The phrase used by the cook seemed particularly suited to Panyu as both water and earth were very much in evidence in the semi-rural setting of the factory.

Sometimes pairings of two characters are phrases in themselves such as "wind and cloud", a state of affairs that is stormy and changeable; "mountains and water" traditional Chinese landscape painting; "cut sleeve", implying homosexuality after a Han Dynasty (206 B.C. to A.D. 220) emperor who cut off the sleeve of his imperial robe rather than wake his lover; or "clouds and rain", a euphemism for sex.

The two characters in the Chinese word for "contradiction" *maodun* literally mean "spear shield" after a story from the Warring States period (475-221 B.C.) concerning a man with a surprisingly bad business sense for a Chinese person. At the same time as trying to sell a shield which he boasted was "so strong nothing can pierce it" he also offered for sale a spear "so sharp it can pierce anything". According to the story the man had no answer when an alert if literal-minded bystander asked, "what if I take your spear and pierce your shield with it, what then?"

Although the cook had been speaking in broad terms when she said I wasn't used to the water and earth, implying I hadn't acclimatized to local conditions in Panyu and by extension China, I felt the problem was more geographically limited in scope. It could be narrowed down to the water and earth in the factory kitchen or even more specifically to the water and earth in my bowl on the table at that very moment. But I did not want to be rude ("enter village follow custom" after all) and thought it would be tactful to go with her explanation.

"Eat a bit more," the cook said and then added to the room in general, "he's thin".

And thin I would remain unless I could get a more

substantial and appetizing meal. The possibility of doing just that arrived in the form of a local clerk called Li Yi who came up to Min and I while we were washing our bowls at the outside tap and invited us for a barbecue that evening in a nearby park. Li Yi said they would bring along some vegetarian food for me.

My stomach was already rumbling with anticipation but in the meantime it looked as if we would be contemplating another slow afternoon of "familiarising" ourselves with the factory. One thing I had ascertained in these wanderings, despite hunting high and low, was the absence of anything resembling the sexy underwear I had seen in Clara's siren catalogue, though I had learned that the baggy garment on the shop floor was called a sleep shirt.

That afternoon there was a flurry of excitement in the office and Michael told us to go to the classroom in anticipation of a factory visit by the U.S. Consul General from Guangzhou. Min and I did as instructed and found the room full of company employees seated at the shaky desks, keeping a nervous eye out for mosquitoes.

Michael handed out some papers, produced a piece of chalk, drew some work study symbols on the blackboard and sat back in his chair gazing into space. On hearing voices and the creaking of the stairs he stood up slowly and launched into a lecture about how to represent the movement of workers and materials in work study diagrams. The sound of feet grew louder and the Consul's party were suddenly spilling into the room, apologizing for interrupting the lecture.

"That is quite all right," said Michael.

The Consul was escorted by a group of people

from the Hong Kong office including Bart Ryder, the general manager, and Chris Twist, CEO.

"This is where we train our work study engineers from all over the world," said Bart gesturing round the room. "It's an intensive course but our guys like a challenge! The training we give our people here in Panyu results in a huge increase in manufacturing potential for the company as a whole."

The Consul nodded politely but without any great interest. It was probably a good thing Michael had not kindled a fire in his belly to find out more about work study. Had he approached our desks he would have been as surprised as I to see that Michael had not handed out training material but a page from a puzzle book entitled "coffee break turkey shoot". As our intensive training was being described I was counting the feathers on a cartoon turkey's bottom trying to spot the difference.

Michael had already put down his chalk and was wiping the symbols from the board before the Consul and his party had finished negotiating the staircase and departing the building. His expression was unreadable and I couldn't tell what he felt about his part in the performance. At least it gave us something to do for the rest of the afternoon till the bus ride back to the Panyu Hotel, after which we grabbed our coats and walked to the park a few minutes down the road.

It was still rush hour and the streets were as busy as during the morning with a stop-start flow of small vans and motorbikes hooting and beeping each other. Bright lights and neon illuminated pedestrians crossing the roads warily as heavier trucks rattled by.

We passed a butcher's stall with whole pig's heads

in the window, thin purple-red sausages and rows of tongues, hearts and glistening livers. Further on a shop sold jars of alcohol with dead snakes coiled at the bottom, preserved like specimens in a science laboratory. Some were decaying, the skin lifting upwards like fraying cloth. Around us we heard the sing-song sounds of Cantonese.

Two local women from the second floor office were waiting for us at the gates of the park and as dusk fell they took us along a path that skirted a small boating lake. Midges danced in the air above faintly rippling water that reflected nearby lights.

We crossed a patch of grass, walked past some straggly bushes and emerged in a large barbecue area with tables and seats for many separate parties. Small trees were dotted between them. The tables were concrete discs with a cone-shaped hollow for the coals, leaving a rim on which to put plates and cups. While we waited, Li Yi and her colleagues opened bags and boxes, prepared the food, cleaned large barbecue forks by wiping them in a sandy area nearby, and lit the fire.

I was watching the food closely in an attempt to identify something I might be able to eat. The concept of vegetarianism as familiar to people in the UK had proved new to the waitresses in the Panyu Hotel. The night before I had explained at length that I did not eat meat, fish, fowl, prawn, squid, snail or any other living creature that ran, walked, flew, crawled, hopped, swam, propelled itself or slithered, or in short demonstrated any form of animation raising it above the level of a vegetable. I was sitting back in my chair, sipping jasmine tea and congratulating myself on my use of Chinese, when the soup arrived. Unmistakeable

73

chunks of meat floated and jostled against the sweet corn, bobbing and rolling insolently in the swell. The seconds passed.

"This soup has meat in it," I said finally, after exhaling a deep and calming *qigong* breath. I looked the waitress in the eye and informed her of the error, waiting for her to snatch the bowl back in embarrassment and return shamefaced to the kitchen. But she glanced casually down at it and shrugged, saying "it's only a little bit of meat."

"I told you that I do not eat meat. I am a vegetarian," I said after a long pause.

"It's only a little bit. Why can't you eat such a small amount?"

"I do not eat any meat, whether the piece is big or small."

She pouted, a disarming, child-like gesture. I had at last made myself understood and was prepared to be magnanimous in victory. A new bowl of soup would suffice, no apology was necessary.

"Well you should try the meat. You might like it," she finally retorted, turning to say something to Min in Cantonese and afterwards returning to the kitchen with a brisk step. "What did she say?" I asked Min, who was smiling despite the seriousness of the situation. "Has she gone to get another dish?" But the waitress was not going to bring a replacement bowl of sweet corn soup; instead she dispensed some domestic advice to Min: get him used to the taste of meat by giving him small pieces at first, then make them progressively larger as he is gradually weaned from his vegetarian diet.

The food for the evening's barbecue was contained

in two steel buckets and when the lids were raised a tremendous smell of raw meat wafted across the barbecue pit. Pork, chicken and squid were in abundance, but just as I thought I was to be a spectator only, I was handed a bottle of beer, a bag of ten hard-boiled eggs, a loaf of bread and slab of cake.

The atmosphere was relaxed and friendly and we learned a new Cantonese word *nung* meaning "burnt". The meal was accompanied by loud belches of appreciation and I manoeuvred the eggs with skill between sizzling and dripping pieces of meat amid laughter at my eccentricity. Later we walked back to the hotel and saw Orion's Belt shining bright and timeless above our heads.

7 Dey got more mah lee dan you!

The first week in China stretched to two and then three as we adjusted to life in Panyu. Though we were in the south of the country there were frequent reminders of life in Beijing. The early morning music video of the dancing teenage girls was soon replaced by a podgy taxi driver in a black leather jacket who sang hoarsely but vigorously about working as a driver in the capital.

My memories of Beijing taxi drivers were mixed due to an innate conflict over payment of fares that existed between members of their profession and foreign students. As *liuxuesheng* or students studying abroad we were entitled to use RMB in almost all of our financial transactions instead of Foreign Exchange Certificates (FEC). The latter were compulsory for foreign tourists, diplomats or overseas Chinese and had to be used in designated shops or hotels. Though 1 FEC was nominally equal to 1 RMB, in practice there was a black market for the certificates as they could be used to purchase goods or services not available in ordinary shops or to people with RMB only.

As students we carried a "Special Treatment Card" granting "Exemption from the Payment of Foreign Exchange Certificates". Informally this was known as a "White Card" after its colour, though in appearance it was more of an off-white beige. On the document was a photograph of the student, passport number, nationality, expiry date (August 30th 1989 in my case) and a stamp by the State Administration of Foreign Exchange. In theory production of the card entitled students to legally pay in RMB.

Taking a taxi could be a hassle involving first an argument over the meter being "broken" and then lengthy negotiations to cut down the driver's proposed fare, usually an over-optimistic figure intended to set him up in retirement. Producing a White Card at the negotiating stage could result in the driver suddenly losing interest and refusing to take you anywhere. Taxi drivers saw foreigners as the bearers of glad tidings in the form of Foreign Exchange Certificates and an announcement at the end of the trip that payment was to be in RMB would cause a sudden chilling of the atmosphere at best, and often resulted in angry shouts and recriminations. Where possible I took the bus in Beijing.

The White Card also had to be produced when buying train tickets and I was once stopped as I disembarked at Beijing Railway Station. I was separated from the ranks of thousands of fellow travellers by a young woman of about my age, perhaps a year or two older, wearing a large green army coat with a furry brown collar. She spoke Chinese with a strong Beijing accent and I missed most of what she said, but I picked up that she wasn't happy about my ticket. She ordered me to follow her as if it was an arrest and we passed through a side door into a private area separated from the rest of the station. We followed several deserted but warren-like corridors and finally stopped at a small room where a number of railway staff sat drinking green tea out of old Nescafé jars.

They detained me for a while but finally let me leave after I produced my Beijing Foreign Languages Institute student ID card and White Card; or maybe they were just fed up with the effort of speaking to me as my comprehension of the Beijing accent was limited. A strong accent could completely transform or truncate words such as *dir* (meaning "place") instead of the standard Mandarin word *difang* or *jinr wanr* instead of *jintian wanshang* ("this evening"), adding to the difficulties of an already challenging language.

In Panyu I had no White Card and though FEC were still officially in use (they weren't removed from circulation till 1994) we were able to pay for things in RMB and often Hong Kong dollars too. Black market money changers operated openly in Panyu swapping Hong Kong dollars for RMB as they had done in Beijing changing FEC to RMB.

Many foreign students in Beijing changed money despite it being a criminal offence as it was a means of stretching limited finances further. There was great demand for FEC from local people and the phrase "change money" followed me round the streets like a greeting, from Beijing to Shanghai and back again.

Money changers could trick the unwary in any number of ways such as inserting blank pieces of paper into a stack of notes or the more subtle variation of folding a note in half and counting it twice; or they demonstrated marvellous sleight of hand and while performing a final count of the money would spirit a wad of notes away into thin air. Some used less finesse and mid-transaction would shout "police! police!" snatch the FEC and run (Jackie Chan aficionados will recall a similar ruse adopted by Iron Head Rat in the 1978 classic "Drunken Master").

Just outside the Panyu Hotel was a stall run by a neatly dressed old woman with three gold teeth and a face scorched brown by years in the sun. There were a few token packets of cigarettes in front of her, apparently for sale. When changing money she would check the street for police, produce a calculator, rapidly work out how much she would give her customer for his or her Hong Kong dollars and hand over wads of RMB in exchange. Two youths loitered near the stall and chased away inquisitive onlookers. In Panyu there was evidently a thriving underworld and on local news we often saw pictures of people arrested for crimes of violence, drugs and prostitution.

We soon stopped using the Panyu Hotel restaurant for breakfast as the morning menu was too rich and oily for everyday consumption. It was a special occasion menu that people eat on holiday and then spend weeks regretting. In any case it was busy in the mornings and we could never get served in time to catch the company minibus, so instead we ate our breakfast in the hotel bedroom. Our preferred meal was pot noodle, crisps and "Lucky Fuk" preserved fruit from a supermarket across the road. For variety we had sticky cakes and mandarin oranges from a fruit stall nearby.

The tap water wasn't drinkable but the room was supplied with thermos flasks of piping-hot boiled water we used for the noodles and added to powdered milk for morning tea and coffee. We bought two mugs decorated with the characters for longevity and happiness, and bowls and spoons for the factory canteen.

Due to our high consumption of noodles, tea and coffee we used more hot water than most guests and the hotel staff soon recognised our voices when we rang for more. They spoke good Mandarin but I used Cantonese whenever possible. On one occasion I was about to give our room number but the woman said, "you're 701 aren't you?"

"How did you know?" I asked.

"Your voice is very distinctive," she replied in Mandarin and I heard laughter at the end of the phone. It was probably my Chinese tones giving me away again. In Chinese altering the pitch or tone of your voice can change the meaning of a word, a difficult concept to put into practice for a person brought up speaking English or another non-tonal language. The four tones in Mandarin were hard enough but Cantonese has between six and ten depending on the approach. I opted for six as a starting point as ten seemed an extraordinarily high number more suited to a gifted musician than the average language learner. In any case I had discovered that in practice Chinese people could usually understand me from the context and combinations of sounds, even if the tones themselves were not completely accurate.

One of the most difficult Chinese language challenges for a foreigner is keeping to the correct tones when in a heightened emotional state, such as when explaining the meaning of the White Card to a taxi driver who demands FEC or the finer points of vegetarianism to a waitress who insists that a meat diet would be more appropriate.

After breakfast we ran through the grounds to catch the company minibus at the main gate of the hotel. Li Yi the clerk and John, one of the work study engineers, would usually be there first and we exchanged the Cantonese greeting for good morning, *"jo san"*.

The bus would arrive minutes later and Li Yi who was small and burly shouldered her way on first. John deferred politely and was invariably last to climb aboard. Tall and thin with glasses, he was the typical intellectual student and looked out of place in the factory. His eyesight had been ruined by too much studying in poor conditions. When he took off his glasses to rub his eyes, he sat blinking for a while, naked and exposed, as if he had just emerged from a dark cellar into piercing sunlight. Gangling and with lighter skin he stood out from the locals who were small and compact with tanned and healthy faces.

John came from Hunan, one of Guangdong's neighbouring provinces and the birth place of Mao Zedong. He spoke Mandarin with yet another variety of accent difficult to understand, pronouncing "h" as "f" and interchanging the letters "n" and "l". When I first spoke to him he said he came from "Fulan" and I assumed it to be some small town or village I had never heard of. It was only after I'd got used to his accent that I realised he meant Hunan Province, population 65 million. He was proud of his origins and had a snobbish attitude towards the local people and the Cantonese language which he refused to learn.

One night he invited us to his home, a company flat five minutes' walk from the hotel. He lived on the third floor above a shop that sold Chinese medicine and the entrance and alleyway were filled with wonderful pungent smells of dried herbs and other aromatic ingredients. The smells were so strong and unusual that they almost blurred across the senses and I imagined them as colours, browns, oranges and yellows. I lingered by the entrance, inhaling deeply. In the stairwell statues of household gods watched over doorways from behind heavy metal security shutters.

Panyu was apparently one of the four richest counties in China and Charlotte, the other local work study engineer, complained that visiting Westerners often failed to realise how wealthy local people were. This irritated her and I heard her say to one such person in her strong Cantonese accent, "huh! dey got more mah lee dan you". Charlotte was probably in a position to know this for a fact as more than once I heard her bluntly asking foreign staff how much money they earned.

John lived in his flat with another company employee and they shared a communal dining area and kitchen. The toilet was a hole in the ground and reminded me of my student days in Beijing but at least it had a door that locked.

The sparse furniture was old and battered and the

flat had the unloved feel of temporary student accommodation. John's bedroom was a dark lair without windows, lit by a dim reading lamp standing on a table next to an unmade bed. A science fiction picture of a spaceship against an airbrushed sky was hanging on one wall and his clothes appeared to have been ejected round the room onto all available surfaces by a wardrobe now gaping loosely open. On the pillow of the bed was a copy of "The Brothers Karamazov", neatly bookmarked with only a few chapters remaining.

He was one of millions of Chinese people obsessed with learning English, a passport to well-paid jobs with foreign companies. In his case it had already paid off as although John's flat was basic his living conditions were considerably better than those of most people in China. The toilet was not a deluxe model but I had visited areas where houses did not have them at all and occupants had to trudge to a communal latrine down the street. In other cities I had seen parents and children sharing a bedroom and whole families living in one room. As a student I visited Min's dormitory in Shanghai that she shared with six others. You could cross the room in a single step; the only space a person could call their own was the bed with its semi-privacy behind a mosquito net.

Many of the machine operators came from Hunan, in search of better paid jobs, as did Anne now working as a Production Manager but initially employed as an interpreter and assistant to Steve, the director of manufacturing. "Welcome, welcome," she said when first meeting us, displaying warmth and interest in marked contrast to Lenny. She was small, in her forties, often smiling and like John similarly preoccupied with the study of English. She relished conversations with native speakers, savouring her words as she spoke them, often asking me obscure questions about English language and literature.

Unlike John she had no objection to learning Cantonese and had acquired the language as a matter of survival. She told us of early frustrations with local machine operators and line supervisors who refused to work with her, complaining that they couldn't understand her accent. She practiced Cantonese until they could no longer use this excuse but her accent was peculiar and they often teased her about it. She had recommended John for his job and they spoke together in incomprehensible Hunan dialect.

When Anne arrived at the factory Charlotte was already well established as the main interpreter and initially there was some friction between the two, but by the time we arrived there was no hint of past conflict and on most days they shared a table at lunchtime in the canteen.

Charlotte was in her early twenties and had completed a two year language course at a college in Guangzhou. Like many young people in China she wanted to go abroad and was considering New Zealand or Australia but was having difficulty passing the necessary English proficiency exams. Her knowledge of the written language was lacking but at work she had no problem expressing herself.

She had a round bright face and ink black hair that fell over her eyes in a spiky fringe. In addition to numerous snacks and food products, the drawer beside her desk contained hair bands, brushes and face cream that she applied each morning on arriving at work.

The other daily ritual for Charlotte was a nap after lunch. This was a well-established habit for many people in Chinese institutions but a custom unfamiliar to senior management from England. Usual practice was to put your head down on the desk cushioned by your arms, close your eyes and drift off to sleep surrounded by a room full of similarly dozing colleagues. The second floor office with its noisy international atmosphere and English managers who did not understand the unspoken "do not disturb" implied by the position of desktop repose was not conducive to Charlotte's afternoon beauty sleep, and she became notable for long after-lunch absences. They eventually tracked her down to a partially concealed corner at the back of the third floor office where she was sleeping soundly on a big reclining office chair.

Charlotte had strong feelings about some of our colleagues, largely based on their appearance or status within the factory. She was intolerant of John and one of the Filipino work study engineers called Pete who was "too short". When in a bad mood everyone else suffered and if she felt wronged she would sulk at her desk with her jacket collar pulled up round her face.

She was generally treated with indulgence by the Filipino women who sometimes depended on her to sort out problems that required a native speaker. If she was in an uncooperative mood the atmosphere in the office would turn icy. Charlotte would mutter the patronising term *Ban Mui* (literally "Filipino younger sisters"), widely used in Hong Kong to refer to the

Filipino women working there as maids and nannies. The Filipino women would insult her in return, questioning her professionalism. Definitely a time to vacate the office and go for a walk on the shop floor.

*

The monotony of factory life was broken by Bart Ryder's arrival from Hong Kong. An early Christmas dinner for line supervisors and office staff was to be held at the Panyu Hotel. At the restaurant large circular tables were set in place for the meal. Behind them was a small stage and karaoke equipment.

Bart was accompanied by an American called Martin Goldman whose job involved scouting out locations for new factories. He had been looking at sites in North China and Vietnam in a constant search for cheaper labour. The service in the Panyu Hotel was slow and Martin was visibly impatient, tapping his hand against the table. Suddenly he tipped back his head and roared the word *xiaojie* ("miss") as loudly as he could. The line supervisors hushed and a disgruntled waitress came over to our table and said that the food was already on its way.

The starter was sweet corn soup followed by a main meal of crab. Within no time bright pink claws, segmented legs and other crustacean detritus littered the tables. While I was filling up on peanuts and *kiutao* I became aware of a tugging at my elbow and turned to see a little girl holding up a bunch of red roses. In Panyu beggars regularly singled me out on the street but it was the first time I had been approached in the hotel. Looking round further I saw a motionless adult beside a pillar watching silently but with a fixed intensity that was disconcerting. I told the girl I did not want to buy a flower.

After the meal Bart handed out Christmas bonuses for the line supervisors in traditional red envelopes. It was an old Chinese custom but not one I had seen practiced in Beijing. Many old traditions rejected by the authorities in the post-1949 period proved to be deeply rooted within the Chinese psyche and given a chance were beginning to resurface. A newer tradition I was pleased to forgo during the meal was karaoke. Mercifully the equipment on the stage had remained unused and the nearest we had got to karaoke had been Martin's drawn out shout of frustration for the waitress.

"You guys, come with me," said Bart after the meal, leading the way out of the restaurant, along the main road outside the hotel and then down an alley. He climbed some steps and went through a doorway above which flashed the Chinese characters "*ka la*" and the English letters "OK" in pink and blue neon. We emerged into a dark room with a small stage at the far end and the dreaded karaoke equipment. A young man in a white shirt was muttering into a microphone, a lament of some kind, perhaps that he had never learned to sing, while behind him on a TV screen a woman in a swimming costume posed beside a pool.

"Have you ever done karaoke?" Bart asked me.

"No, and I don't intend to either."

"That's what all the *gwailos* say at first. That's what I said, but even I do it now. You'll be up there before long," he added, filling in his choice of song on a slip of paper.

Karaoke had swept across the whole of China and in Panyu some hotels and night-clubs even had private rooms where individuals could sing behind closed doors (a good thing actually). On television karaoke subtitles appeared with the theme music for soap operas and even with advertisements for household products.

While much karaoke was regular wholesome entertainment, if torturing the ears of innocents can be called that, it also served as a front for prostitution in many places and businessmen would expect more than just a merry sing-along from the karaoke hostesses. Bart treated us to a rendering of "Let It Be" that refused to let me be and Johnson belted out a song that made thought as well as speech impossible. In one of the few pauses for breath during the evening, Anne, realizing I had eaten next to nothing at the Christmas meal, ordered me a double helping of fried bread. As I was finishing it off the Filipino women entered our table for a joint performance and I went outside for a breath of fresh air. I found a place to lurk among some Panyu youths playing video games in a nearby arcade.

When I returned I saw again the little girl who had been selling flowers at the hotel. She and the accompanying adult had followed us across the street and this time targeted Bart who bought all her flowers and handed them out to the women present. The party broke up after midnight and we strolled back to the Panyu Hotel. The temperature had dropped and there was a chill in the air.

8 Try and see

Bart and the others returned to Hong Kong, and seeing the ease with which they came and went, Min began a relentless campaign for a response from Office Head Wang. He had said he would contact us after reporting to his superior in Guangzhou but we heard nothing more so Min telephoned him at work and home. Min spoke to his wife, daughter, mother-in-law, a succession of relatives and colleagues and finally Mr Wang himself. He told her he had been too busy to contact his superior and that we should apply for a border pass from the Public Security Bureau in Guangzhou. As Min had permanent residence in the UK there was no need for her to obtain the pass, but Wang would not budge and had nothing else to add. It was possible the PSB might be able to assist in some way so we told Michael we would be going to Guangzhou to sort things out. He looked unhappy that we would be out of his jurisdiction for a day but we were still unoccupied at the factory and I thought a change of scene would do us good.

The next morning we set off in the direction of the bus station but halfway there a battered minibus pulled alongside and a youth shouting "Guangzhou! Guangzhou!" pulled open a sliding door and dragged us inside. The minibus was full but instead of setting off for Guangzhou we circled around Shiqiao looking for more passengers. The youth was like a predatory shark, nervous energy reflected in his eyes flicking up and down the streets as our vehicle crawled along in first gear, engine revving loudly. People were bundled quickly aboard as if they were sardines to be packed. Finally, overloaded, we accelerated away from Shiqiao.

We learned later that these minibuses often operated illegally and were frequently stopped by the police due to their dangerous practices. No one in China wore a seatbelt and there wouldn't have been enough to go round anyway due to the number of people squeezed onto each seat. The minibus was symbolic of any number of businesses in China, from small entrepreneurial start-ups to vast corporations, demonstrating commitment, long hours, hard work, and due consideration for the law; they'd considered it and decided it didn't apply to them.

Profit was master and depended on two factors in the minibus transport business; squeezing a record-breaking number of people into a vehicle and completing as many journeys in a working day as possible, the latter achieved through "speed, speed and more speed" as Rod had said to us at our interview in London. This was more than a mantra to the driver, it was his raison d'être and if he couldn't keep his foot flat down on the accelerator his whole body began to shake. No concept of traffic safety clouded his brain and he was single-minded in the objective of reaching Guangzhou in the fastest time possible.

The minibus was rough and ready, the steering wheel and foot pedals seeming to have been transplanted from an arcade simulation. The driver tore along the road as if we had multiple lives to spare. Cyclists appeared in front of us like clusters of dots on a TV screen. They grew in size as we approached, then swerved off to the right and left as we accelerated up behind them and charged through their wobbling ranks.

The 18 kilometre journey to Guangzhou cost five RMB and lasted one hour. Buildings beside the road were rough and unfinished but the area was thriving and we saw signs of wealth and prosperity everywhere. Along one side of the road for ten minutes we saw nothing but row upon row of furniture stores selling endless sofas, chairs and tables.

The land was a casualty of the new development and the countryside all around was disappearing beneath highways and road works. The major road to Guangzhou was wide and flat and marked on our local map simply as a highway under construction. Panyu County had once been covered in small hills and along sections of the road scarred remains were visible, gouged away to flatten the land. Some hills had been sliced down the middle as if by a giant guillotine, one half removed completely and the remaining portion a cross-section with different strata of reddish soil visible and a thin layer of grass at the top, tree roots sticking out into space.

At the northern edge of the county stood the Luoxi

Bridge linking Panyu to the city of Guangzhou. It climbed into the sky and lifted itself in a gentle curve above squares of flooded paddy field and the sluggish Pearl River. Crossing the bridge the traffic slowed to a halt. Unhappy with the speed of the queue our driver's leg twitched with impatience. Seeing a gap open up two cars ahead he pulled out oblivious to oncoming traffic, accelerated forwards and wedged the front of the minibus into the space, jostling another vehicle out of the way. The traffic started to move again and he stepped on the accelerator to make up for lost time.

The driver was equally at home on either side of the road and not in the least concerned about being the odd man out in the sense that he was travelling in one direction and everyone else the other, until he found himself facing a heavy truck thundering towards us from the other end of the bridge. At the last minute realizing he didn't have the acceleration to make the spot in the traffic ahead he had identified as rightfully his, he braked sharply and swerved back into the space he vacated seconds before, except it was no longer a space but a rapidly diminishing gap. These were the days before anyone had even considered the concept of automobile collision avoidance systems but a startled scream of panic from the back of the bus served just as well to alert our driver to a large army vehicle inches from our left rear side. It was sucked in towards us till the inevitable bang and crash of colliding vehicles.

There was a brief tussle as the truck and minibus entangled in the middle of the road and we ended up being pushed briefly towards the railings of the bridge. As we were bulldozered towards a drop into clear blue sky, which would have deprived the company of its two promising new graduates, to use a four-character phrase previously alluded to, the farts rolled and the piss flowed. I should have been able to predict the response of our driver, his solution to all ills: depress accelerator until foot encounters resistance in form of floor, depress some more. The vehicles separated and he held onto first place as we tore off the bridge. We drove for another twenty minutes (I have no memory of that last part of the journey) and arrived in the sprawling outskirts of Guangzhou.

Legs shaky we hailed a taxi. The new driver, apparently a clone of the man we had just left behind, adjusted his shades, turned up the stereo and tore off into the thick traffic, cutting up four vehicles with one twist of the wheel.

But soon he was forced to slow down as we joined buses and trucks crawling in lengthy traffic jams while suicidal cyclists choked in hot fumes and dust. Guangzhou could barely cope with the volume of traffic and it seemed that if one more vehicle was added the streets would seize up permanently. Ugly iron bridges and flyovers crossed different corners of the city but were as packed as the stagnant roads below.

The driver switched channels and we listened to traffic announcements on Guangzhou radio station. It started with a cheery jingle *"hoi sam chut moon, ping on wooi ga"* ("happily leave your house, safely return home"). The traffic news that followed was an endless list of roads through Guangzhou that had ground to a halt because of traffic jams. Even the city ring road was blocked.

It wasn't so crowded on some of the smaller, older side streets and the Public Security Bureau was in a quiet lane shaded by dust-covered trees with clusters of aerial roots hanging high overhead.

The Bureau was dark inside with a broken bench and other furniture leaning against one wall. A young man looked at Min's passport and said that there was no problem, she could leave China without any difficulty and didn't need a pass. This was a great relief but the issue still remained of convincing Office Head Wang that Min was entitled to leave the country.

"Would you be able to contact the Lianhuashan border control and explain that I'm able to leave the country?" asked Min.

"No, I can't do that," he replied. "We don't have anything to do with them."

"Could you write a letter or some kind of document saying that I can leave?"

"No, but I can give you a copy of the rules and regulations."

He opened a drawer and produced a booklet which he folded open and handed to Min. Sure enough it said that a Chinese person who was a permanent resident in another country could leave China freely. It had been surprisingly easy to get this information in black and white from the Public Security Bureau and it seemed impossible that Office Head Wang was not aware of it. Min had the idea of going to a public notary to make a registered translation of the English words of her permanent residence visa in case it was a language issue causing the difficulty. A translation would save face for any border official who could not read the English and combined with the rule book it might even convince Office Head Wang.

We queued for an hour at the public notary office only to be told that they were not permitted to make translations of visas or similar documents. Lying on a desk was the card of a private translator and we walked to his office a few streets away. I was grateful Office Head Wang was not with us as the elderly translator had problems with the phrase "indefinite leave to remain" translating the word "indefinite" as "not definite" and by extension "not permanent", resulting in a translation that deprived Min of her permanent residence status and would have kept her waiting at the border for a very long time. She politely offered an alternative translation which he accepted without a murmur and was happy to type out for an exorbitant fee.

When we arrived back in Panyu (by a large public bus) Min telephoned Office Head Wang and read him the relevant passage from the book of rules and regulations.

"Ah. It's like that is it?" he said.

"Will I be able to leave via Lianhuashan?" asked Min.

Wang thought for a moment and then said, "try and see" ("*shishi kan*").

"What do you mean 'try and see?' Will I be let through or not?"

"Try and see," said Wang again.

The conversation went round in circles with Wang finally suggesting that we leave China via Shenzhen, the Special Economic Zone sharing a border with Hong Kong. It would be a roundabout route that would take a full day's travel rather than a couple of hours.

"If I can leave China via Shenzhen, why can't I go through Lianhuashan?" asked Min.

"We have an internal regulation," said Wang.

"What internal regulation? You didn't mention it before."

"We have an internal regulation stating that only businessmen and foreigners can leave China via Lianhuashan."

It was the old "internal regulation" ruse and Wang played it like a trump card. If what he said were true, and we had no way of knowing whether it was or not, there would no point going to Lianhuashan to "try and see".

His attitude brought to mind an ancient Chinese pun on the word *guan*, which as a noun can mean an official and as a verb can mean to control or manage. The full phrase *bu pa guan zhi pa guan* (literally "no fear official, only fear officiation") warns that officials with direct control over you are the ones to worry about. It seemed to be true in our case and from then on we decided not to trouble Office Head Wang again, to forget Lianhuashan Port and to attempt to exit China via Shenzhen.

Only some time later did it occur to us that the alacrity of Mr Wang's visit to the factory had been prompted by the thought of an early Christmas bonus. His plaintive request for a conference room would have given us more privacy to discuss the finer points. No wonder he was disappointed.

9 Of the 36 strategies the best is to run away

"Well. Can we start the class now?" asked Michael one morning several weeks after our arrival, referring to the work study course Bart had spoken about in Hong Kong.

The weather had turned cool and the sky was a pale grey rather than the bright blue that had first greeted us at Lianhuashan Port. While Michael unlocked the door I watched the ornamental raft floating in the factory garden pond, moored by a length of blue wire. Chunks of grey rock, fissured by the elements, stood in the water, bonsai jammed into the cracks and crevices. The factory garden was surrounded by a high brick wall but near the classroom was a padlocked gate through which I could see a section of the road. A woman walked past in green wellingtons carrying a plastic bag with vegetables from the market; close behind her came a man wearing a Western-style suit jacket and jeans, then three cyclists riding abreast and a sputtering tractor and a van. More people followed on foot or slowly pedalled by, the flow of their passing unbroken and relaxing to the eyes and senses.

Michael's course was finally starting as the group of long-awaited Sri Lankan work study engineers had arrived in Panyu: Matthew, tall and well built, features normally set in a fierce frown of concentration; Pilla, small and sinuous with an almost comical crafty expression; and Gopal, older, bearded, bespectacled and altogether more serious. Alfred, a Chinese man from Hong Kong was also waiting outside the classroom. His face was set in a careful neutral expression, body language suggesting a man who would much rather be somewhere else. He seemed to studiously avoid talking to any of the Sri Lankans. John the work study engineer from Hunan was also taking the course and some of the Filipino work study engineers from the second floor office.

"Now can we start?" asked Michael after we had trooped up to the classroom and seated ourselves at the ramshackle desks. Following introductions and a long preamble he finally began the topic of work study. "Now, you know, work study is in fact having a very long history. Is anyone knowing when work study begins?" He spoke slowly, pausing after every word, the soothing inflectionless tones of the master hypnotist. Heads were already beginning to nod but not in answer to his question and he continued, "of course, work study you know... was being used to build those... you know those... how are they being called?" There was a long pause. "Pyramids. They are being called pyramids. Of course you know... the Egyptians are not having stopwatches," chuckled Michael.

An unwelcome tingling began at the back of my jaw

but I suppressed the feeling and tried to distract myself by looking round the room. John appeared to be studying his desk closely, presenting the crown of his head to Michael and the front of the classroom. His head jerked strangely as he unsuccessfully battled an emerging yawn. Matthew was less circumspect; he sat upright at his desk, mouth wide open yawning cavernously and audibly. I too felt the inexorable build-up of wave after wave of juddering yawn, each suppressed, but the next more powerful, break-out imminent.

"Oh, I should have said. This course on work study techniques will be involving two weeks of lectures followed by a three hour exam."

"Uh?" That woke me up fast as suppressed memories of assembling beehive frames and cleaning light fittings surged to the surface. "And then you will be doing a project using the work study techniques you have learned. But where am I talking to? Ah yes…"

It was going to be a long morning and I found my attention wandering again, until my leg started itching. I had received the first of many bites from one of the monstrous mosquitoes that shared the classroom with us. The creatures were everywhere. I saw them out of the corner of my eye, launching themselves off furniture and floating towards me; or they crawled up from under the desk and I discovered them sticking like drawing pins to the undersides of my hands and forearms.

"…but seriously you know. Much, much later there is an American gentleman who is called Frederick Winslow Taylor. He is going into the factory one day and, you know, this fellow Frederick Winslow Taylor is a very clever gentleman. He is noticing the worker is not working efficiently, he looks very carefully and he is thinking to himself, 'I can be eliminating the wasting of time and motion.' Then he is doing experiments and that is the origin of work study."

Michael spoke solidly for two hours until one of the Filipinos suggested it was time for a coffee break. Walking back to the office trying to clear my head I found myself talking to Gopal. With years of experience in the garment industry he had worked as a factory manager in Sri Lanka. He was surprised at my lack of industry qualifications but said work study was a good place to start, and added, "you really have to love work study to do it well. I love work study. Do you love work study?"

"No," I replied in my still numb state.

"You are joking," he replied wagging his finger at me. I was too weary to refute being the humourist he seemed to take me for.

The coffee break consisted of hot water from one of the thermos flasks kept at the front of the office. Charlotte was having a picnic at her desk with a whole range of snacks and dried fruit and dried meat in little packets spread out around her. Afterwards we shuffled back to the classroom.

"I am a tool," said Michael surveying the room with his unhappy smile. The morning lecture had not been the best known to man but I thought he was being hard on himself. Kudos to him though for some serious soul-searching while we were on our coffee break. It was the first morning after all and he could only improve with practice; never mind that Bart had described him as the top work study lecturer in

Southeast Asia. I was about to offer words of encouragement when he said, "you are a tool, you are a tool and you are a tool", picking out individuals with a pointing finger. By the time he had finished he had called everyone in the room a tool.

"Yes, we are all tools. Work study is the tool of management. We just give advice. We say, 'look, you can do it this way, or you can do it that way.' But we can't tell the management what to do."

Though relieved for his sake that Michael thought of himself as the right kind of tool I found the "us and them" attitude to management surprising. I thought Min and I *were* management and this was supposed to be a management training course.

"Now, before the break, we are learning about Frederick Winslow Taylor. But now you know for the work study engineer the most important article is this."

My jaw dropped open again, this time in disbelief as Michael proceeded to demonstrate with great deliberation how to wind a stopwatch. "We turn the button like this, and then like that, like this, and then like that. Now, the most important task for the work study engineer is using the stopwatch to time the operator performing the operation. We press this button to start the watch and this button to turn it off. Now always remember to wind your stopwatch. Now we practice the use of the stopwatch."

Could this possibly get any worse? Michael crossed the room and came back with a makeshift wooden board with coloured light bulbs attached to it. It looked like a DIY traffic light. So this was what he got up to in his long hours alone in the classroom.

"Now you must use the stopwatch to time for how

long the light bulb is lit."

He flicked a concealed switch and a red light bulb went on. There was a click as our stopwatches started and the sound of ticking filled the silence. The red bulb went off and a blue light came on and then a green, and then the blue followed by the red, and so it went on, and the sound of a petrol engine drifted up past the factory wall followed by a burst of laughter. There were shouts in Cantonese, a friendly greeting between a man and a woman, perhaps on the way back from the market. A mosquito whined past my ear and landed on my clipboard bringing my attention back to the empty columns I had neglected to fill in. Michael stood before us, immobile and infinitely patient, flicking switches and checking times against his stopwatch. I swiped at the mosquito which slid out of the way on an erratic path towards the window and freedom. I felt like jumping out after it, jumping into the boat in the garden and rowing frantically away.

It wasn't till late in the afternoon that Michael despatched us to the shop floor to practice timing the operators at their sewing machines. As usual I was struck by the constant buzz and hum of activity compared to the relaxed pace in the office and classroom. I hadn't been standing there long when I saw Rod Highbury walking towards me. Normally a visit from Rod or someone senior from Hong Kong would be preceded by announcements, gossip and frantic preparation, but no one had mentioned he was coming to the factory. He was casually dressed and wearing blue canvas boating shoes as if he had jumped off a yacht.

"How are you getting on?" he asked. I didn't tell

him I had just learned how to wind a stopwatch but spoke about my plans for learning more Chinese. Rod asked me how long I'd lived in Beijing and I explained it should have been a full year but we were evacuated home early due to the student demonstrations and subsequent events occurring on and around Tiananmen Square on June 4th, 1989.

"Ah yes, Tiananmen Square," he said.

In late May of 1989 I had been staying as an unofficial guest at the foreign students' dormitory of Fudan University, Shanghai, home to another 20 Leeds students from my year. Arriving in Shanghai or Beijing the first thing a student would do was to seek out friends from the course with a spare floor or bed to sleep on. It was often the latter as students travelled frequently and widely around China without too much concern for whether it was holiday or term-time. Initially the Chinese university authorities ignored or were unaware of these informal sleeping arrangements but in the uneasy atmosphere of the Tiananmen demonstrations they began to tighten up.

The foreign students' dormitory in Shanghai was in a separate compound even more isolated from local Chinese people than our university in Beijing. To the elderly guard who watched students coming and going we all appeared to look alike and he rarely stopped anyone at the gate to check ID. The guard sat in a reception area next to the only telephone in the whole building.

I had assumed the identity of an English friend, Chinese name Zhang Yuehan, who was often away but had recently come back from his travels. Shortly after his return, two phone calls were announced minutes apart and unknown to each other we both went down to answer using his Chinese name. Seeing two people within the space of a few minutes both claiming to be Zhang Yuehan but who didn't really look that much alike and were wearing completely different clothes was enough to alert the old man.

"How can there be two Zhang Yuehan?" he asked, not unreasonably, as my friend went down to answer his telephone call.

"*Mei you*," replied my friend, a useful negative expression, much in vogue in Beijing at the time, usually indicating the lack of whatever it was you wanted, or simply denial. But the old man was not to be put off and as he seemed serious about running to earth Mr Zhang's mysterious doppelganger, I packed my things and bought a ticket for the long train ride back to Beijing.

I hadn't been in Beijing for the build-up of the student demonstrations in Tiananmen Square but the atmosphere had been tense in Shanghai with surging crowds of protestors in the streets by day and students marching round the universities at night. The latter were accompanied by the sounds of smashing glass as students threw bottles across the streets in defiance of Deng Xiaoping, the Chinese word for bottle *ping* having the same sound as the last character in his name.

I left Shanghai on June 2nd and it seemed a good time to return as we had the impression that things were settling down in the capital even though the city was still under martial law. As the train pulled into Beijing railway station the next day I saw that soldiers had set up tents along the side of the railway track and were occupying railway carriages. The station was chaotic and the usual taxis were absent but I negotiated a lift back to the Beijing Foreign Languages Institute with some *getihu* entrepreneurs. They took me on a roundabout route along unfamiliar streets in the back of a battered vehicle, the Chinese equivalent of an old green Land Rover.

A notice on the door of the dormitory building at the Institute said that students were strongly advised not to go to Beijing city centre and in particular to keep away from Tiananmen Square. The bloody events that began that day on the evening of June 3rd and continued into the small hours of June 4th were widely reported by journalists at the time. I remained in the Institute during that period and only left later that day following a visit by a member of staff from the British Embassy. He advised us to relocate there for our own safety as amidst the chaos there was a growing concern that China was on the brink of civil war. He told us of a rumour that one of the Chinese armies might enter Beijing, and if soldiers came through the Institute there would be no way of ensuring our safety. A bus was waiting outside and it would take us to the Embassy but we had to decide fast; there was no time to pack anything and there wouldn't be a second chance.

Some Leeds students decided to stay but I didn't like the possibility (and in the unpredictable atmosphere of Beijing at the time it didn't seem remote) of being at the mercy of armed soldiers invading the campus.

On the ride to the British Embassy I saw burned out trucks at intervals and on one occasion we were forced to turn round and find a different route because of a road block of piled up vehicles. When we did finally arrive we discovered that those students who had remained behind had changed their minds. They now wanted to leave as well. They had time to pack some things and a friend arrived with some of my Chinese dictionaries. One of them was a "reverse" dictionary enabling a Chinese word to be looked up by the second character rather than the first. It was a favourite of mine and had been a present from Min. It was generous of my friend as he had less room for his own things; not only that, but as my room was locked he had climbed round the outside of the building to gain access by the window.

The British Embassy was swarming with activity and in an outside forecourt staff were hurriedly burning piles of documents. Dense smoke poured into the air. Though camp beds had been set up on the floor there wasn't space for the crowd of Leeds students and in groups of two or three we were assigned to different members of Embassy staff. James, our host, took us straight to a bar in the foreign diplomatic quarter where a group of English people were speculating wildly and some very confidently about the imminent civil war (which ultimately never happened). The bar had a colonial Evelyn Waugh feel about it and was removed from life as I had experienced it till then in China. None of the people there spoke any Chinese other than being able to order a beer, and that shakily.

Later James led the way back to his flat, an enormous apartment by any standards, and the sense of unreality I had felt in the bar increased all the more. The many kitchen cupboards were packed front to back with bottles of alcohol but there was no food to be seen. In the main room floor to ceiling shelves were filled with books on modern history and politics.

James said that he had to return to work and left us with the run of his flat, a fridge full of beer and a VCR player with tapes. We tried a couple of films but neither appealed and we went out to sit on the balcony to watch tanks turning and manoeuvring on a long straight road. The evening was quiet apart from the crackle of intermittent gunfire. Shortly afterwards there was a phone call from James. He said that if we were sitting outside we should come back into the building as there were reports of soldiers shooting at people on balconies.

The next day we were evacuated to Hong Kong from a desperately overcrowded and tense Beijing airport. People of all nationalities were hurrying to leave China. It came as a surprise to Min to learn that I was in Hong Kong and ever since she has referred to my tactical withdrawal from Beijing as *taozou* or "running away".

A day or two after that we were back at Heathrow and disembarking after a short talk warning us that we would be facing TV cameras and the press. It wasn't until six months later that I was able to return to Shanghai to marry Min.

As I began my Tiananmen Square anecdote Rod interrupted and said, "you've met Martin Goldman haven't you? He was there during the Tiananmen Square demonstrations. He got shot you know. Right here on his face." Rod pointed vaguely at his temple. "You can see the scar."

He strode off and stopped to inspect some

garments hanging on racks, his face reddening and his body language indicating dissatisfaction with what he saw. I prepared to time the operator I had selected but the basket beside her machine was empty and she was chatting to the worker behind her. I went back to the office for a break and a cup of warm water.

10 Rating

"Now we are going to practice rating," said Michael one morning some time later. The term was familiar to me from the work study course we had been sent on in Nottingham.

I was beginning to appreciate the common sense logic involved in garment making, after all a basic human skill dating back thousands of years. Unlike electronic equipment for example, where only an expert fully understands the function of each component, the garment assembly process was easy to grasp and visually satisfying as the colourful pieces came together in their journey from one end of the factory to the other. Start with a roll of cloth, take to cutting room, cut into shapes, bring to shop floor, sew pieces together, iron, place on rack and there was a finished garment assembled in front of your eyes. Sometimes it was like a scene from a Zhang Yimou film as swathes of bright colour dominated the shop floor, saturating the eye and vision.

There were business and sales aspects as well: produce sample for customer, agree price, receive main order, complete within time frame, freight finished garments, get paid, make big profit and be happy (the latter referring primarily to the mental wellbeing of owners, managers and directors). Large profits depended on low operating costs, hence Martin Goldman's search, head wound and all, for cheaper labour in China and beyond; or to borrow metaphors from the catering industry, the more of the cake the workers consumed the less there would be for the aforementioned persons to enjoy.

One function of work study is to determine a worker's rate of pay for completion of a single operation, such as sewing together the front and back panels of a garment. The pay rate is determined by using a stopwatch to time the operator completing the task while actual daily pay will depend on the total number of completed items.

Even I with my pre-Neanderthal grasp of maths could comprehend that if I was a worker it would be in my interests to take it easy when being timed on an operation. If I knew I could actually perform a task in 15 seconds but was timed at 20 seconds or greater I would have leeway for a more relaxing day, or if feeling motivated could try to earn more than usual. (On the other hand I might have a problem if the work study engineer determined that the operation should be performed in 10 seconds.) Some workers, on seeing the approach of a person with a clipboard and stopwatch would therefore ease up on the speed and move into cruise control.

But if only it were that simple. Frederick Winslow

Taylor or one of his successors had come up with the concept of "rating" to counter a worker slowing down deliberately or trying to manipulate the time produced by the stopwatch.

The rating is a percentage adjustment to the stopwatch figure based on the work study engineer's impression of how hard the person is working. Say the ideal rate of work or expected performance of a worker is 100% but the engineer believes that person only to be working at 60% efficiency, then the stopwatch time would be adjusted down by that percentage. So for example a stopwatch time of 20 seconds would become 12 seconds and this figure would be deemed the correct time for performing the operation. If the percentage adjustment was wrong due to a mistake on the part of the work study engineer, the worker would be unable to earn the anticipated amount for a day's work.

All workers are expected to work at 100% efficiency but how do you teach a work study engineer to recognize this ideal rate of work? Michael had the answer.

"Now, you know, I have ordered some rating videos from America, but still they have not arrived. We will be using these." He fumbled in his pockets and produced a pack of playing cards. "I would like you to give me a rating," he added, dealing the cards out into four equal piles.

I admired Michael's ability to make do with whatever he could get his hands on. A pack of cards was a stroke of genius though it was difficult to shake the feeling that we were at casino training school instead of a garment factory.

"Pretend I am a worker, operating a sewing machine, or ironing garments. Any operation will be doing nicely," he clarified.

I looked at Michael dealing cards like an automaton and tried to visualize him as a young woman sitting at a bench operating a sewing machine. A great leap of imagination was required.

"Now you must rate me according to your assessment of my skill, concentration and speed just like I am the worker. Remember that is how you perform a rating, on those three things, skill, concentration and speed."

Michael was not the most practiced of dealers and when he speeded up to 100% his technique resembled the game where you try to throw cards across the room into the bin, most of them usually ending up on the floor. Had we really been watching a sewing machine operator she would have put random stitches all over the garment and sewn herself into her own clothes.

"See, that is how it is being done."

A worker would have to be very skilled and fast to maintain the 100% mark. To get a rating of just 70% she would have to be working very efficiently and smoothly.

"Now I want you to spend the rest of the day practising time studies. You must go to the shop floor with a stopwatch, time and rate a worker performing an operation. Now always remember to wind your stopwatch."

Crossing the courtyard I pushed through the glass doors onto the shop floor and was enveloped in warmth and noise. Piles of fabric from the cutting room stood near the door and sewing machines stretched in clattering rows to the far end of the building where finished garments were pressed and packed. Fluorescent tubes flickered above the machines and radios blasted out Cantonese pop music. The shop floor was awash with the purples and blues of partially assembled garments spilling from plastic baskets onto the ground.

I chose to time study an operation called "overlock facing", overlock being a looping stitch that stops edges fraying and the facing an extra piece of material used on the front of garments for strengthening and appearance. The worker was a girl of about seventeen and she sat with a radio close to her seat. Most machine operators were in their late teens and early twenties and though some looked very young, sixteen was apparently the minimum working age.

There was so much background noise that I could only hear the radio when I was very close, but I recognised the cheery jingle from Guangzhou traffic news and learned that the roads were as blocked as ever. The operator looked up briefly and then quickly away. Work study engineers from Michael's course were positioning themselves strategically on the shop floor and I saw Gopal walking towards me.

"The workers are much better in Sri Lanka," he said shaking his head as he walked past. He stopped to talk to Pilla who was standing such that it was not apparent which individual out of a group of workers he was observing for his time study.

I turned back to the operator but felt intrusive standing there with my stopwatch and clipboard. Unlike some workers who managed a very blank look when they felt themselves under observation, the girl in front of me looked uncomfortable. She stopped what she was doing (attempting to cut some thread with a pair of blunt scissors), turned her head and adjusted her hairband. As she did so a ray of mid-morning sunlight shone through her hair and tinted it the faintest of reds.

My mind wandered to the popular Chinese hit "Descendants of the Dragon" written in the seventies by Taiwanese lyricist Hou Dejian and belted forth at tremendous volume by Stanley at Bart's karaoke evening. According to one memorable line of the song, descendants of the dragon (i.e. of China) would forever be those with "black eyes, black hair and yellow skin".

Looking round the shop floor I observed that the word "black" failed to adequately describe the varieties, tones and shades of Chinese hair. While some women had hair that really was coal black throughout, others had additional subtle natural shades of blue or burnt sienna reds, usually only visible against the light. Looking back at the operator I speculated as to what village she was from and about her prospects in life. Her skin wasn't really yellow either, more of a warm brown that set off beautifully a gold earring in her left ear.

"Any problems?" said a voice and I jumped into the air, startled to see Michael who had come up silently behind me and was looking at the unmarked paper on my clipboard. The operator glanced up at him, collected together the pieces she had completed and tied them into a bundle, which she then passed forward to the woman in front of her.

"They are not supposed to be doing that," said Michael looking impassively at the back of her head. "Now you know the object of work study is to maximise productivity. To maximise productivity in a garment factory, workers should be spending all their time on sewing and not wasting time with tying and untying bundles." He paused for breath. "Anyway, I will let you continue with your time study."

Michael moved away but the girl didn't resume her sewing. Instead she got up, stretched and walked off leaving me facing an empty seat. I heard shouts of "*sik fan ah*" ("time to eat") and in twos and threes the operators went off to the canteen for lunch.

It looked busy at the other end of the shop floor where three young men were pressing garments. I moved over and watched them as they worked. They rapidly folded and positioned the items of clothing as they ironed them. The ironing boards had a noisy vacuum device beneath them operated by a foot peddle which sucked the garment flat making it easier to iron. Bubbling and hissing water was fed to the irons along rubber pipes.

"Tell me," said Michael. I jumped again, once more startled by his silent approach. From the 1970s series "Kung Fu" featuring David Carradine I was familiar with the concept of walking on rice paper and leaving no footprints, a technique known in Chinese as "*qing gong*" or "light kung fu", and here was Michael demonstrating something very similar, in a factory of all places. I checked out his footwear: flat sensible soles but nothing too unusual.

"How are you rating that young fellow doing the pressing?" The presser's hands were flying, he was concentrating hard and he looked as if he was doing skilled work. I replied that I would give him a rating of 100.

"Oh no. You are too generous," he said. "Workers can pull the wool over your eyes you know. You see the way he is working? Unnecessary motion. He just is looking as if he is working very fast. Remember, a rating is not just about speed. It is also about skill."

This was adding a layer of subtlety beyond me. I thought the man looked as if he was moving very fast because that was exactly what he was doing, yet here was Michael saying it was merely illusion. I had a lot to learn.

Our lunch break started at half past twelve as usual and after two fried eggs (thanks to Min's intervention with the cooks), a bowl of rice and some greens I was ready to have another go at my time study. The workers had returned to the shop floor but the girl at the overlock machine had run out of work and was clipping her nails with a pair of sewing scissors. There was no knowing when she would start again so I went over to a second overlock machine on another line where the operator had a full basket of fabric waiting to be sewn.

Michael had told us that before starting a time study the first thing to do was to become familiar with the method the operator was using and decide on the "elements". When a new order came into the factory, particularly for a style of garment not produced before, line supervisors, senior work study engineers and production managers would work out how to produce the item based on the resources to hand. As with "assembling beehive frames", construction of the garment would be broken down into different operations. Each operation was then further divided into separate elements for the purposes of timing with a stopwatch. When making a collar, for example, the first element might occur where the worker picks up the two pieces of fabric, aligns them together and positions them under the foot of the machine ready to sew.

The intention behind work study is to make every aspect in the process measurable and for this to work each machine operator must follow an identical method. Although the operator on the second overlock machine was doing the same operation as the previous worker her technique was different. She lifted a bundle of fabric from the basket, placed it on her lap, untied the knot holding the bundle together and then picked up the individual pieces and ran them through the machine. She didn't have a pair of scissors but after each piece snapped the thread with her fingers. When she had finished she tied the completed pieces into another bundle and passed them forward.

The whole cycle took about twenty minutes and initially looked straightforward but she had no fixed method of working and sometimes did it one way and sometimes another. One of the Filipino work study engineers told me that some workers would deliberately add variety to their technique in order to confuse the person doing the time study. I didn't know if that was happening in this case but the constant changes made it hard to judge where one element stopped and the other began. It made timing with a stopwatch difficult. Eventually I thought I was familiar enough with her movements, including the occasional variation of technique, and was ready to begin.

I started my stopwatch and focused on the operator's fingers. Michael had said to watch the movement of the hands when finding the elements. Though I wasn't a natural at performing a time study, it was going well so far. I had filled in many rows of figures in the columns on my clipboard. But then with a loud shout another operator came over and interrupted the woman I was watching. She stopped working and a brief conversation followed. I thought it was interesting that they were speaking together in Mandarin and not Cantonese. They must both be from another province, most likely Hunan. I lost track of where I was, the numbers on my time study incomplete. I had also made another mistake. I had been concentrating so hard on timing her movements that I had forgotten to give her a rating. I couldn't do so now. It was considered bad form for a work study engineer to add a rating after the event.

On my next attempt she introduced a new method that I had not seen previously that afternoon and the time study fell apart again. She stopped tearing the thread with her fingers after completing each piece; instead she let the completed pieces remain connected in a chain until the cycle was finished and then pulled the bundle out of the basket and separated them all in one go. Where was I supposed to write that down? On my next attempt she was distracted by a bundle of fabric pieces that came sailing through the air and hit her squarely on the back of her head. "Aiyah," she shouted and jumped in surprise. She turned round to shout something at the culprit and I heard laughter from some of the other operators. More general chat followed, very sociable, but my figures were a mess.

Something new or unexpected popped up with every attempt I made, the minutes turned to hours and before long the end of the afternoon was in sight. One batch of fabric remained in her basket and I had a final chance to complete a successful time study. I set my watch ticking and focused my whole attention on the movement of her hands. On this occasion it was finally coming together. There were no interruptions from boisterous colleagues, the operator was in a hurry to finish and she introduced no unexpected variations. But suddenly the hands on my watch were no longer moving. Frantic shaking did not help and too late I remembered Michael's words, "now always remember to wind your stopwatch".

*

Another Christmas meal was announced, this one a Friday evening end of year celebration in Hong Kong. The second floor office staff (excluding John, Anne and Charlotte who weren't free to travel outside China) would leave by ferry from Lianhuashan late in the afternoon. Min and I, following Office Head Wang's proposed travel itinerary, would set off in the morning on the scenic route from Panyu to Guangzhou railway station, then go by train to Shenzhen, and take another train to Hong Kong.

We arrived at Guangzhou railway station late in the morning and made our way past dense crowds and long lines of people waiting on the forecourt outside. There was barely a gap to squeeze through and after descending from the taxi we took a roundabout, zigzagging route into the station building, avoiding the densest groups of waiting travellers and their piles of luggage. The building was grand but diminished by the mass of humanity swarming within it. The sheer volume of people obscured architecture, swamped stairways, blocked doorways and hid signs to platforms and ticket offices.

We pushed our way through endless queues that stretched and turned, and just when we thought we had reached the end, folded and twisted back on themselves, or bisected other lines causing cul-de-sacs and dead ends. People stood immobile as if they had taken root where they stood and crowds of peasants occupied wide areas of floor, asleep in groups across sacks and bales of goods. Their faces, framed by matted unkempt hair, were darkened by the sun to the colours of the earth: umbers, ochre and sienna. Wrapped in coarse shapeless clothing they were returning to an interior a world apart from Guangzhou.

I was pursued by beggars and a disembodied voice "thank you sir, yes, thank you sir, yes" spoke in my ear and followed me from the station forecourt until we stumbled finally on an office selling tickets to Shenzhen. The earliest was for 6.30 that evening and we resigned ourselves to arriving late in Hong Kong. Then by chance, the crowds having shifted, we discovered a second office previously obscured where we bought tickets for a train leaving within the hour.

A young Indian man with a briefcase popped up behind us and with a desperate, crazy smile asked, "this train Shinjin? This train Shinjin?". His suit was crumpled and his hair dishevelled, a wayfarer who had wandered the station for long days and nights. We directed him to the right queue but later saw him lost again, turning and bumping erratically through the crowds, knocked about like a ball in a pinball machine. Min went forward to intercept him and took him to the waiting room for trains to Shenzhen.

A guard on the door checked our tickets and suddenly we were inside away from the noise, heat and crowds. We sat on covered armchairs next to a palm in a large pot and I caught my breath, able to reflect simultaneously on the benefits of privilege and the four-character phrase meaning crowds of people, *ren shan ren hai* ("people mountain people sea"). A rough sprawling ink painting of the mountains in Guilin dominated the wall opposite. It was in the impressionistic *xieyi* style of freehand brushwork in which ink is applied spontaneously and loosely, allowing shapes and meaning to form as if by themselves. Another method of Chinese painting, known as *gongbi* takes the opposite approach and emphasizes outline, meticulous drawing and fine detail.

A loud whistle indicated that it was time to board the train and we entered a spacious compartment with large comfortable seats. We pulled away from Guangzhou and picking up speed cut through fields of smoking bonfires and groves of silver bamboo. In the distance were small hills with cultivated terraces and beside the track stretches of banana trees and sugarcane.

We rattled past blocks of flats and muddy pools, and a river where peasants in fluorescent colours shovelled sand into barges. Stations came and went, the landscape changed and we entered Shenzhen where the buildings were bigger and newer and there were crowds of young professionals. They wore suits and spoke into mobile phones.

Finding the Shenzhen border took time as the railway station was undergoing reconstruction. Outside, road works dominated every corner. Buildings were covered in bamboo scaffolding. Street names and signs were obscured by planks and boards.

After retracing our steps several times we eventually arrived at the border control area and joined the queue of travellers for Hong Kong. The official looked at Min's passport and pointed away with a dismissive gesture. I assumed that this was where our journey was going to end and had visions of Office Head Wang wagging his finger at us reprovingly over Min's lack of a green card. But it was just a case of being on the wrong floor, so we went downstairs and queued again in two separate lines, one for Chinese people and one for other nationals. Min was let through with no more than a passing glance at her passport and I joined her on the other side of the border. It seemed as if we had been worrying for nothing.

But on the Hong Kong side Min was ordered out of the queue by a brusque border officer. "This is just a transit visa," she said with a frown of irritation. "Where's your plane ticket?"

"What plane ticket?" asked Min.

"You're in transit. You must have a plane ticket."

It was unfortunate that the company personnel department had only managed to obtain a 48 hour transit visa for Min, valid for three entries only. As she was still travelling under a Mainland Chinese passport, albeit with a UK permanent residence stamp, Min needed a visa for any trip into Hong Kong. This wasn't a requirement for me as Hong Kong was a British colony at the time and my passport was automatically stamped for a year's stay.

While still in England we had asked the company personnel department to apply for a multi-entry visa that would allow Min to travel regularly between China and Hong Kong. The man summoned to the Hong Kong Immigration Office to verify and support Min's application was none other than Bart, to his surprise and ours, and the result was a confused general manager and a visa not conducive to frequent business trips to company head office.

"Where's your plane ticket?" repeated the border officer. "You're in transit. You must be flying to a second country. Let me see your plane ticket," she said again, the look of irritation entrenched.

"I'm not flying anywhere. I'm coming to Hong Kong for 48 hours and then going back to China."

"You've got the wrong visa. You can't enter Hong Kong unless you have a plane ticket to a second country. Where's your plane ticket?"

The two opposing points of view to the discussion at hand, namely Min saying that she didn't have a plane ticket and the officer saying that she must have a plane ticket, a variation of "oh yes I do, oh no you don't" fuelled a lengthy debate in which determination from both sides made up for lack of substantive content. Eventually the officer wearied, snatched Min's passport, unlatched the door to her cubicle and went off without a word of explanation.

Other border officers appeared and asked again about the non-existent plane ticket, as if Min had concealed it on her person all the time and was just winding them up for the fun of it. Half an hour later the original person came back, thrust the passport into Min's hands without a word, turned and stamped off.

We ran to catch a train to central Hong Kong and squeezed into a compartment crowded with people laden with goods and livestock. One shopper returning from China had bought quilts, vegetables and a live chicken stuffed into a tiny basket. We entered the New Territories and sped past tower blocks and skyscrapers surrounded by thriving trees, palms and bright green plant life.

Checking into our hotel we dropped off our suitcases and departed again immediately, taking the MTR (Mass Transit Railway) to the Sheraton Hotel. It had been a full day's travel but we finally arrived with a minute or two to spare.

The party took place in one of the Sheraton's banqueting halls where all cutlery, plates and serving dishes were said to be of solid silver. I didn't verify this but did notice that tables at the side of the hall were piled high with buffet food and exotic dishes I couldn't have named in any language. We had been told it was casual wear but some of the women looked dressed for the catwalk with unusual combinations of clothing, such as one who wore a leather jacket above a skirt like a ballerina's tutu.

At our table Michael told me with his unhappy smile that drinks had to be paid for at the bar. He unfolded a purple party hat and positioned it on his head. At each place were small metal objects that made a clicking noise when you pressed them between finger and thumb. Michael picked one up, inspected it carefully and clicked it in Pete's face saying, "ha, ha". Pete returned the compliment with a click of his own and an equally unconvincing "ha, ha" back.

"Look, they are having a whale of a time," said Michael, pointing at some of the Hong Kong staff. He and Pete had found the clicking objects to be of limited entertainment value but this was not the case with our local colleagues. They threw themselves around the room like demented crickets or crept up behind one another and clicked furiously at unsuspecting eardrums, roaring with laughter all the while.

Equally energetic were the Filipino women in attacking the buffet. Plates disappeared under pyramids of salad as they went up for third and fourth helpings. Most of them were of medium height down to petite but they could eat extraordinary amounts of food and remain slim. They came to the factory each day loaded with carrier bags of dishes cooked in advance by a maid employed by the company, as well as biscuits, bread, spreads and other snacks and drinks. Min learned that this extra food was covered by a company expense system that applied to all expatriates working in Panyu, including the two of us.

Min's discovery was well-timed as we were low on cash due to the rushed banking arrangements made on our first stopover in Hong Kong. Immediately on arrival I had applied for a Chinese visa and had to leave my passport at the China Travel Service for processing. This meant that we had to open a bank account in Min's name using her passport. We ended up with a highly effective savings scheme as Min was restricted from travel to Hong Kong by the visa issue, while I on the other hand could go there anytime but couldn't withdraw money from the account as it wasn't in my name.

A bellowing from the stage indicated the beginning of the evening's karaoke competition, and looking up I saw Johnson holding the microphone like a pumped-up teddy bear, treating us to a reprise of "Descendants of the Dragon". Not all contenders favoured the bold full-frontal assault; some were like professional performers with wispy voices and well-timed gestures, the clenched fist and the look of anguish. Then it was Bart again and I had the look of anguish.

The karaoke went on and on but finally appeared to be over, calm descending on the hall. Then it began again, solos giving way to a couple's competition, the contenders favouring slow romantic songs, gazing into each other's eyes and bowing deeply when finished. Once more it appeared to be over but started yet again, this time chorus groups for anyone requiring further punishment.

Bart had bought beer for everyone on our table not realizing that the majority didn't drink for religious or other reasons. His generosity didn't go to waste and after a while a reassuring stimulus-deadening wall interposed itself between me and the outside world.

Later Rod announced the results of the karaoke competition and read out the winning numbers of the raffle in Cantonese, a mastery of language greatly appreciated by the local staff. "You've won a camera," said Pete and I was propelled towards the stage. I aimed carefully at Rod's outstretched hand, took a swipe at it, connected, shook it heartily and returned to my seat. Pete looked at me sadly and said, "you must be a very lucky person, uh? I would like to win a camera." I said I had never won anything in a raffle before and Pete cheered up. A few minutes later Min's number was read out. She had won a top-of-the-range microwave oven. Pete shook his head resignedly.

The next day we returned to Panyu, leaving the microwave behind as the duty on it would have been as much as the item itself originally cost. Joan said that we could keep it in her office until we decided what to do with it.

We took the ferry back to Lianhuashan with the other returning staff but this time were among the first off the boat. I recognised the same woman who had meticulously written down the details of my Walkman and she looked at me suspiciously as I produced the new camera. We went through customs fast this time as she and the rest of Wang's staff were more interested in a man who was travelling into Panyu with three shiny red and white motorbikes. He had my sympathy.

11 Quality number one

The cool weather turned colder and the leaves in front of the hotel changed to yellow brown. Rows of pot plants at the entrance died overnight, killed by the sudden temperature drop. There was no central heating in the hotel and after work we warmed ourselves up with steaming hot baths. In the factory work study engineers showed a sudden enthusiasm for the warm and inviting shop floor. The canteen became an ice-cold vault and lunch was hurried and silent.

Standing outside the classroom we waited for Michael to arrive with the key and start another morning of lectures. It was raw and drizzly and the temperature hovered a few degrees above freezing. For the Filipinos and Sri Lankans it was a new experience and they shuffled and stamped in the chilly air. Pilla was lean and he stood shivering, his teeth chattering uncontrollably. Matthew pinched my coat between finger and thumb and asked whether I had bought it locally and if we ever had snow in England. When Michael appeared he was wrapped in a thick ski jacket. His nose was running and he trod heavily up the stairs towards the unheated classroom.

"You know," he said as he crossed the room. "I have been discussing with Lenny, and he will be arranging for heating. But for the time being we must be making do and tighten our belts."

"Now why do people work?" he asked a minute later, the question escaping him like a sigh as he leant back in his chair and withdrew into his jacket. It seemed rhetorical as if Michael was pondering his own circumstances, but then he said, "go on. I mean I am asking you the question why do people work? Why?"

"For money," said Pete.

"Yes. Good. But you know, why are people wanting to earn money?"

"So they can buy things," said one of the Filipino women.

"Yes. Very good."

"People are wanting to earn money so they can be keeping up with the Jones's. They are wanting a higher standard of living. What else? Why also do people work?" There was a long silence. "Advancement! People work because they are wanting advancement."

The joints of my fingers ached and I heard Pilla's chattering teeth behind me but Michael had forgotten the cold and was emerging from his jacket.

"Now we know why people are working. So therefore we can understand how we can motivate workers. How can we be motivating workers?" No one replied and Michael continued. "Rewards. Yes. We can motivate the workers by rewards. Okay. So what are the different types of rewards? Well, you know, we have material and social rewards. Who can give me some examples of material rewards?"

"Money," said Pete.

"Yes," said Michael. "Or, for instance, a luxurious car, medical benefits or company accommodation. These are all rewards of a material nature. Okay. We have looked at material rewards. Now, who can give me some examples of social rewards?"

"Money," said Pete.

"What? No. Money is material. By social we are meaning such things as promotion, recognition and appreciation. If people are not being appreciated they will not work well."

Michael's one-sided discussion continued until lunch time. His talk about motivating employees with company rewards and benefits, and more specifically company accommodation, made good sense to me. We had been living out of our suitcases in the Panyu Hotel for more than six weeks instead of the two Bart had mentioned when we first arrived. I telephoned him in Hong Kong to find out what was happening about the accommodation.

"Hey there," said Bart reassuringly. "I guarantee we'll have you guys in your own place in two weeks' time."

On the other side of the office Anne the production manager from Hunan Province was talking to a short man with tinted sunglasses.

Anne had been cheerful at our first meeting but her usual workday demeanour was troubled. She had originally been employed in a three year position as personal assistant and interpreter to Steve, the director of manufacturing. For someone who enjoyed speaking English it was the ideal job. It was also important work as Steve was in the process of implementing major changes in the factory. The only cloud on the horizon was a jealous Charlotte who had a strong infatuation for Steve and didn't welcome another woman monopolizing his time. Charlotte felt the same way about Steve's wife, fortunately out of harm's way in Hong Kong and ignorant of schemes afoot to supersede her.

Unfortunately for Anne Steve left China to work abroad after only one year and she became redundant. She accepted the alternative position of production manager but disliked it because there was no opportunity to use her language skills. Anne continued to practice English with native speakers whenever she could and was deep in conversation with the new arrival.

From his nondescript blue anorak and general dress sense, both similar to my own, I guessed him to be English. He looked as if he was in his early forties. Unlike me he had a booming cheerful voice that filled the office. He said his name was Bernard and when I asked the nature of his job he threw up his hands in a gesture of helplessness and said, "don't ask, don't ask". I didn't ask anything further and his face assumed a solemn expression. "Seriously now, quality consultant. Factory's been having some problems. Here to sort them out."

Rod hadn't been happy with the quality of the garments he inspected during his surprise visit to the factory. His solution was to launch Bernard at the problem, optimistically employing him on a short-term contract in the hope that the quality issues could be sorted out in a matter of weeks.

Lenny the factory manager was not jumping for joy at the arrival of Bernard; in fact he was nowhere to be seen. While Anne loved speaking to foreigners, Lenny was somewhere at the other end of the spectrum and would find working with Bernard a challenge to his fledgling social skills. If our arrival was anything to go by, Lenny might not even know of Bernard's appointment. It must have been a blow for him to have the chairman and owner of the company turn up unannounced and roundly condemn the state of the factory, ranting about low standards and poor quality on the shop floor.

Bernard had never been to China before, said he spoke no Chinese and had not been assigned an interpreter. But no matter; his cheerful can-do attitude and resolve to turn around garment quality was like an optimistic wind blowing through the dusty and forgotten upper reaches of the company canteen. He was also staying in the Panyu Hotel and after work we took him to one of the local supermarkets to equip himself with a bowl and spoon for the factory lunches. As we walked I asked him what he thought of the company.

"Brilliant!" he said. "Some excellent people at the top. Really nice guys. Amount that Steve knows about manufacturing is frightening. Then there's Martin Goldman. Great businessman, computer whizz kid too. And of course Chris Twist, real professional. I've worked for much worse companies than this."

We stopped at the main road outside the Panyu Hotel and watched the motorbikes and buses pouring past. Min had grown up in Shanghai and was an expert at judging the speeds of oncoming vehicles. She slipped across with perfect timing, leaving the two of us hoping for a more substantial break in the traffic. I would usually wait for a large group of people to build up and then cross with them as they overflowed into the road clogging up the passage of cars and other vehicles. Motorbikes were predominant and they doubled up as taxis, or were used as family vehicles by young couples with small children. It was rare to see anyone, adult or child, with a helmet.

As usual Shiqiao was buzzing with activity in the evening. The opposite side of the road was a mass of colourful neon advertising restaurants and karaoke. Near a taxi rank was a small unlit sign that seemed out of place. Stencilled white characters on a plain blue background said, "one couple must only have one child". It was gradually becoming concealed by newer neon and after dark would fade away to invisibility. The sign reminded me of the large red characters I had sometimes seen from train or bus windows, daubed along walls in remoter areas, political slogans from an earlier era.

In the supermarket Bernard bought coffee, skimmed milk and boxes of hot chocolate sachets. He had found the canteen water and earth problematic too and stocked up on pot noodle and bread. His eye was caught by bottles of spirits and wine behind a glass counter.

"You know I'd really love to try some Chinese wine," he said in English to the shop assistant with a wide grin. From past experience I could have told Bernard that female employees in a state-run department store don't generally respond well to British charm or gallantry, or for that matter any attempt at social interaction. Her face impassive she looked across at Min and asked in Chinese, "what does he want?" While not delivered in the warmest of tones it was a fair question as Bernard was leaning forward, elbows on the counter, grinning wolfishly at her and exclaiming with interest over the variety of wines on offer, but giving no indication that he wanted to buy anything.

The shop assistant turned her head away and looked back towards the book she had been reading. It lay face down on a stool next to a jam jar of slowly steeping tea leaves.

"Is he going to buy or not?" she asked Min again a few minutes later, ignoring Bernard who had both elbows on the counter and was making observations as to bottle size and the colour of the labels. I told Bernard that I didn't think the wine would be what he was expecting but he was determined to give it a try. Finally he bought a bottle and the shop assistant turned her back on us, resuming her book.

We moved away and as we did so heard Bernard's voice booming out. "Look at that!" I turned round and saw him back at the counter, one buttock perched on its edge. "Is that Champagne? That says Champagne doesn't it? How much is it?"

"25 RMB," said Min.

"That is cheap! Look at the size of the bottle. Got to give that a try."

Interrupted from her book again, the shop assistant stood up slowly, eyes focused on an imaginary object miles behind us, features blank and emotionless.

"I think she had the beginnings of a smile there," said Bernard to me as Min bought the drink.

We returned to the Panyu Hotel for our evening meal and in one of the smaller restaurants chose a table overlooking a flat green pool, the mirror-like surface broken only by occasional clusters of shiny water lilies.

Bernard enjoyed the fragrant chrysanthemum tea and when the pot was empty Min removed the lid and balanced it on the rim indicating that we were ready for a refill. Another custom in Cantonese restaurants is tapping the table with index and middle finger to thank waiters and waitresses when they pour tea or put dishes on the table. The custom originates from a story about the Qing Dynasty Emperor Qian Long who reigned from 1736 to 1795 (and was in power during the unsuccessful McCartney Embassy to China in 1792 by which England hoped to improve conditions for trade).

According to the story Qian Long enjoyed travelling incognito in the south of China with only a small entourage for company (rather like Rod on a surprise visit to the factory). On one occasion the Emperor, thoroughly immersed in his role as member of the proletariat, sprang up and poured tea for his aghast travelling companions. To prostrate oneself in the normal manner would have blown the Emperor's cover and aroused the imperial ire. On the other hand the gesture could not be ignored. A quick-thinking member of the group had the idea of expressing his respect and gratitude in a symbolic finger kow-tow; not the British two fingers such as Lord McCartney might have wished to offer the Emperor after the failure of his trade mission, but a discrete tapping of the table with the first two fingers to show one's thanks.

Min ordered sweet and sour pork for Bernard and I had a cashew nut stir-fry. We also had egg fried rice, fried steamed bread and fried noodles, washed down with Qingdao beer. The latter is named after the city in Shandong province where it is produced. The brewery was built by the Germans who occupied Qingdao in 1897.

"Tell me about losing face," said Bernard as we were eating. "I mean are the Chinese really worried about losing face or is that just a cliché? Am I going to have to be very careful what I say in the factory?"

I thought this unlikely to be an issue for Bernard, though the fact of his appointment, through no fault of his own, could be viewed as a loss of face for Lenny. Whether Lenny saw it as such would depend on his own psychology. Some Chinese people were relaxed about "face" while others were uptight. The latter, those individuals to whom face is important, i.e. those who "*ai mianzi*" (love face), are often encountered in social situations rather than at work. For example they will go to any lengths to avoid you buying them a drink or paying for a meal even if it is clearly your turn (ideal people to know for the backpacker on a budget). Life should be simpler in the factory where social status or standing would not be an issue during day-to-day work.

After the meal Bernard suggested we go to his room to try the bottle of wine he had bought. Clothes and belongings were scattered around the floor and on the table beside the bed was a half-read thriller and a

Spanish phrase book.

"I know. I have come to the wrong country," he said in reply to my comment. "When I was interviewed by Chris Twist he told me I'd be in Guatemala. That's why I've been learning Spanish. Never expected to end up in China."

I pondered this as Bernard poured the wine into two bathroom mugs. Advertisements on Chinese television had become more polished since my first visit, particularly those for beer, wine, and other alcoholic beverages. Typically a well-dressed individual would be sitting in a plush armchair, the camera zooming in on the look of extreme, almost reverential (often orgasmic) satisfaction as he or she sipped the drink. Bernard's reaction was quite the opposite. He grimaced when he took his first mouthful and started back in his chair until brought up by the back of the seat. I asked him why he had left England.

"To find work. Made redundant. We were at a management meeting and were told some cuts were going to be made. Said whatever happened, needn't worry, our jobs would be safe. Two days later I was out. Way they did it that upset me."

Bernard's face fell and he looked unhappy. Absently he took a drink from the mug and started again in surprise.

"Couldn't you get another job in England?" asked Min.

"No. Garment industry finished there. In terms of cost, how can we compete with factories here? Tragedy. England built the garment industry but now it's finished."

It was a melancholy topic, the decline of Britain's

industrial past, and I changed the subject by asking him what he thought of the factory.

"Complete mess and quality of the garments is abysmal. Lots of work to be done. Recession in the States catching up with them. Lot more competition now, can't get away with selling poor quality garments anymore. Quality has to be better. Amazing the rubbish they've been turning out and their customers have been accepting."

"Rod said they hadn't been affected by the recession."

"When did he say that?"

"When he interviewed us."

"Would do wouldn't he."

Bernard continued before I had time to reflect on his last comment. "In Sri Lanka I worked on quality with the factory manager over there, a really nice guy. Improved things no end. But had problems from Bart." Bernard's face assumed a look of weariness and he swept his hand down in front of his face as if brushing aside something unpleasant. "He would arrive at the factory with Rod and the others, walk about looking for problems with us following him. Used to go like this on the machines and lights." Bernard held up his index finger, wiped it across an imaginary surface and inspected it as if looking for dust. "No need for that. All part of the same team. I said to the factory manager 'not taking any more of this, following Bart around like a schoolboy'. So I went back to the office and sat there waiting for him."

12 The ghost boy is coming

In Michael's last lecture he had returned to the theme of motivations and, unlike Pete who remained tightly focused on the financial, I surprised him by my interest in the Chinese language and Cantonese. It was one of the reasons I had come to Panyu. Bearing in mind the discussion with Rod at the interview in London, I had not expected to find myself in an office where English was so predominant, great learning environment though it was for John, Anne, Charlotte and anyone else who cared to brush up on my mother tongue.

I was beginning to suspect that if I had told Rod my motivation for coming to Panyu was to learn the language of the Kalahari Bushmen he would have said "no problem", detailed the tribes in occupation of the factory garden and asked me how soon I could leave England.

To improve my Chinese Min and I visited one of the department stores in Shiqiao and bought a cassette recorder and some Cantonese tapes. These were designed for children (perfect material for language learners as the words were so clear) and featured stories about literary figures, politicians and famous inventors. According to the introduction on the back, frequent listening would "increase your child's wisdom and develop problem-solving abilities". Many of the stories were taken from ancient Chinese history, but some were about Mao Zedong and another concerned Lenin and a friendship he had developed with a beekeeper. There were also stories about Watt and Eddison and a Chinese inventor who discovered the saw blade through his observation of the teeth on a blade of grass.

Other tapes consisted of narrated dramatizations of American cartoons and I learned a vocabulary too specialised for daily factory life which included phrases like "if you touch my brother you're history!" The tapes were a good start with a wide range of vocabulary but I also needed a teacher and was keeping my eyes open for likely candidates. So far I hadn't found anyone.

One cold morning a few days later Michael greeted us with his usual "can we have a class now?" Sitting through weeks of his lectures had not been easy. I was holding it together, just, but the intellectual rigour of those sessions had eventually cracked Alfred the factory manager from Hong Kong. At the end of the previous day's class Pilla had been questioning him too closely about his experience in work study. Coming after a day of punitive Michael lectures this was too much and he shouted "enough, enough" and stormed out of the room. "These Hong Kong Chinese, they are so arrogant," said Pilla. Michael made a quiet comment and Pilla looked down like a chastised schoolboy. But he looked up again almost immediately with a lopsided smile.

Alfred was absent today, not for the first time, and Michael noted his truancy unhappily. Then he brightened. "Now I am pleased to say we have installed the heating." He pointed to three tiny fan heaters hanging from the far wall. Crossing the room, he switched them on. "Oh dear!" he said as the ceiling lights went off and we were plunged into semi-darkness, each of us suddenly alert to the mosquito menace lurking under the desks. "The fuse has broken you know. I will go and discuss with Lenny."

Half an hour later Michael reappeared. "You know. Lenny said the electrician is not in the factory. We will stop classes until we have heating. But you can start revising for your exam which will be at the end of the week."

I had learned that John was doing Michael's course for the second time, a mind-boggling concept, and as we walked back to the office I asked him whether he still had a copy of the old exam paper. Michael hadn't handed out any past papers for our revision but I didn't want to be completely unprepared. John dropped the paper on my desk later in the day, furtively, as he walked past where I was sitting. The questions looked straightforward but would involve rote-learning a large number of work study definitions. For the next week we were busy in the evenings after work committing work study terminology to memory.

By the day of the exam the heating had finally been resolved to Michael's satisfaction. He hovered near the three fan heaters. "Of course, you know, we had more problems. The electrician would not want to come. He did not come for a long, long time. But when he did come finally, you know, he has brought the wrong size plugs. So then he went away and we cannot find him again." Considering the man was an employee of the company this was all very relaxed and enlightened, though perhaps some plug identification training would be advantageous when he next elected to come to work.

"But now anyway we have installed the heating and all is ship shape and Bristol fashion you know," finished Michael. He stepped forward and cautiously switching on the heaters one by one, pausing after the click of each switch. There was a barely audible whirring noise. The engineer had done a heroic job but the classroom was large and airy with cracked windows and no door. It was fortunate that the worst of the cold weather would soon be over.

"Well, anyway, this is the examination," said Michael handing out the paper. "You can start now. You are having three hours."

*

"There's a message for you from Bart," said Charlotte one morning a week later. I assumed it to be the news that finally we would be moving out of the Panyu Hotel and into our own accommodation. The company used a DOS based e-mail system called cc:Mail running on the only computer in the second floor office, and most news entered the factory via this route. One or more of my colleagues had a communal spirit when it came to cc:Mail and treated private e-mails as a form of public bulletin board. My message had already been read and I reflected that perusing other people's mail was a great way to keep abreast of what was happening in the factory.

"We are undertaking a major upgrade of our inventory control system," said Bart's message. "The Panyu warehouse is the most critical asset we have to support this upgrade. As part of the upgrade I would like to conduct English classes for some of the staff at the warehouse. Would you be interested in giving lessons? If you are interested please contact Rupert Choi the warehouse manager."

Though the role of peripatetic English teacher hadn't featured prominently in my job interview, the chance to put distance between me and Michael's teaching was not an opportunity I was going to squander. When I mentioned Bart's proposal to Michael his unhappy smile became an unhappy frown. "No one is telling me anything of this," he responded and went off to telephone Bart.

Meanwhile I gave Rupert Choi a call to ask when I should start the teaching. There was silence at the end of the telephone. "What teaching?" he asked in a strong Cantonese accent and, unsurprised that Bart had left someone else out of the loop (which was in actual fact more of a straight line between two individuals, Bart at one end and me at the other) I explained the plan to teach English to the warehouse staff. Rupert was frank concerning his colleagues' English abilities. "Dey dong no nudding, dose guys. Dey dong even no de ABC."

The habit of pronouncing an English "th" with less than strict precision is not unique to Cantonese speakers. In fact many a young Englishman or woman, particularly those inhabiting the nation's capital, may pronounce "nothing" as "nuffink", "with" as "wiv", "thick" as "fick", and so on. A further variation may be observed among Chinese speakers from Shanghai or other parts of China who pronounce "th" as a "z" sound, resulting in "zey" and "zat" in place of "they" and "that".

Rupert remained unenthusiastic about the proposed English teaching but we agreed that I would visit the warehouse to give a trial lesson in two days' time. I told Michael about the plan and he said, "oh no, but we are having a class then, you cannot be doing that". When it came to the timetable for his lectures, Michael played his cards close to his chest. He would materialize silently at random times and ask "can we have a class now?" To my knowledge no one had ever replied in the negative and as far as Michael was concerned it was a good system. For the rest of us it made planning a hit and miss affair. Michael was looking very unhappy and went off to telephone Bart again so I spoke to Rupert and re-arranged the date.

I thought Michael might be suffering from a variant of cabin fever, "factory fever" perhaps. He seemed bored and irritable, quick to take up arms against any perceived threat to his authority. Much as we were a captive audience to his teaching, he himself was a captive of the factory, isolated in his classroom during the day and returning at night to share a flat with Lenny and other colleagues with whom he had little rapport.

It wasn't till several days later that I climbed into the company minibus for my first trip and English lesson at the Panyu warehouse. Warming rays from the sun made the bus a pleasant drowsy temperature and I sat listening to the sounds of laughter and shouting from the kitchen. The gardener was watering a collection of bonsai trees and beyond the factory wall cyclists and motorcyclists pottered past. The structure we had seen from the third floor on our first day in Panyu was taller. It rose from the dust in layers of reinforced concrete and steel. Workers in brightly coloured clothes scrambled like ants across its surface, pushing heavily loaded wheelbarrows, climbing up and down bamboo scaffolding.

Ah Ling the driver jumped on board, nodded a greeting at me and reversed full speed out of the factory gates into the oncoming cyclists and other traffic, forcing them to stop suddenly or break like a wave around him.

One of the most characterful forms of conveyance I saw all over Panyu was the versatile *shoufu tuolaji* "hand tractor" or "two-wheel tractor". These vehicles were used predominantly for transporting goods but could also power agricultural machinery. Comprising two wheels only, a powerful engine and operated by a clutch system at the end of a pair of handlebars instead of a steering wheel, they looked like a small version of the front half of an ordinary tractor without the cab and back wheels. Coupled to trailers of varying sizes they were the tugboats of the muddy tracks and pot-holed roads around Panyu and hauled loads many times their own weight and size. Usually the driver was exposed to the elements but some models had a small roof for protection from the rain.

Hand tractors chugged and spluttered along at the pace of a fast cyclist and in speed could not compete with Ah Ling who cut across their path as he lined himself up on the road outside the factory.

There hadn't been a significant rainfall since our arrival and the water in the nearby pools had receded leaving an expanse of black mud. Opposite were shops and fruit stalls. Small wooded hills and dusty trees formed a backdrop behind them. We continued along the road as if returning to Shiqiao but then turned left and set off into new territory. After passing rows of grey buildings with more stretches of mud in front and stagnant, rubbish-filled streams, the road widened, emptied of other traffic and cut away through scrub land.

We followed an endless factory wall, whitewashed and stark, topped with broken glass. In the distance clusters of graves were dotted among green trees and a solitary pagoda stood silhouetted against the sky. Driving further we passed a factory complex called the South China Tyre and Rubber Company. It stood alone, the only building for miles around. Beyond its walls heaps of bricks and bags of sand were strewn among the tangled grass and weeds. Blue-jacketed peasants sprawled among them.

A sudden patch of greenery came into sight and I saw a man squatting beside a muddy pool holding a water buffalo loosely by a tether. Ancient trees clamped to the earth by as many roots below as there were branches above grew on raised banks on either side of the road. Further along we rattled past a group of houses where yellow flowers stood on a window sill and were bright against the dull greens and greys of the landscape.

We drove between rows of pale trees that lined the road and were either dead or dormant. Then we descended a hill and travelled past coal heaps and quarries with crude stone smashing equipment, wheels and rubber belts jumping and turning, grey dust flying, rocks crunching.

A cluster of new houses appeared, each several stories high with flat roofs and balconies decorated with flowers. For a while we followed a large river that snaked into view beyond a bend in the road. Hundreds of ducks swam on its surface among unloading boats and barges. Nearby, small hills were being removed piece by piece, the earth disemboweled. Huge vehicles shifted the red soil, bumping round the Martian landscape.

Ah Ling had an intercom in his bus for communication with the factory and the warehouse. Static crackled as he turned it on and announced my arrival. *"Guai jai lai le! Guai jai lai le!"* "The ghost boy is coming! The ghost boy is coming!"

Our eyes met in the mirror and he looked embarrassed. "You don't mind, do you?" he said to me in Cantonese. "You're too young to be an old ghost so you must be a young ghost, a ghost boy."

Whether he was asking if I objected to the lack of seniority he had accorded me in ghost hierarchy, or if it was the term "ghost" itself I might find disagreeable, I did not pursue as I was more concerned that we were travelling at considerable speed in a forward direction while Ah Ling had turned fully in his seat to face me at the back of the bus, and was apparently waiting for an answer. Had I taken time to fully express my views on the topic there would likely have been two ghosts in the vehicle instead of one and Ah Ling might have been better informed to answer the question himself.

After a few more minutes' drive he pulled up at a raised loading area in front of a green building surfaced with countless chequered tiles. Through a pair of sliding steel doors I saw row upon row of cardboard boxes and packages stacked neatly beside numbered pillars stretching back into the gloom. There was no sign of Rupert or any of his staff and I went to look for the back door.

Climbing down from the loading bay I walked past another warehouse, this one under construction and covered in bamboo scaffolding. Nearby were the usual items that accumulate on building sites the world over: wheelbarrows, tools, heaps of broken bricks and bags of cement. Less usual was the tumble-down shack, clothes and bedding hanging out to air and a group of labourers sitting around a fire. I assumed them to be migrant workers from one of the poorer provinces in China. As they caught sight of me and stood up for a better look, I found the back entrance to the company warehouse. Walking down a short corridor I emerged into an office area. It all looked very new as if the floor had just been put down and the walls painted a day or two before.

A small baby-faced man wearing baggy jeans and a blue sweat shirt, the latter stained around the collar, introduced himself as Rupert Choi the warehouse manager. We eyed each other in silence.

"Well. How can I help you?" he asked without much warmth, and then added, "de worker here, dey wery busy, not much spare time learn English".

Rupert was wary of me and I explained that the plan to teach English to his staff had originated with senior management in Hong Kong. He asked me for more details and though I was used to Cantonese accents it took me a while to work out that when Rupert said "butt" he wasn't referring to anyone's backside but to the general manager Mr Bart "Butt" Ryder himself. I tried speaking to Rupert in Cantonese but he preferred English. We went round in circles discussing how often I should come to the warehouse. The times convenient for me were not convenient for Rupert's staff; those convenient for Rupert's staff were not convenient for me. Then Rupert mentioned another company bus that travelled back from the warehouse to Shiqiao every evening and we were able to arrange some times that suited everyone.

"What will you teach today?" asked Rupert.

I asked what would be useful for their work. He thought for a moment. "Maybe some names of de people in Hong Kong. Yes. Someone from Hong Kong make de telephone call, dey dong know who it is. Den maybe teach dem some colours, den day of de week." Rupert's face fell. "But dey dong even know de ABC."

"How about I start with the ABC?"

"Yes. Wery good. Yes, and den you can teach dem how to read de packing form."

"And how about lessons for you Rupert?"

"No. I too busy." He pointed at a young man sitting at one of the desks nearby. "De boy will show you de conference room where you can teach."

The conference room was well-suited to teaching

with a clean and tidy if Spartan appearance. There was a whiteboard on one wall and no windows to distract either teacher or students. The door opened and my new students entered. Their ages ranged from late teens to late twenties and maybe even early thirties. I would have found it difficult to guess precise figures. Chinese people had the same problem with me. The first time I went to China as a student I was 21 and more than once my age was guessed as 15. Three years older in real time I was even younger in the perceived time of other people's eyes. Some of the women in the factory had decided I was 12 and well below the legal age of marriage in China. This fuelled gossip and speculation as to the relationship between Min and me. According to the old women who packed garments at one end of the shop floor, we were brother and sister, even though Min was Chinese and I quite clearly not a descendant of the dragon.

I spoke some simple English to the warehouse staff sitting in front of me but they didn't appear to understand so I changed to Mandarin. I told them my Chinese name, *Lu Si,* a transliteration of my English surname. By coincidence the Cantonese pronunciation of this name is a homonym of the word for teacher *lo see*. After a few jokes on the theme of calling me "teacher teacher" (*lo see lo see*) they settled on calling me *laoshi* which means teacher in Mandarin.

Despite Rupert's pessimistic assessment most of the students had a rough idea of the English alphabet. Two or three knew it almost perfectly and some of the others knew the beginning and end but faded in the middle. I wrote the alphabet on the board and we went through the letters together. "N" and "l" caused problems. Many Cantonese speakers make no distinction between these sounds and the basic Cantonese greeting for "hello" can either be pronounced *"nei ho"* or *"lei ho"*. Unlike English, changing from an "n" to an "l" sound doesn't necessarily change the meaning, particularly if the tone is correct.

I wrote the words "no" and "low" on the board and read them out several times pointing to each as I did so. Then I read one out at random and asked them to say which it was. Half the class could manage if they thought very carefully before answering. It reminded me of the problems I had trying to distinguish Chinese tones.

One woman called Li Sanmei (age anywhere between 20 and 35) could understand Mandarin but couldn't speak it and had a very strong local Cantonese accent. The other students helped communication between us by translating her Panyu Cantonese back to Mandarin. Li Sanmei couldn't distinguish between the words on the board and instead watched my face intently for clues to help her guess the answer. She turned the exercise into a game of poker and I tried to out-bluff her by reading the same word several times with a neutral expression. "What are you looking at him for? Why don't you listen instead?" said one of the others.

The ride back to the hotel was in a faster vehicle than the usual minibus. We had a new driver and he looked about 12 as well, wearing a large pair of trainers, jeans, black T-shirt and sunglasses. He drove fast and I spent much of the journey in free fall as we jolted over bumps in the road or swerved past slower traffic beeping madly. Cantonese music blasted from two speakers in front of the vehicle and the bus was filled with shouting and joking between the driver and his friends. As I sat bouncing around on one of the back seats I reflected that this had been the most enjoyable afternoon's work since arriving at the factory. For an instant, like a sudden view of the China everyone expects to see, framed against the orange sun I saw the roof guardians on a traditional Chinese gateway. It was just for a second as we zoomed crazily past like a vehicle in a cartoon, leaving a trail of noise, music and dust.

13 Where is that fellow Alfred?

One day without any big fanfare Michael casually mentioned that we had all passed the work study exam. The paper from John had helped considerably as Michael set exactly the same questions again, the only difference being the date at the top of the exam sheet. Well on the way to becoming a company-qualified work study engineer I could finally put assembling beehive frames and cleaning light fittings behind me.

Michael's lectures were almost over and all that remained was the completion of a two week project. The aim was to analyse processes in the factory using work study techniques and to suggest improvements in working methods.

For the project Min and I worked with Alfred from Hong Kong. He told Min that he had joined the company two months before to work as a factory manager in the Philippines. Instead he found himself on Michael's work study course. Bart's response to any new employee was to direct them to Michael's classroom. It functioned as an effective holding pen while the company decided what to do with them.

We only saw Alfred intermittently during lectures as following his outburst of temper with Pilla his attendance had been sporadic. The absenteeism was a thorn in Michael's side and his "can we have a class now?" was often followed by "where is that fellow Alfred?" a frown of annoyance creasing his forehead. We occasionally bumped into Alfred in the office or on the factory floor. Once I found him with a cup of green tea at a machine chatting to a group of workers. Another time he sat surrounded by colourful pieces of fabric making himself a pair of boxer shorts, fully absorbed and working like a craftsman.

While this activity was calming for Alfred the effect on Michael was less therapeutic and did little to ease his factory fever. Arriving to let us into the classroom he would perform a quick head count and noting Alfred's absence with a grim pleasure would interrogate us as to his last known whereabouts. Leaving us waiting for his return Michael would head off at a brisk walk (the equivalent of a sprint for him) in the direction of the last known sighting, whether it be shop floor, cutting room or even the factory garden. Often Michael's intelligence was bad and half an hour later he would return saying, "you know, I can't find that fellow Alfred anywhere. Where did you say he is being?"

Then someone would suggest another location and Michael would set off again. Small and about the size of the average operator, Alfred was difficult to spot, particularly if he was head down at one of the machines adding to his wardrobe. Hiding in plain sight in this manner brought to mind lines of strategy from the Art of War by Sunzi: "if near seem far, if far seem near" (*jin er shi zhi yuan, yuan er shi zhi jin*) or to give a more interpretive translation, "when near feign that you are distant, when distant feign that you are near". Commentators sometimes make a case for applying the Art of War to the business environment and seeing the game of wits unfold between Michal and Alfred I saw their point.

Sunzi was a military strategist and contemporary of Confucius living around 500 B.C. during the Spring and Autumn Period of Chinese history (770-476 B.C.). Written in succinct classical Chinese but accessible to modern readers with the help of explanatory notes, Sunzi's manual on war is an oft-quoted classic. Caution may be needed in applying the Art of War to a business setting, however, as some content is specific to warfare and the military, i.e. fighting in the mountains, crossing marshes, attacking cities and killing generals. Other sections contain tactics that would be more suited to individuals running organized crime groups rather than to legitimate businesses. Chapter 12, for example, is devoted to arson or "Attacking by Fire" and lists the five methods of doing so, the first of which is *huo ren* "burning people".

Less brutal but no less intense was the pursuit between hunter and quarry, Michael and Alfred, that played itself out across the varied backdrop of factory garden, concrete staircases and lines of sewing machines on the three shop floors. Alfred was often a step ahead and I thought Michael might have benefitted from the wisdom of the "36 Strategies", that other major classic of Chinese military thought and warfare. While Sunzi's Art of War can be dated to a specific period of history, my copy of the "36 Strategies" was vague about dates, stating that the stratagems and ruses contained within it were probably collected into book form sometime in the Ming or Qing dynasties, a period covering around 600 years. Alfred's technique of disguising himself as a machine operator was a textbook example of Strategy No. 21, "golden cicada casts off its shell"; the one place you wouldn't look for a former Hong Kong factory manager would be sitting anonymously among a crowd of female workers.

Michael didn't quite have the hang of Strategy No. 13, "beating the grass to startle the snake". He would enter the shop floor dramatically by one set of doors and flush out Alfred who then exited at the far end, Michael failing to notice the speedy departure of his quarry. To use Art of War terminology it was the "terrain" that was against Michael on these occasions as the two sets of doors provided a constant and frequent escape route for Alfred. The same concept is covered in Strategy No. 22, "shutting the door to catch the thief".

It became a dreadful game of hide and seek with dire consequences for Alfred when occasionally collared by Michael, who it had to be said, though lacking in strategy, almost made up for it with his rice-paper walking and the extraordinary silence with which he could materialize in different corners of the factory. Such were the rules that if Alfred were successfully run to earth he would return without protest to face torture behind enemy lines: "now we can finally be starting the class".

But the game wasn't always predictable. One morning Michael announced the start of lectures in his usual way but on arrival was visibly out of breath and shaken. The pursuit had taken the two players to the very gates of the factory and there Alfred had broken the rules. "I just saw that fellow Alfred getting into a taxi cab at the factory gate," he said panting as his breathing returned to normal. "I am calling loudly but he cannot hear me. How can he not hear me?"

Soon, however, the Alfred thorn was removed from Michael's side. A few days into our project Alfred told Min he was going to Sri Lanka that afternoon as Rod wanted him to look at some factories there. We would miss him. Alfred was knowledgeable about the garment industry and had been patient in answering Min's questions about the work processes we were analysing for the assignment.

As it was only two of us we picked a simpler garment for our work study project, a red chemise and the nearest thing to lingerie I had seen yet. We had to time-study all the different operations required to make the chemise and then do a scale drawing showing the positions of machines, pressers and examination boards. While assessing the number of operations involved I became aware of Michael wandering up and down the shop floor between the lines of operators as if looking for someone. Eventually he came over to where we were standing and stopped beside us. "Oh you know," he said. "I cannot find Alfred anywhere. Where can he be?"

I explained that he was on his way to Sri Lanka but Michael thought this an example of English humour.

It did not surprise me that the great communicator Rod had not thought to tell Michael that Alfred would no longer be one of his students. I repeated what we had learned earlier in the day, that Alfred was leaving Panyu and would not be returning to the factory.

"I will find him. I am having it up to here with him. I will report him to Lenny."

He wandered off still searching and we began our time studies. Fourteen different operations were needed to make the chemise, including pressing, examining and packing. The garment consisted of front and back panels and thin shoulder straps. Each of the latter started off as one long piece of fabric about an inch wide. After being fed through a sewing machine attachment called a "folder" the fabric emerged as a narrow band.

I asked the old woman operating the machine if I could measure the length of strap she was about to feed through the machine. She had gold hoop earrings, hair pulled into a tight a bun and a face deeply lined by the sun. I spoke to her in Cantonese and she reacted to my question with a look of fright. An amused crowd of machine operators and line supervisors formed round us and I repeated my question. Someone said to her, "he's speaking Chinese", and she finally understood what I was saying. The majority of people in the factory had never spoken to foreigners before and were surprised to find that, once over their initial shock, they could understand what I was saying.

A lot of Mandarin was spoken in the factory by workers from provinces other than Guangdong. These people were far from home and understood less Cantonese than I did. Despite the number of

Mandarin speakers in the factory I still wanted to improve my Cantonese and eventually found a teacher. His name was Xiao Song and he worked in the quality department in the third floor office directly above us. The problem with Xiao Song wasn't so much that he was cripplingly shy but that he couldn't speak Cantonese.

I was unaware of this to start with and progress seemed rapid because I found it so easy to converse with him. Cantonese spoken in Panyu and to a lesser extent Guangzhou differed in pronunciation from that of Hong Kong. The language spoken by Xiao Song didn't resemble any of these regional variations and after a week or two I realised that he was easy to understand because his version was basically Mandarin with a heavy Cantonese intonation. He was originally from Shanghai but had lived locally for quite a few years and picked up his own version of the language. It was like trying to learn French from an English person speaking with a comedy French accent but no actual words of French. I finally discovered how little Xiao Song knew when I needed help with one of my Cantonese tapes, and found that all the words I didn't know he didn't know either. It was one of the tapes designed to "increase your child's knowledge". Unfortunately it showed up Xiao Song's lack of knowledge and I wasn't convinced by the way he shook the tape recorder around and looked at it accusingly, suggesting there was something wrong with the sound.

In return for Xiao Song teaching me a version of Cantonese spoken by a demographic of one individual I had agreed to teach him English, and because he was so desperate to learn I didn't feel able to stop the arrangement. Eventually I just taught him English and we forgot about the Cantonese. We did the lesson during siesta time in the third floor office. Heads twitched awake as Xiao Song repeated after me "please can I have my red umbrella".

But finally I thought of Charlotte. It brought to mind the Chinese 14 character phrase about wearing out iron shoes looking everywhere for something but finally finding it right in front of you. Her Cantonese was beautifully clear and in return for English lessons she helped me with Cantonese on Tuesdays, Thursdays and Saturdays after work.

Min hadn't spoken any Cantonese since the age of ten but was fluent soon after our arrival and only needed to learn specialist garment industry terms. Charlotte taught us the Cantonese for common sewing operations such as "overlock facing, hem facing, set pleats at waist, insert front and back straps, insert two labels and tack facing", and the names for the different types of stitch, "top sew, bluff stitch, overlock stitch and lock stitch". By now I knew what they all looked like.

Charlotte had been responsible for almost all the translation work in the factory and gave us a reference manual she had translated into Chinese for the machine operators. It had been put to one side and forgotten about but now her work wasn't wasted. It described the different components of a sewing machine, how it functioned and how it should be maintained. It wasn't riveting bedtime reading but helped Min and I with the knowledge and vocabulary needed to communicate in the factory.

*

That evening all the restaurants in the hotel were full. The main one was booked for a wedding, and Min, Bernard and I went in search of another eating place. Some people from the wedding party were hanging bright red strings of firecrackers at the front gate of the hotel and we stayed to watch them set off. The noise was thunderous, especially the final explosion that echoed round the courtyard and left our ears ringing. We walked past heaps of burnt paper littering the ground like empty cartridge shells. Out on the street I was accosted by a crowd of unkempt, grimy children who pulled at my coat and asked for money. As we continued they fell away one by one and returned empty-handed to a man standing in a nearby doorway.

In one of the gleaming new shopping centres we found a place to eat, a restaurant that was also part night-club and karaoke bar. Sawdust from recent carpentry work in the corridor had yet to be swept up and the furnishings looked as though they had been unpacked the day before. The chairs gave off a strong smell of clean new fabric.

A waitress came over to our table and spoke in English. Originally from Hunan Province she had recently finished a two year language course and was employed to take orders from foreigners who couldn't speak Chinese.

In the past looking for work in other parts of China was almost impossible due to a strictly enforced *hukou* household registration system. Without a local residence registration a person couldn't work in a state job or enjoy a state pension, healthcare or other benefits. One of the few legitimate ways to move to a different part of China was to find someone in that area who wanted to move to your current location and swap *hukou* with them. These days the *hukou* system was less restrictive as people could find work in other cities with private companies independent of the state. For an employee such as John it didn't matter in the short term that his *hukou* was outside Panyu because the company provided accommodation and a salary high by Chinese standards.

We ate our "Italian noodles" (spaghetti) and toasted cheese sandwiches without talking as music blasting from speakers all around the room was deafening. There was a brief respite after the sound system was turned down and the strobe lights stopped spinning. Then the television screens, numerous and difficult to avoid no matter where you sat, showed a violent film from Hong Kong. Diners roared with laughter as a man was shot at point blank range in the testicles while beneath the screens toddlers scrambled over the furniture and bar stools. After the film the karaoke set appeared but for once the singer was a professional and he danced with energy and rhythm to a popular song from Hong Kong.

As we came out onto the street we heard the screech of skidding tyres followed by a crunch as a man on a motorbike crashed into the side of a taxi. His bike was a wreck. Half of it was jammed under the car but he pulled himself out, limping badly. It was the second accident we had seen in one day. In the morning a young woman went over the handlebars of her bike and landed on the road in front of the company minibus. Ah Ling shouted abuse at her, stabbing at the windscreen with his index finger. She picked herself up with a stoical look and ignoring him brushed the dust from her jeans.

When we returned, the Panyu Hotel was still busy with the evening's wedding banquet. The hotel and grounds had been quiet on our arrival several months previously but now were flooded with guests from other areas of China. Sociable groups sat in their pyjamas with bedroom doors wide open, chatting volubly into the small hours. We were often disturbed by people ringing the bell or knocking late in the evening. When I opened the door they jumped back awkwardly as if they really had seen a ghost. The telephone often woke us at all hours of the night.

"Wei?" I would say, picking up the phone, my voice croaking sleepily.

"Wei?"

"Wei? Who d'you want to speak to?"

"Wei? Who are you?"

"Who are you?"

"What work unit are you from?"

"What work unit are you from?"

"Are you Old Zhang?"

"No. I'm not old Zhang."

"Aren't you Little Li then?"

"No."

"Third Uncle?"

"No. I think you've got the wrong number."

Slam! The phone would be put down without a word. It happened frequently and eventually Min arranged for hotel reception to block out all night time phone calls. But we couldn't do anything about our fellow guests knocking on the door at odd hours and I phoned Bart to find out what was happening about the company accommodation. I received his usual guarantee that we would only have to wait another two weeks. Initially I had been pedantic and overly literal, taking "two weeks' time" to mean 14 days or in the region thereof. Now I realized that Bart had a flexible approach to language and, depending on context, many meanings could be ascribed to that deceptively short time period such as "sometime in the future", "never" or even "not now, I'm busy".

14 You speak Chinese no?

The project continued and with the time studies for the chemise completed we set to work on a scale drawing of the factory. Where was Hercules when you needed him? It should have been an easy task but there were no measuring tapes. Michael suffered from constant attrition in all his things; items were missing, hadn't turned up when they were supposed to, or when they did, were broken and unusable. The measuring tapes had disappeared from the store room ("oh, I am giving them back there") and all we had to measure the considerable area of the shop floor was a twelve inch ruler. As I crawled around I received some odd looks from the women operating the sewing machines. With my backside on the ground, in the air, and always in the way I didn't cut a dashing figure, but after two hours I had mapped out most of the floor with the location of the various machines marked in place.

I went back to the office to join the other work

study engineers for a coffee break. Like Min and I the Sri Lankans didn't have their own desks and we all congregated round a large oval conference table at the back of the room. Bernard was sitting nearby making a telephone call, nodding occasionally and looking thoughtful. During these breaks I would have some odd conversations with my Sri Lankan colleagues. They spoke English fluently but with different stress or emphasis that could make communication between us hard work, such as their habit of using the word "no" to mean "yes". Matthew touched my arm and said, "you speak Chinese, no?"

"Yes," I said. "I do."

"You know Chinese words, no?"

"Yes."

"No?"

"Yes. I can speak Chinese."

"You help me, no?"

"Yes. I'll help you."

"No?"

"Yes."

"Please. How to say "rice" in Chinese? How to say "egg"? And how to say "receipt"?"

Matthew said that they were staying in the Hotel Miramar on the other side of Shiqiao and that the staff there couldn't understand English. Incomprehension was mutual, or to use the Cantonese phrase it was *gai tong aap gong* "chickens talking to ducks". Pilla and Gopal were vegetarians and often ended up with no more than a bowl of rice for their evening meal. This explained their increasingly gaunt appearance as the weeks went by. Min added other basic foods and dishes to Matthew's list, Chinese in one column and

English in another so that in future they could point at what they wanted.

Bernard came over and said, "been on the phone to Hong Kong. Martin Goldman let go. Don't know why. Maybe cost too much. Maybe no use for him at the moment. Or personality clash. Who knows?"

I saw worried faces round the table. The "letting go" of such a senior person in the company was disquieting.

After the break I went back to the shop floor for the next stage of the project. Michael had asked us to indicate on the diagram the movement of the garment as it was put together by the operators, and to confirm whether it followed the approved method of travel. This should have been agreed by the work study department, production managers, factory manager and line supervisors before starting production.

The factory used an approach called the progressive bundling system whereby the garment was assembled in stages as the different pieces moved from the back of the shop floor to the front. In theory each worker finished the piece she was working on and passed it forward to the operator sitting directly ahead of her. That person then passed it forward and so on. A garment or bundle of partially completed pieces was said to be "travelling" when in transit between different operators. The aim was to cut travelling to a minimum so that workers spent as much of their time as possible sitting at their machines sewing.

Planning the layout of machines and the movement of the garment was a scientific process. It was like kitchen design where it would be inefficient to have the kettle on one side of the room and tea on the other. Making one cup would be mildly inconvenient but making hundreds would be very uneconomical as most of one's time would be spent walking to and fro between the kettle and the tea. The same principle applied in a factory. The more that travel time could be reduced, the more efficient it would become.

I took up a position at the end of the line where I could see the whole process of the chemise being assembled from beginning to end. A minute or two later an operator with a stack of partially finished garments under one arm ambled past me and on towards the other end of the shop floor, stopping en route to greet friends and shout comments at other workers. A while later she arrived at her destination and tossed the garments into a basket for another person to start sewing.

She wasn't the only one working in this way. Other machine operators often strolled the length of the shop floor to see if their next pieces were ready. If they weren't, they would find someone to talk to (usually another operator with work to do) hang around for a while, then potter back to their machines. A few minutes later they would get up and come back for another look. Sometimes by the time they got back to their seats the next garment pieces would already be waiting for them, having arrived by an alternative route.

Michael had told us to focus on the travel time of garments but said nothing about flying time. Sometimes an operator would stand up, shout at someone further down the shop floor and then launch a bundle of garments into the air. Very occasionally the right person would catch it. We hadn't been taught a work study symbol for this but a small representation of an aeroplane seemed appropriate. After two or three hours' observation I saw that while garments generally started at one end of the shop floor and ended at the other, in-between they took a varied and scenic route, enjoyed the odd vacation in quiet backwaters off the regular itinerary and occasionally went by air, stopping at a variety of unplanned destinations.

Assembly of the chemise wasn't an example of work study perfection but by all accounts it represented considerable progress over practices existing when the company first acquired the factory two years before. Since then the company had invested a lot of time and money in improving it. As factory manager during that period Steve was responsible for modernizing the working environment, but had to struggle against a general unwillingness to embrace change among machine operators and other employees. Local cleaners had reached the comfortable conclusion some time ago that cleaning anything in the factory was a waste of time since dust would just blow in again from the street. This meant a good lifestyle for these employees as no one was so indelicate as to question whether, in that case, there was any point having cleaners at all. Steve's solution was to strike a deal with the cleaners whereby he would mop a patch of the shop floor himself and if it remained free from dirt the next day they would agree to keep it clean in future. The floor stayed clean but overall progress must have been slow if he had to justify to everyone why they should do their jobs.

Cleanliness was a priority even before

manufacturing quality, as dirt and dust could easily be transferred to delicate fabric carelessly dropped on the ground. But dirt was only part of the problem; it wasn't unusual to see an operator leaning over and away from her bench for clearance, raise a chin delicately and then spit mightily on the ground. Sometimes I would suddenly become aware that there was less friction between shoe and floor than anticipated and only a frantic wind-milling of the hands would keep me upright. I also heard of another cause of damage to garments. In colder weather some operators sat at their machines wrapped in items of clothing they had been working on, resulting in a garment that was second-hand before it even left the shop floor.

We also heard stories about entrepreneurial workers who set up a side-line business selling company goods in a local market. It gave a totally new meaning to travelling, as the method study diagram would have shown the completed garment heading towards the window where it was dropped to a co-entrepreneur sales rep in a quiet lane below and then continued onward to the local market. This emerging business was brought to a halt after the company bolted shut the factory windows overlooking the lane.

The new layout for the progressive bundling system had involved another change in lifestyle not welcomed by all parties. It's far pleasanter to have sewing machines arranged in a circle with someone to talk to on either side instead of a straight line where all you see is the back of another person's head. For a while a number of operators demonstrated a willingness to take on extra work by re-arranging the machines into a circle whenever Steve left the factory. Each morning Steve would move them back himself and eventually his persistence must have paid off because the machines were now in straight lines permanently.

My method study on the chemise showed that to some extent this was a cosmetic change only as garments were still following a circuitous route. The system wasn't running according to the principles advocated by Mr Frederick Winslow Taylor and I doubted that Rod, Steve, Bart or anyone else proposing work study as the answer to the company's production problems would be pleased with the reality of the shop floor. Bart, general manager, advocated work study like an evangelist while Lenny, factory manager, enjoyed punning on the fact that work study didn't "work". Perhaps Bart should sign Lenny up for a couple of months of Michael's lectures to help him see the error of his ways. In the meantime Lenny ignored the use of work study in the factory as best as he could and got on with what he considered more useful labour. He didn't waste energy opposing the Filipino work study engineers but instead acted as if they were invisible, as if one day he would look round and they would all be gone. It was a passive non-confrontational approach that brought to mind Taoism, Laozi and the principle of following the path of least resistance. It seemed to help Lenny as he was less stressed than when we first arrived.

Like water, that substance much lauded for its physical properties by the ancient Taoists, Lenny's philosophical approach to work study trickled downwards from high to low. It was imbibed willingly by Ah Ban, the production manager from Hong Kong, and by many of the workers too. Ah Ban was a graduate of no lesser an institution than the company university itself and after completion of Michael's course was promoted from work study engineer to production manager. But to the surprise of many he then "dismantled the bridge after crossing the river". He turned his back on the teachings of guru Michael and abandoned his former work study colleagues to form a close alliance with Lenny instead.

This didn't make things easy for the Filipino work study engineers who expected to work closely with the production manager in the various stages of producing a finished garment. They already faced considerable difficulty in that they didn't speak Chinese. While doing the method study I had observed Annette, one of the Filipino work study engineers, attempting to communicate with a worker who had introduced many personal and creative variations to the approved work study technique.

A number of operators stopped work and watched Annette's elaborate mime with interest. But how do you express with gestures something like "sewing on the collar should be operation number five not 25", "the tension on the sewing machine is wrong causing the fabric to wrinkle", "why are you wandering around with a stack of fabric under your arm?" or "by the way you shouldn't spit on the floor, that man keeps stepping in it"? It was difficult enough even with a knowledge of Mandarin as operators could be deliberately obtuse. On one occasion I saw a garment passing overhead like a rocket, launched from some distant point far behind me out of my field of view. I asked the operator who caught it where it had come from. With a helpful expression she pointed to the woman sitting immediately behind her and right in front of me.

Annette's attempts to communicate on this occasion were not helped by a surprise visit from Ah Ban. He had descended from the third floor, his normal area of responsibility. The operators were distracted by the sight of him handing out small presents and trinkets to other workers and line supervisors.

Ah Ban seemed to get on well with local staff. This wasn't always the case in dealings between Hong Kong and Mainland Chinese. Relations could sometimes be strained due to cultural and political differences arising from the circumstances of history, i.e. the British claiming Hong Kong and turning it into a colony after the First Opium War. Some mainlanders (particularly those further north) took the stance that people from Hong Kong had sold out and were not true Chinese, while certain Hong Kong Chinese held mainlanders in disdain for their backwardness and poverty.

Although growing up with different political systems, the Hong Kong Chinese managers and local workers did share a culture in terms of the Cantonese language, albeit with minor differences in pronunciation. Where there was no shared language, such as between the Filipinos and the Hong Kong Chinese, or the Sri Lankans and the Hong Kong Chinese, there was very little in the way of communication or productive working relationships. There were also communication problems between the Hong Kong Chinese and the English, the two major powers of the company.

"What the...? Don't believe it," said a voice behind me. Bernard strode past. "Ah Ban, there you are! Management audit, waiting for you, time to start."

Management audits were a crucial step in the quality control system Bernard was trying to implement in the factory. The aim of the audit was for key personnel to review garments that had already been passed as of satisfactory quality and were ready to be shipped to the customer.

In the day-to-day running of the factory, whether or not a garment met quality standards was up to examiners who carried out a final quality examination on each item as it came off the production line. A poor quality garment delivered to the customer meant at the very least that something had gone wrong with the garment examination process. But this was not necessarily straightforward as garment examiners were subject to various pressures such as workers complaining or making comments if too many garments were sent back. The examiners needed the support of the line supervisors who in turn needed the support of the production manager, in this case Ah Ban. The management audit was an opportunity for line supervisors and the two production managers to work as a team and to reach a consensus as to whether the quality was adequate or not.

"No. I not go. I too busy," said Ah Ban.

"Has to be done you know," said Bernard after a pause, tapping his watch. "*Now*. People waiting."

"No. I too busy." Ah Ban turned his back on Bernard, handed out the rest of his gifts and hurried from the shop floor.

"Don't believe it. Just don't believe it." Bernard

swept his hand down in front of his face in a characteristic gesture of dismissal; it was beginning to appear more frequently. "As bad as Lenny. No help from him either. Think he only translates half of what I say." He threw his hands in the air. "How the hell do they expect me to do my job? Bloody ridiculous. Need a full time interpreter with me all day long. Otherwise all a waste of time and might as well go home. This company, I don't know."

*

The afternoon exhausted itself and we climbed onto the bus for the familiar ride back to the hotel. Ah Ling followed a winding route round the centre of Shiqiao, dropping off the office staff at different points along the way. He beeped continuously from the minute we entered the traffic to our arrival back at the hotel. He had a well-developed technique of driving to within inches of pedestrians and cyclists, looming over them and sounding the horn in their ears. When the person leapt astonished into the air and then turned round, Ah Ling glared furiously and stabbed his index finger audibly and repeatedly against the windscreen. On one occasion, following a particularly enthusiastic burst of beeping, Steve exclaimed, "she's a poor little old lady on crutches." This was translated for the benefit of Ah Ling who laughed uproariously.

Each day we travelled home in the evening rush hour against the background sounds of bicycle bells, beeping and shouting voices. We used to pass a local toy factory as hordes of female workers finished a shift and poured out through the gates, overflowing into the road where they stood chatting in circles. Panyu was definitely the place for a young single man and I had recently learned that Hunan John had found himself a local girlfriend. It explained his sudden acquisition of basic Cantonese despite his earlier prejudice against the language.

Ah Ling drove on and the Filipino women descended from the bus at the entrance to some flats, followed by Anne, Charlotte and the rest of the office staff. They walked a few paces and disappeared down an alley or merged with the crowd and became invisible. We drove past a small night market where the stalls were lit by glowing lamps, then continued past the Shiqiao Middle School and the local cinema.

Shop owners pulled down the shutters of their stalls and sat on small stools as they prepared the evening meal. Rich cooking smells filled the air and wafted into the minibus. We followed the road to the Miramar Hotel where the Sri Lankans were staying. It was a big yellow building that looked as if it had seen better days, dusty and shabby compared to the Panyu Hotel, our destination and the last stop on Ah Ling's circuit.

15 Do you mind sharing?

Spring Festival was approaching, the most important holiday of the year in China and a time for families to reunite. During the run up to the celebrations the whole country slows down in anticipation. The factory was no exception. It ground to a gradual halt a week before the official holiday was due to start. The workers disappeared and their machines fell quiet.

For the holiday we planned to visit a relative of Min's in Shenzhen and fly onwards to Shanghai. Anticipating a country on the move and crowds of people swamping all forms of public transport over Spring Festival, we went to Guangzhou Railway Station to book our seats to Shenzhen in advance. Recently the news had featured a story about commuters killed in a minibus crash on the road out of Panyu and this time we took a large public bus. Behind us sat visitors from Beijing and they remarked with surprise at how wealthy the area was. I enjoyed listening to Chinese spoken by people from the North.

Beijing accents had a richness and tonal quality generally lacking in Mandarin spoken in the South. To many of the latter, growing up at home with another dialect such as Cantonese, Mandarin was effectively a second language.

Guangzhou was more crowded and chaotic than before and the station was hectic. Inside, faces were drawn and the atmosphere was tense. Noisy crowds surged before each ticket window. A lucky absent minority would be able to get seats without visiting the station as some work units or employers could obtain tickets for staff through unofficial connections.

As a foreigner I was able to buy our tickets almost immediately at a different window. Our short queue was separated from the one beside it by thick metal railings. Looking over I saw people crushed and packed into long lines snaking back without an end in sight. Around the tiny ticket window was a protective system of iron bars in which people fought and struggled to keep their place. Policemen in green uniforms balanced on railings above their heads and shouted at anyone trying to barge the queue, banging their batons furiously against the bars (their angry yelling was constant as quite a few railway customers seemed oblivious to the idea that a queue should be joined from the back). Buying a ticket was a traumatic event and I saw one man literally crying with relief when he finally had one in his hand.

Back in Panyu, calm and sedate in comparison, we stopped off at the hotel for lunch before returning to the factory. We had been living there for several months and though quiet when we arrived, it was now banqueting season and the restaurants were often fully booked in the evenings. Returning after work we were turned away from one dining-hall after another. Sometimes every restaurant in the vicinity of the hotel was packed too and we would go back to the room for a bowl of noodles and a packet of crisps. It began to feel claustrophobic with its windows that didn't open and our suitcases and belongings occupying the floor, desk and every other available surface.

It was time for another call to Bart. Anyone listening to our telephone calls would think we worked at a property company rather than a garment factory as our sole topic of conversation concerned the elusive accommodation. The last time we spoke Bart had said, "you guys will be in company accommodation by Spring Festival, and that's a guarantee." By now I understood that when Bart said "that's a guarantee" he didn't mean "guarantee" in the sense of giving an assurance or undertaking an obligation; in fact what he really meant was "that's not a guarantee at all" but that didn't have quite the same punchy, upbeat ring to it.

This time when I dialled Bart's number there was an uncomfortable pause at the end of the phone, followed by, "hey! Why don't you guys go find yourselves a place?"

"What about the company accommodation?" I asked. There was another long pause.

"Yeah. We're working on that one... look I'm due in a meeting. If you need any other help give me a call. Great! Bye."

Hong Kong had a well-developed landlord and tenant property industry with estate agents on every corner. Shiqiao, centre of Panyu, did not. In such circumstances what was needed was local connections and Anne offered to put the word around the factory that we were looking for somewhere to live.

Our project was coming to a close and all that remained was some activity sampling and two method studies. Activity sampling involved walking along the line of machine operators at random times and noting what each person was doing (Michael told us to vary the times so that workers wouldn't be able to predict when we were coming). The object was to make a rough estimate of what proportion of an operator's time was actually spent sewing.

"Now," said Michael, "what you are looking out for is handling fabric, cutting thread, changing needles, sewing, waiting for work, talking and idling."

I discovered a few extra activities such as spitting, brushing hair, trimming fingernails with sewing scissors, sleeping on work desk and reading books. The sample showed that a very small percentage of the workers' time was used for sewing. A significant amount was spent waiting for work and the factory seemed less busy than on our arrival.

Our next task was a method study of the packing room. This was a small square area at the back of the shop floor with an entrance normally concealed by racks of hanging garments. The packing room was the final stop for a garment before if left the factory. After it had been pressed and examined for quality it would be packed, taken downstairs and put into cardboard boxes for shipping.

A group of elderly women worked in the packing room and their job involved collecting the examined garments from the racks outside, folding them and packing them into plastic bags. The sight of me in the entrance way with my 12 inch ruler, clipboard, pencil and disarming grin did not give rise to a hearty welcome; instead, scowling and muttering greeted my appearance. But I had a job to do and once again a scale drawing of the workplace was the first requirement. I spent quite some time crawling behind racks of garments or balancing on the table trying to avoid the women's hands and their jam jars of green tea leaves.

"He can speak Chinese," one of them said to the others after I had asked her about the method they were using.

When a foreigner speaks Chinese, no matter whether it is a basic greeting such as "hello" or a sentence of more complexity, he or she can usually expect compliments, congratulations and words of encouragement. I've even had people clap their hands in delight.

"What are you doing in here?" she asked with a frown.

I started to explain that the aim was to look at the efficiency of their working methods and to come up with improvements. But then it occurred to me that having been witnessed crouching awkwardly on the ground while measuring the length of the shop floor with a 12 inch ruler I was unlikely to be persuasive on the subject of efficiency. Nevertheless I continued with my explanation as well as I could until I was interrupted.

"Who has reported us? What's wrong with our work?"

"Uh? What? No one. Nothing."

"Who has been complaining about our work?

Come on, who was it?"

The women stopped packing garments and took it in turns to question me closely, grim-faced, sleeves rolled up, trying to discover the identity of the person who kept reporting them for sloppy work. I did my best to explain the situation but the first woman, dissatisfied and disbelieving my response, asked, "then why do so many of you come in here watching us work?"

That made me think. To Michael the packing room was a sort of work study training ground, sandbox or play area for us to cut our teeth on, but no one had mentioned this to the people working there. Streams of students from the course had subjected the packing room to a similar scrutiny and it was enough to make anyone feel uncertain about their job. I attempted to explain that this was an exercise only but they weren't convinced and turned to get on with their work. The racks outside bulged with garments waiting to be packed.

It gave me a chance to analyse the working methods of the packing room. Looking round I saw that despite the number of work study engineers passing through it and writing up reports on how efficiency could be improved, there were still a few basic problems to be addressed. The main issue was simply that the room was full of rubbish and broken pieces of furniture. We suggested a good clean-up (though I hoped it wouldn't be me having to justify this to the recalcitrant factory cleaners) and designed a system of racks and baskets for storage of garments after they had been packed. Some of the baskets would have wheels and the elderly workers could slide them down ramps so they wouldn't have to waste time or effort walking across the room; alternatively they could kick the baskets to a specially prepared storage area.

I was pleased to leave the packing room behind and its atmosphere of understandable paranoia to start the second method study and final part of our project. We chose to look at a simple operation that involved the worker measuring the width of fabric to be used as collars. The process seemed inefficient as the worker had to keep picking up and putting down a tape measure. We suggested that the operator wear a ring on her thumb on which was glued a small piece of card against which she could measure the collar. This would save time because she wouldn't have to stop to pick up the measuring tape. One thing we had learned from the company was the importance of a name and we referred to this solution as the "Ring Systems Measurement Package".

*

A few days later one of the local office staff told Anne that she knew of a friend with a flat to let. We went to have a look after work and were welcomed by a large family who lived in a cosy place dominated by a large television and some very new furniture. It would have been cosier still had Min and I joined them as the "flat" we had come to look at was more of a lodging in the form of two additional rooms off to one side and a shared bathroom and kitchen. Access to the rooms was gained by walking past the television through the family's main living area. It occurred to me that living with a Chinese family would be good for my Cantonese but it wasn't quite what we were looking for.

We visited many flats in Panyu of all shapes and sizes. Anne had put the word out very successfully and anyone who knew of anything vaguely resembling four walls, a floor and ceiling stepped up and volunteered their own, a friend's or a relative's living space for our consideration. Almost all were unsuitable but eventually we heard about a flat in good condition belonging to an acquaintance of one of the payroll clerks. It had been recently renovated and looked to be perfect. Situated eleven flights up it was light and airy with balconies on three sides and open views into the distance over the whole of Shiqiao. It had a clean new kitchen and we both looked forward to home cooking and a meal other than pot noodle or restaurant food.

The only problem was the price. Charlotte, who had taken us round the flats and made introductions, told us that the proposed rent of 1,500 RMB a month was more than double the usual rate, inflated because I was a foreigner. We made an offer of 700 RMB. No knowledge of Chinese was necessary to understand the owner's pantomime of shock, disbelief, disgust, pity for our ignorance and finally dismissal of such a ridiculous offer. A day later he accepted the price.

I phoned Bart to tell him the news. After a short pause and some deliberation he agreed that the rent was reasonable and authorised us to go ahead with it. Unlike Bart I had no financial training or MBA but I thought RMB 700 was a bargain compared to the amount the company was paying for us to live in the

Panyu Hotel. At the current rates two nights in the hotel would pay for a month in the flat. Three weeks at the hotel would enable us to rent the flat for a year.

But ultimately it was all in vain. Later that afternoon there was a call from Joan Wong, Hong Kong office personnel manager. She told Min that we couldn't move into the new flat; the company had plenty of accommodation and it would be a waste of money to rent more property. Min explained that we had spent a lot of time looking for somewhere to live and mentioned the cost savings for the company if we moved to the flat, ready as it was for immediate occupation. But Joan was adamant that ample "quarters" were already available and it was out of the question for the company to rent another property. Bart kept his head down and proved as elusive as the accommodation itself.

The days passed, Spring Festival loomed, but there was no indication that our time in the Panyu Hotel might be drawing to a close. Min gave Joan another call. Slight problem, the accommodation in Panyu was fully occupied after all; a group of company drivers were living in the flat supposedly available for us and they quite liked living there and intended to continue doing so. Joan was untroubled by this turn of events and announced a plan to visit Panyu in a few days with one of the company accountants to "assess the situation". This was an unusual move as Hong Kong managers generally avoided trips to China where possible. Those working on the mainland for any length of time received extra "hardship pay" as compensation. "Times changing, worried about costs," said Bernard.

The next event in the company calendar was the Spring Festival meal for the office staff. I, however, was not in a celebratory mood and would not be the life and soul on this occasion. The ongoing saga of the accommodation was frustrating enough in itself but also seemed symbolic of a general failure of the company to follow through with what had been promised at interview. A few teething problems at the beginning were perfectly understandable (general manager, personnel manager, factory manager not expecting us, no company flat, wrong visa for Min, etc.) but questions remained as to what we might expect in terms of actual work with the company in the future. Was Michael's course really part of a trainee management programme and what would happen when it came to an end? So far I was more English teacher than manager and I had a growing conviction that when Chris said they would "train me up to represent the company in transactions with the Chinese government" he had just made the remark up on the spot, riffing with Rod, as it were. It led me to wonder how much of that interview was on the spot improvisation between the two of them. Maybe it had all been a little too easy.

The meal took place at an entertainment complex half an hour's bus ride from Shiqiao, in the middle of nowhere, situated at the end of a long drive that wound past a power station. The decor was new and tacky and the facilities included restaurants, a laser disco, go-kart track and foot massage parlour. I had never seen anything like it on my previous visits to Beijing, Shanghai and other cities across the country.

The go-karts proved noisy and exhilarating and

were easy to control if you had previous experience at driving a real car. The staff were only vaguely concerned that one or two of the party had trouble walking in a straight line, but they shouted at John who went shooting up the grass bank backwards, wheels spinning and clods of mud flying everywhere.

At the meal I shared a bowl of bean curd with Pilla and Gopal, who despite Min's list of Chinese phrases for ordering food still looked thin and hungry. In Panyu bean curd was either smooth and jelly-like or served in a sloppier form with a ladle. I looked forward to having the chewy variety available in Shanghai known as "dried bean curd" or *doufu gan*. It was often served in strips and fried with soy sauce and ginger.

Back in the factory on the last day before the Spring Festival holiday we waited for Joan to reach her conclusions about the available accommodation. With the workers away there were no time studies to be done and for many in the office the holiday had already started. Bernard was about to finish at the factory, his short term contract coming to an end. He sat back on the conference table, an audience of largely male Filipino and Sri Lankan work study engineers around him.

"Best massage ever had," he said shaking his head. "Bart took me after the meal. Six hundred dollars." I reached for my calculator and discovered that the combined cost of the massage for Bart and Bernard would have paid for Min and I to live for almost two months in our flat. "Very thorough massage. Beautiful girls!" he continued and shook his head, looking round at the wistful expressions of the others, separated from wives and girlfriends for many long months. "For an extra hundred dollars we could… you know…" He raised an eyebrow and grinned, his expression an experiment between nonchalant man-of-the-world and a new bad boy Bernard. "But I'm not saying, not saying".

Joan Wong wasn't saying either. After spending the day looking round the various flats that the company owned or rented from local landlords, she said she needed to go back to Hong Kong to "review the situation". We pressed her on what accommodation was actually available in Panyu. Joan said there was plenty of room for everyone if a bit of reshuffling and squeezing up was done, particularly if we had no objection to sharing. If we didn't want to share it might take longer to sort out our own flat. Alarm bells sounded at the word "sharing". I doubted that Joan herself, Bart or other married couples employed by the company were living in Maoist style communes in Hong Kong and I said that we would wait for our own place. Joan was vague about when this might become available but we did manage to get a commitment from her that it would happen "sometime after Spring Festival".

The next day Min, I and Bernard checked out of the Panyu Hotel and the two bills came to a staggering amount. "Made a few calls," said Bernard, commenting on his telephone bill, comfortably in excess of £1,000. The hotel initially asked for payment in cash but the accountants at the factory turned pale at the request and said there was never that much to hand. Preparations were made to bring the money across in suitcases from Hong Kong but at the last minute the hotel staff agreed to accept a cheque from the factory. We said goodbye to Bernard and wished him well in his search for another job in the garment industry, whether in China or beyond.

16 New spring sweep the dust

Having secured our possessions in the hotel strong room we took a taxi to Guangzhou railway station. We planned to travel once more from Guangzhou to the Shenzhen Special Economic Zone but this time fly onward to Shanghai for the Spring Festival holiday.

Firecrackers are set off across China during the celebrations and at the station our bags were searched thoroughly. "It is strictly forbidden to bring easily combustible, explosive and toxic items onto the train" said a sign in large white characters against a red background. Bangers igniting accidentally could set fire to whole carriages causing death and devastation. Photos in the station showed the consequences in grisly detail.

On the way to the waiting room for the Shenzhen train we passed an endless queue of people travelling back to Hunan Province. I thought of John standing somewhere along its length, fighting for a space so that he could get home to see his family. Our waiting room was virtually empty as the Shenzhen Special Economic Zone was closed to the majority in China. Only those with the correct travelling papers would be allowed across the border.

The train pulled away from the station as dusk was falling. Leaving the company and thoughts of work behind we rolled past high rise buildings and flats. The elevated track gave a bird's eye view of the streets of Guangzhou and we watched people eating out on the pavements beneath us. Cyclists rode home along dark lanes past the neon lights of dance halls and karaoke bars.

On our previous trip to Hong Kong we had passed rapidly through Shenzhen but now we had time to look around properly. The centre of Shiqiao was well developed but Shenzhen was a whole city of gleaming high-rise buildings, wide streets and spacious parks. The shops were crammed with consumer goods and it seemed more like Hong Kong than mainland China. One of Min's relatives told us that 10% of Shenzhen's inhabitants were millionaires in local currency.

We visited a theme park called "Splendid China" with detailed 1:15 scale models of famous buildings, monuments and historical sites across the country. It was then the practice to charge foreigners different rates and my ticket (paid in FEC) was four or five times the price paid by Min. Once inside I picked out miniature versions of my old haunts in Beijing. After the theme park, Min's relative drove us to an empty beach a couple of hours from Shenzhen. We sat on the sand and watched the sea. It was unexpected and surreal.

Stepping onto the plane the next day we left behind

the sounds of Cantonese and instead heard the softer tones of Shanghai dialect. Belonging to a group of languages known as *Wu*, Shanghai dialect or Shanghainese is spoken in the eastern coastal provinces of Zhejiang and Jiangsu. It is as different from Mandarin as Cantonese and is incomprehensible to people from other areas of China.

Before returning to Shanghai to marry Min I had learned enough Shanghai dialect to get by. The only book on the subject in Leeds University library was written by a missionary 100 years previously. The phrases were for a lifestyle long since vanished and I couldn't very well go around calling people "boy", so I advertised in the Chinese department for a teacher. The only person to respond was from Ningbo, an ancient port in Zhejiang about 80 miles south of Shanghai. He told me that he spoke standard Shanghai dialect and twice a week we met and converted my Mandarin textbook into Shanghainese. Occasionally when I repeated phrases without mistakes he shook his head and laughed as if he couldn't quite believe what he was hearing.

When I next visited Shanghai, Min's relatives were amused by my weird Ningbo accent but at least I could follow basic conversations. Before starting lessons my teacher said he had some film acting experience but he was a chain-smoker with a large round face and didn't look like silver-screen material at all. A year or two later I was astonished to see him in a small walk-on part in the 1987 epic film "The Last Emperor" directed by Bernardo Bertolucci.

I continued to learn Shanghai dialect after returning to Leeds but my Ningbo teacher had moved on and I advertised once again. Shanghai dialect varies across the city and surrounding area but to my ear it all sounded more or less the same and subtleties were lost. In the past, people who spoke with a north Shanghai accent were apparently discriminated against and could find it difficult to marry outside their own community. I was told that a man with a Suzhou accent might be considered overly effeminate. My second teacher never said what part of Shanghai he was from but when I used some of his expressions I was informed by Min that people she knew didn't say things like that. She had learned Shanghai dialect after leaving Guangdong Province at the age of ten but spoke without any trace of a Cantonese accent.

The plane journey from Shenzhen to Shanghai was a two hour flight. Service was rudimentary with air hostesses literally throwing the boxed meals along the rows at passengers. One man had been sleeping peacefully but was jolted instantly awake by a food box landing squarely in his groin.

A "passenger's opinion card" handed out before disembarking showed that service was an area they were keeping an eye on. "Respectable Passenger: You are greet welcome!" it said and invited people to comment on whether aspects of the service were "good, general or bad". These included "active and warm attitude", "adopt civilised words", "regular service process", "delicious dish" and "clean dining tool". The English was easier to understand if you had some knowledge of Chinese and reminded me of a notice I once saw above a litter bin that said "No Disorderly Tossing". In this case "regular service process" was probably the appropriate column for a comment to the effect that lunch should not be bounced off a passenger's testicles.

As the plane began its descent a woman next to me started praying with her hands clasped tightly together. She didn't stop until we came to a halt, landing at the new Shanghai International Airport. Leaving the plane we were numbed by a blast of icy air. We were 700 miles north and back in winter.

With no central heating, living conditions were hard for people in Shanghai. The constant cold was a new experience for me. In Min's home we wore layers of inner clothing and kept our coats on all the time, even during meals.

Some local people had unusual ways of coping with the weather conditions. On television I saw two men who could control their body temperatures and seemed impervious to cold. In front of a TV audience they were shut into a freezer with transparent sides while the temperature inside was gradually lowered. The men sat unperturbed in single layers of clothing, occasionally answering questions from an interviewer who opened a plastic flap in the side to talk to them. Containers of water beside the men froze in front of the cameras a long time before the experiment was stopped due to safety concerns.

Staying with Min's family again it was as if the company had never existed. I was taken back to the time I had spent in Shanghai as a student visiting from Beijing. Living in a Chinese household for weeks with no English spoken or any contact with other foreigners, I had been completely immersed in Chinese life and culture. Such isolation from the Western world would be almost impossible today due to developments in telecommunications, mobile phones, the internet, shopping centres, consumerism and the substantial international community now living in Shanghai.

That past way of life, the tail-end of post-1949 communist, socialist China, has effectively disappeared along with the buildings around Min's old neighbourhood. The latter were flattened for new infrastructure and re-development. Whenever I hear the Chinese national anthem today I vividly recall that brief period as I woke to its sound each morning. The first few bars were loudly broadcast across lanes and alleys from a local school as the children arrived for classes. It was always followed by a strident male voice, similarly amplified, counting up to ten while students performed their morning exercises.

The national anthem was also broadcast every day before the evening "news". The programme featured endless optimistic reports of increased grain output, steel production or other industrial and agricultural achievements. But Western TV shows were already appearing and there was a period when "Moonlighting" with Bruce Willis and Cybill Shepherd, dubbed into Chinese, was on television several times a week.

Another early purveyor of Western culture in Shanghai was the US crime series "Hunter". The story followed the work and life of a homicide detective and his female partner. I was questioned closely about Hunter's lifestyle. What caused most concern among the older generation of Min's family wasn't his readiness to shoot people but his casual sexual relationships. Unfortunately Hunter was taken as the norm for all Western males.

Min's family said that we had both lost weight since we saw them last (*"ni shou le!"* "you're thinner!") and they were determined to fatten us up before we returned to Panyu. I enjoyed the home cooking. It was unlike any Chinese food I had ever eaten in England, but as I didn't have meat with my rice they were concerned I wasn't eating enough.

Food is a major topic of conversation among Chinese people, bordering on an obsession, and I was quizzed in detail about what I had eaten over the past few months in Panyu. I could barely remember what I had eaten on the flight up from Shenzhen (we were both questioned closely about this too) but following the lengthy discussion Min's uncle made a bulk order of local baked beans, her mother bought different types of *doufugan* (dried bean curd) and her aunt made potato cakes. She fried these in a wok in the tiny kitchen at the back of the flat.

It surprised me that Min's uncle could buy baked beans locally as in England Min had looked at the English staple food "baked beans on toast" with incomprehension and an unwillingness to partake that I associated more with the British abroad. She was the same with the humble potato and that wonderful preparation known as "mash".

In the two or three years since our last visit to Shanghai there had been many improvements in the standard of living. Flats in the locality had welcoming wooden floors instead of cold cement and large air-conditioning units stood ready for the heat of summer.

Previously there was no hot water but now a gas boiler had been installed in the kitchen. On an earlier visit, unused to living without central heating, I made the mistake of washing my hair in icy cold water over the large trough-like sink. Afterwards I developed an awful, splitting headache.

Most households had neither fridge nor freezer so shopping for vegetables was a daily necessity. The local market was simply an empty space in front of a nearby block of flats where peasants from outlying areas sold their produce. They spread it on the ground or sold it from the back of pedal-powered push carts. On the way we passed a group of elderly people wrapped in thick blue coats sitting on chairs brought outside to catch the feeble rays of morning sunlight. They stopped talking and watched as we walked past. I heard the phrase *nga go nying* ("foreigner" or literally "outside country person"), three words of Shanghai dialect that every non-Chinese visitor would learn to recognize soon after arrival, whether studying the language or not.

The vegetable sellers at the market were good-humoured despite squatting in the road all day in freezing conditions. Their faces were red and their fingers chapped and in some cases swollen and shapeless. One man wrapped in a quilted blue army coat selling *doumiao* (pea shoots) said he recognised me from three years before. He wanted to know about our relationship and, commenting that we were too young to be married, concluded that Min must be my interpreter. Min's response to remarks like this was usually to smile but not say anything. The man next to him was selling potatoes, *yang se yu* in Shanghai dialect with the literal meaning "foreign sweet potato". "Ah!" he said. "Of course. Foreign sweet potatoes for the foreigner!"

Occasionally Min would be subject to verbal abuse for being in the company of a Westerner and sometimes it just seemed better to let people believe she was my interpreter. One of the few places it was possible to avoid comments and excessive attention from people who had never seen a foreigner before was the Peace Hotel on Nanjing Road. It was a favourite haunt of ours when I visited as a student from Beijing. It had a small coffee bar just inside the foyer with comfortable armchairs next to semi-tropical potted plants.

At the time ordinary Chinese people weren't allowed into many of the major hotels in the country (another unspoken regulation) but there were no such restrictions on foreigners and those accompanying them. Finding privacy was difficult enough for young Chinese couples but was almost impossible where one party was a foreigner. I was grateful for the quiet of the Peace Hotel foyer and coffee bar.

We decided to stop off at the Peace Hotel for old time's sake after having a look at some of the nearby bookshops. As I descended from the bus at Nanjing Road a voice in my ear said, "hashish? You want hashish?" Turning I saw a man with distinctly non-Chinese features and assumed him to be from Xinjiang in the North West. I replied in the negative and he said, "okay, American, very good", as if that explained my lack of interest in his merchandise. Walking along Nanjing Road I often had encounters like this, but they were discreet and usually Min would be unaware they had taken place.

The bookshops had improved though some were

still run on the old basis where the books were kept behind counters and the customer had to ask bad tempered shop assistants to pass them across. They got up sighing and cursing and either threw the book at you or slammed it down on the counter. Ease of shopping was not helped by the system where you had to go and pay for the book at another counter, then return to pick it up again and show proof you had just paid for it.

But there were also newer shops where books were more accessible, and each time we went back to Shanghai there was more variety and sometimes even improvements in the quality of service. On this occasion we bought a *Ci Hai* ("Word Sea") encyclopaedia for a few pounds.

The Peace Hotel was much the same as before but RMB instead of FEC was accepted without question. The rule prohibiting ordinary people was no longer in force and everyday Shanghai shoppers browsed round new counters of goods in the lobby.

16 or 17 years later on a visit to Shanghai we returned to the Peace Hotel for a drink but found the doors firmly closed. They were partially hidden by scaffolding and had been boarded up for renovation. Shanghai was now dominated by shopping centres, fast food and brightly lit bars, and I felt nostalgic for the shabby, faded gentility of the Peace Hotel as it was in the late 1980s and the haven of quiet it had been for us. Leaving the Peace Hotel behind we walked along Nanjing Road to another distinguished old building of the same era, the Shanghai Art Museum. After admiring the works on display and in need of a coffee break we followed an old sign up some stairs and

along a corridor. At the end of another passageway we emerged into a dimly lit seating area. There, dusty pot plants stood next to faded old sofas. On the opposite side of the room was a disused bar, several stacks of chairs, a door marked "private" and a bell to ring for service. A man appeared after a short wait, took our order and returned a few minutes later with our drinks. No other customers strayed into the room while we were there and we had our tea and coffee in an atmosphere of timeless quiet and peace unusual for central Shanghai. But like the Chinese tale of the "Peach Blossom Spring", when we came back a few days later we could find no sign of the dusty old room.

The roads near the Peace Hotel were busier than before with re-routings and diversions as stretches of the city were dug up for the new subway system. Whole blocks of housing were being swept aside for its construction. Buses were slow and a bicycle was still the best way to travel round Shanghai. Wrapped in a thick coat and scarf I was anonymous and blended in with other cyclists as we left main roads and turned onto smaller streets lined with spreading plane trees. One evening we went out to watch some Chinese opera and as we cycled back at night the roads were empty apart from the two of us, the only sound the swish of our tyres as we passed by.

Cycling around Shanghai always brought an unusual look of happiness to Min's face. The bikes were single-geared and heavy but quite a speed could be reached on some of the roads, particularly when descending the long, gently sloping bridge near her flat. She was a fast cyclist from years of riding across the city from home to university and back.

Young women travelling on overcrowded public buses would often be subjected to both surreptitious and blatant groping attempts. Cycling was one way of avoiding this, though even then some men attempted to hassle women by following too close behind. Cyclists faced other more predictable hazards too but these were diminished if they were familiar with the streets. In the middle of one cycle lane a concrete pillar reared up suddenly without warning. Its sharp corners were blunted in places by the dents and pockmarks of countless previous impacts. Another danger of cycling in China was the occasional mega-pothole which could swallow both bike and rider.

The unimpeded view from a bicycle was a good way to appreciate housing in Shanghai, from the grandeur of 19th century buildings constructed in the foreign settlements after the Treaty of Nanking (1842), to ragged lean-to shacks of boards and corrugated iron, built against walls or on the flat roofs of existing buildings.

In the old foreign concessions we saw French villas, English country houses and rows of terraced housing with pedestrianized back alleys between them that reminded me of the streets and architecture of England. Originally designed for one household they were now home to three or four families. I saw parents and their children living in a single room, sharing a bathroom, kitchen and communal cooking areas with other inhabitants of the same building. Overcrowded but built to last, their thick walls blocked the noise of traffic and the existence of the world outside.

In one house we visited near Nanjing Road an old couple lived in one tiny room. Decorated with paintings and calligraphy it was another haven of quiet after the frantic crowds and shops. A white narcissus stood on a window ledge and caught the sun, where it would be minutely appreciated as it opened over the passing days.

Other structures, such as the shed-like dwellings assembled from planks, flower pots, sheets of metal and old roof tiles, were dark and grimy and brought to mind the world of Dickensian London. Many Chinese people I met believed that London was still a city of gloomy fogs and pea-soupers but I saw more in China to make me think of that aspect of Dickens's England than anything I ever saw back home. The most smoggy, polluted city I visited during that time in China was Chongqing, point of embarkation for a boat trip down the Yangtze River via the Three Gorges, stopping at Wuhan and finishing at Shanghai. The smog in Chongqing was like a dark dusty blanket across the roads and alleys, almost tangible, blurring vision and filling nostrils and lungs with the heavy, acrid smell of coal. Light from windows was instantly swallowed up by the particulate gloom.

Industrial pollution in parts of Shanghai was also an assault on the senses and local people wore goggles and gauze face masks that covered nose and mouth. Factories next to areas of residential housing belched smoke and effluent and returning home we often cycled through zones of dense smog where the air was thick with the smell of burning coal. The chimneys of one factory spewed out a sulphurous yellow substance that flowed like lava down its walls, spilling onto the pavement and street in crusted pools, causing cyclists to divert and pedestrians to cross the road. What had once been a river near one of Shanghai's famous universities was like a road of thick black tar glistening in the sun.

With a bike it was easy to get round Shanghai but occasionally we went by public transport if the weather was bad. Some parts of the city were criss-crossed by an old electric tram system and at night after a fall of rain the wires above the road glinted like a steel spider's web. Cyclists seemed to have no respect for the trams and solitary riders would hurtle out in front of them, forcing the drivers to brake hard.

Commuters risked their lives on a daily basis at a vast sprawling cross-roads and traffic lights a few minutes' walk from Min's home. Drivers rarely slowed as the lights turned orange but instead accelerated to try to get across first. A traffic policeman worked in a tower on an island in the middle of the crossroads and he kept himself busy shouting abuse at cyclists who disobeyed the rules. They would usually first try to ignore him and pretend it was someone else, but the policeman's voice was amplified through loudspeakers and it rose above the noise of the traffic, "you in the white shirt. Yes, you. Stop pretending you can't hear me". The individual would finally turn round and look up at the tower from where there would issue further shouts of righteous wrath.

It was dangerous shooting the lights on a bicycle because the stretch of road was wide and half way across you would find yourself weaving in and out of trucks and army vehicles thundering across your path. The trucks had a hanging metal mesh beneath them to stop cyclists being sucked under but I thought that any collision would probably be fatal. Road users didn't pay attention to the traffic lights in front of them but watched those to the side governing vehicles to the right and left. As soon as these changed they would be away, irrespective of the colour of the lights directly in front of them. Whenever the traffic lights changed there would be a ragged period for half a minute when vehicles travelled in every direction.

While we were visiting Shanghai, people were killed on that stretch of road and the news showed shocking pictures of smashes involving lorries and cyclists. On one occasion some visitors arrived at the flat having just witnessed the death of a young woman. They were upset and gave a graphic description I could never forget.

After our day in Nanjing Road the local streets near Min's flat seemed quiet in comparison but new shops were opening and roadside stalls had constant customers. One of the latest products for sale in Shanghai as well as Panyu was a new toy for children, a variety of blow-up plastic animal with wheels. Looking over the balcony at dusk I saw a small girl tugging along a white rabbit with a light in it. It was a peaceful scene as the child and parent faded into the semi-darkness, the rabbit still visible behind them giving out a flickering light as it was pulled along the road. Old people strolled along enjoying the evening atmosphere while bedding put out to air earlier in the day was brought back indoors. Two children in matching red shoes and coats played badminton in the alleyway between the flats. Smells of cooking pervaded the air. From the main road several hundred yards away the sound of beeping and bicycle bells mingled with the rumble of larger vehicles. Min was cooking in the tiny kitchen and I heard the pop and crackle of greens being thrown into a hot wok. The Chinese national anthem indicated that the news was starting and I sat down to watch it with Min's aunt.

Spring Festival has been celebrated in China for thousands of years. Its origins are lost in myth. According to one legend a demon called *Nian* appeared at the end of each winter and persecuted people, stealing crops and attacking villagers. This happened with distressing regularity until an enquiring mind discovered that fire applied to a section of bamboo tubing would create an explosive bang, loud enough to make any demon jump out of its skin and discourage it from committing further mayhem. From that time on *Nian* or "Year" would be chased away with firecrackers. The Chinese word for firecracker *baozhu* literally means "exploding bamboo".

The explosions started during the day but as New Year approached the nearby popping and banging and distant crackling became a continuous roaring wave of sound. Strings of bangers held at arms' length fragmented in the air with epileptic energy, red paper and copper sparks flying outwards from balconies towards the ground. Children let off rockets horizontally and in showers of greens and reds they arced upwards and fell back to earth. As midnight approached the bombardment of sound reached a resounding climax and looking out into the night I thought of the same noise and celebrations echoing the length and breadth of China.

17 Wunday, Tooday, Feeday, Forday, Fiday

Our two weeks in Shanghai flew past and we returned to Panyu where the temperature had become warm and humid. Back in the hotel room Min hung a calendar on the wall and put a new tea set on the desk, the pot and cups decorated with the Chinese character for longevity. It was almost like home. We weren't optimistic about moving into our own flat and prepared for a long stay in the Panyu Hotel. We would give Bart one more call and after that let events take their own course.

As we rounded the corner to the morning pickup point I heard an unexpected yet familiar sonorous voice. "Quality system not quite there yet, more time needed." Bernard was back, same blue anorak and tinted glasses, talking to John about his surprising re-engagement to finish working on quality issues at the factory.

"Morning, morning," he said when he saw us, looking refreshed after his two weeks back in England.

Charlotte, Anne, John and the others were silent on the bumpy Monday morning ride out of Shiqiao and back to work. We pulled into the factory courtyard past some women standing near the clocking-in machine but there was nothing for them to do that day and by mid-morning they were gone. The factory was quiet apart from the third floor where operators were finishing an old order, and the fourth, where line supervisors chatted in groups.

Lenny and the other senior managers were still in Hong Kong and in the second floor office local staff sat in circles exchanging stories of family reunions or took turns to use the telephone for New Year social calls. Line supervisors wandered in and out greeting friends with the traditional Cantonese Chinese New Year greeting *gung hei fat choi* ("may you become wealthy"). We wrote letters home and while I prepared another lesson for my students at the warehouse Min telephoned Bart and asked him for an update on the flat.

"Hey! I guarantee you guys will be established in accommodation by the end of the week. And that's a guarantee!"

He added that Anthony Cheung, an internal auditor from the Hong Kong office, would be coming to Panyu to lead a reshuffle of the various company properties. Bart was upbeat but we didn't share his enthusiasm. It just seemed like a repeat of Joan's visit.

I was due at the warehouse to teach that day and after lunch climbed into Ah Ling's bus, neatly parked in its usual place on the factory forecourt. He appeared at unpredictable moments and on one occasion drove off without me so I used to arrive a few minutes early.

I came to China with a selection of English classics and sitting in the bus waiting for Ah Ling was an ideal time for reading. The sun filtered through the windows and warmed the bus to a pleasant temperature while outside sounds were deadened by the glass.

I was interrupted by two young machine operators climbing aboard. They sat at the other end of the bus and subjected me to scrutiny, speculating about my age and nationality, and talking about the colour of my hair. But they didn't call me a ghost and I was pleased about that. The bus shook and Ah Ling moved towards the driving seat, warning them to be careful as I could understand Chinese. I thought they would be disconcerted but one of them sat nearer and asked me how old I was and how I had met Min. Not wanting to go into the details of our relationship yet again I simply said that it was *yuanfen* (predetermined destiny). After Min and I were married and visited relatives and friends in Shanghai, people had talked jokingly about the traditional story of the "red thread" by which the old man under the moon ties a red string around the ankles of two people destined to be together. We were given *baihe lianzi tang* (lily and lotus seed soup) the names of the ingredients being auspicious homonyms for a young couple starting married life. *Baihe* means a lily but the sounds of the two syllables are also a contraction of *bai nian he hao* ("one hundred years of happy union"). *Lianzi*, lotus seed, represents the phrase *lian sheng gui zi* ("give birth to many children").

"Why d'you call it predetermined destiny?" she replied, looking at me as if I was a simpleton, and as we drove away from the factory I was obliged to give a full account of how Min and I had met as students.

The two women were travelling to a subcontractor and we set off on a different route from usual. It had rained torrentially while we were in Shanghai and in places the surface of the road had been washed away, leaving deep water-filled potholes that made the minibus lurch and buck, throwing us around inside. At times we slowed almost to a halt as the bottom of the vehicle scraped and grated against rock and tarmac.

We reached higher ground and followed another smaller track to the subcontractor's factory, a vast eyesore of a building at the bottom of a deep hollow, invisible from the road. The slopes that led down to it were covered in thick-stemmed bamboo that grew towards the light, trunks shiny like polished tubing. The factory itself, the road and a supporting wall that held in place the sloping banks of earth, were of pale grey concrete, contrasting with the natural forms and bright colour of the bamboo.

The operators jumped off the bus with a wave and leaving the factory we followed a different route to the warehouse. Its unfamiliarity reminded me of how little I had actually seen of Panyu County. The four-lane road was wide and flat. Young trees had been densely planted on either side and partially obscured paddy fields and the blurred silhouettes of small hills in the distant haze. There was little traffic, mainly small trucks, solitary underpowered motorcyclists and the occasional chugging hand tractor.

We passed a group of female labourers in blue jackets putting the finishing touches to an ornamental archway. I still found it surprising to see women carrying out construction work in China, whether digging up the road or pushing wheelbarrows full of sand and cement. It was heavy work and they rarely had gloves, boots or other basic protective work wear. The traditional archway that they were working on, known as *paifang* in Chinese, straddled a narrow road leading to a small village. *Paifang* are commonly used in China as a form of decorative gateway but also had an earlier commemorative function. In some cases "Chastity Archways" were built to honour exemplary wives who never remarried after the deaths of their husbands.

This one had the name of the village along the top in large Chinese characters and was decorated with the bright orange-yellow roof tiles used throughout the county. We saw them on the buildings at Lianhuashan Port, in the Panyu Hotel, on gateways to factories, on the Luoxi Bridge and even on the pagoda in the factory garden.

Ah Ling dropped me off five minutes from the warehouse and I walked past more buildings under construction. The labourers stopped work to stare, tools forgotten in their hands.

Further on I was met by James, one of my students. He was cycling towards me on a very small child's bicycle. I was quite a bit taller than James but he insisted that I ride the bike to the warehouse, my legs bent awkwardly, knees almost level with my face. For the watching labourers I was enough of a circus act already without the addition of a comedy bicycle routine, but James took my attempts to give him back the bike as a show of politeness and remained insistent, mild but determined. Wobbling dangerously I set off for the warehouse, the bike veering away to the right and left in unpredictable swooping turns.

James, the youngest student at the warehouse and first introduced by Rupert as "de boy" had very little formal education but was very motivated and often got 100% in the tests I later gave them. He was the only person I taught who wanted to use an English name. The others teased him about it, one of them saying in Cantonese, "who needs one of those bloody foreign names?"

Teaching James and his colleagues gave me the full immersion in local culture I had looked forward to before coming out to China. Unlike the factory, no English was spoken at the warehouse and in the Chinese-speaking environment my Cantonese began to improve. I was treated well, enjoyed my time there and felt I was contributing something useful to the individuals I taught as English was such a prized commodity in Panyu. On arrival I was always given a cup of chrysanthemum tea by James. I sat at one of the empty desks in the warehouse office and sipped it before starting the class.

Numbers were gradually rising and in total I had 12 students including office staff and a number of people who worked in the warehouse itself unloading and stacking deliveries from Hong Kong. From the early days of the "ABC" the class had evolved rapidly, mainly because of the dedication and enthusiasm of the majority of the people I was teaching, with one or two exceptions. I had no formal training as a teacher but did have a lot of experience of language classes and thought about effective teaching methods I had encountered over the years. I began by preparing all the teaching materials myself, writing out vocabulary and dialogues in simple English.

Early on it became apparent that as well as there being a great disparity in ability and previous experience with the English language, there was also a range in motivation and willingness to work. A few individuals seemed intent on justifying Rupert's initial scepticism and I suspected that for them it was just a pleasant break in the afternoon rather than a class at which they expected to do anything. I had to explain repeatedly that some work was necessary. It was not enough simply to be in the same room as a native speaker of the target language. One of them, Zhou Yong, still couldn't count to ten or recognize the letters of the alphabet after many weeks. It frustrated the advanced students, who far from encouraging the laggards, made humorous remarks and howled with laughter at their basic mistakes with pronunciation. Their comments were often very funny and I would struggle to control my own laughter.

But the weeks went by and Zhou Yong and several of the others didn't improve. The gap between them and the hard-working contingent expanded exponentially. I thought it unfair on those who were working hard to be held back by one or two with no interest in the subject so I started testing them. Those who failed repeatedly would have to leave the class. The non-working group barely got any marks on their tests and with the evidence in black and white I asked them why they weren't working. Li Sanmei, a borderline case, didn't answer the question but instead launched into a blatantly overblown speech extolling my virtues as a teacher.

"Stop patting my horse's buttocks," I said in Mandarin.

Li Sanmei looked surprised at this colloquialism but she stopped the flattery. Our discussion ended with me exhorting them to make more effort in future. A week later Li Sanmei passed the test but the other marks were still desperately low and I said I would no longer teach them if they failed again. I reported back to Rupert with the marks and my proposed course of action. After our lukewarm start we now got on well; he had accepted me at the warehouse, given me support when needed and even asked me to teach him too (though he was always vague about an actual starting date).

"Okay. If dey English still bad, dey dong pass de test, I fine dem and cut de pay."

This hadn't occurred to me as an option and after more tests and threats Zhou Yong was the only person who hadn't passed. I was relieved to be able to expel him from the class at last, but unexpectedly Rupert intervened, "Dat boy wery lazy, but he really want learn English."

I said that wasn't my impression at all and he was holding everyone back. Rupert looked up at me with an expression half-joking, half-serious; "*Kau kau lei ah*", he said ("I implore you" or "I'm begging you"). I could hardly ignore this heartfelt request and didn't want to cause a loss of face in front of his staff. On the other hand empty threats would undermine my position too, as I had learned from the military strategist Sunzi. But you couldn't always apply Sunzi to modern life. His solutions to lack of effort or incompetence tended to be rigorous and would have landed me in prison. So we agreed to compromise and allow Zhou Yong one more final chance (in reality his fourth or fifth chance at the same basic test). He scored three per cent and Rupert accepted that English wasn't for Zhou Yong after all, the latter leaving the class without suffering any fine or pay cut.

With the students sorted into three groups of varying ability I was able to concentrate on the actual teaching and at this stage I continued to emphasize basic pronunciation. I thought this would be a useful foundation skill that they could build on later. The majority of Chinese people learned English from other Chinese people and had never heard a native speaker talking the language. It was not surprising that pronunciation was a problem area, particularly the "th" sound, an aspect I really had to address considering the frequency of the word "the" in the English language.

For the time being "th" remained challenging but I had a new method to help distinguish between "n" and "l". Confusing these two letters was an issue for native Cantonese speakers but would not generally have caused problems for Chinese speakers from the north of the country. While in Shanghai I had talked to Min's aunt, a professor of English with many years of teaching experience. She said I should explain that the "l" sound comes from the mouth and throat but the "n" is more nasal. This was the explanation my students needed to begin discriminating between the two sounds.

Soon the beginners' class had moved from basic counting to days of the week and months of the year. I used to ask students to recite the days of the week individually. The concept of rote learning was familiar to Chinese people and at school children learn poems, passages of classical Chinese and short stories by heart.

Recently on a local radio show I had heard a five year old reciting a Tang Dynasty (618-907 AD) poem he had been taught by his elder sister, "Quiet Night Thoughts" by Li Bai (701-762).

Before the bed bright moonlight
I believe it is frost on the ground
Lifting my head I look at the bright moon
Lowering my head I think of home

Chuang qian ming yue guang
Yi shi di shang shuang
Ju tou wang ming yue
Di tou si gu xiang

English with its multi-syllable words was difficult for Li Sanmei and she often simplified the sounds so that they were more like Cantonese. When it was her turn to recite the days of the week, aware that I was listening carefully, she would say the words very fast or partly under her breath, hoping I would quickly move on to the next person. As far as I could make out her word for Wednesday was "Feeday" but apart from this anomaly the other days were roughly correct with the major sounds in place. Yet still there was something I couldn't quite put my finger on. I asked her to have another go and speak loudly and clearly this time. Her Monday sounded like "Wunday", the consonant a mystery but vowels both correct; Tuesday became "Tooday", again near enough; "Feeday" we would leave for the time being; "Forday" in place of Thursday was understandable as I knew the "th" caused problems, as did the letter "r" missing from

Friday which she pronounced as "Fiday". "Feeday" was the key and suddenly I understood that she was attempting to say "Oneday, Twoday, Threeday, Fourday, Fiveday", giving a Chinese spin to the English days of the week. It was a logical approach for Li Sanmei as the Mandarin for the days of the week is simply the characters for "week" followed by the numbers from one to six as appropriate, Sunday being an exception.

The beginners group was always brought to a halt by a loud banging on the door from the advanced group, who would not let me overrun by more than a minute or two. In total I taught three different groups of people and the amount of preparation and marking was increasing. The advanced group went through the coursework I prepared so fast that I was constantly having to invent new dialogues and passages of prose. At about the time I realized I couldn't keep up with them through preparing my own teaching materials, James brought in an English text book and we started using that. I supplemented it with some ideas on language learning from a book on teaching that my father sent out from England.

After the lessons I and the other warehouse staff waited at the loading bay for the bus to take us back to Shiqiao. I used to stand watching the nearby builders watching me or watch rock blasting in the distance. A cloud of smoke and the sight of rocks breaking off and crumbling away was followed a second or two later by the sound of the explosion as more local hills were demolished before my eyes.

On one of these occasions a young woman wearing a white track-suit and trainers came over and spoke to me in Mandarin. I assumed her to be one of the warehouse staff..

"Will you teach me English?" she asked.

"Okay," I replied. "But you should talk to Rupert first and then join the class."

"Who's Rupert?"

"He's your boss, isn't he?" I replied, surprised, but then talking to her further discovered that she worked in the sports shoe factory across the road. I said that as she didn't work for the company I could hardly teach her with the others.

"You could teach me after the class."

I said I was too busy. At the factory I was still helping Xiao Song with his English and there were another two people in our office whom I taught during the lunch break. I had found it difficult to refuse their requests for help but it was a commitment I was beginning to regret.

"I'll teach you Cantonese in exchange," she said.

"Sorry. I really am too busy."

"What hotel are you staying in? The Panyu Hotel? What's your room number? I could drop in some time for a chat."

The bus arrived and apologizing again for not being able to help I climbed aboard. On more than one occasion local people had suggested that I set up an English school in Panyu. It could have been a profitable business as there was so much demand for English locally. As I sat down the woman in the white tracksuit slid into the empty seat beside me. I made a show of taking out my book and reading it but she reached over and twisted it round so she could see the cover. Frowning she said, "I can't understand that. I wish I could read English books." Then she continued, "foreigners are very mysterious. I like foreign faces you know. You've all got sunken eyes. Oh, what's that?" She pointing at the lesson material I was carrying. "Can I have a look?" I passed the papers across and tried to focus on my book. "I don't recognise many of these words. I wish I could have a copy."

"Help yourself."

The next time I taught at the warehouse she was waiting with the others for the bus back to Shiqiao. I never understood how she managed to get a free ride back every day but Shiqiao was a small place and everyone seemed to know each other. She had worked through the teaching material and wanted help with some of the more colloquial phrases that she couldn't find in the dictionary. She became a regular feature of my trips to the warehouse and was just one of many people in Panyu desperate for the opportunity to learn English from a native speaker.

18 Lotus Flower Mountain

Michael announced that the course was over and we had all passed, including John this time. I made a few suggestions on the feedback form and Michael's manner grew noticeably colder for a day or two. He frowned at me sternly when we next met. But the Filipinos and Sri Lankans thought the course was tremendous and gave Michael glowing praise. Alfred failed to graduate due to his prolonged absence. He never returned to Panyu after his trip to Sri Lanka.

With work study behind us Min and I were ready to move on to the next stage of our management training, whatever that might be. It would soon be time to call Bart again to find out what was planned, if anything. In the meantime Bernard suggested a trip to Lianhuashan to celebrate our graduation.

"Where's that? Looks amazing," he had said some time ago pointing to a display of photographs in the foyer of the Panyu Hotel. Lianhuashan, it turned out, was more than just the domain and fiefdom of Office

Head Wang. It was also the site of an old sandstone quarry and local tourist spot featuring dramatic man-made cliffs, winding rocky tunnels and pools of lotus flowers. According to our Panyu map there were only a handful of such quarries in all of China.

"Invite everyone, have a party," said Bernard and unintentionally caused loss of face to Ah Ling the driver. Originally we planned to take a taxi but after Bernard invited everyone from the work study course this was no longer feasible. What was needed was something more bus-sized.

Through enquiries Bernard learned that Ah Ling was paid to work seven days a week. He asked Min to find out if Ah Ling would be willing to take our group to Lianhuashan in his minibus on Sunday, a day off for most people in the factory. Ah Ling agreed but then it occurred to Bernard that before commandeering the factory driver and bus he should obtain consent from the general manager. Bart said it was fine provided Johnson did not need the bus on that day. Bernard asked Johnson, Johnson asked Ah Ling (again), Ah Ling yelled long and loud at Bernard. He found it insulting to be asked a second time, as if Bernard doubted he would carry out the task and had therefore informed the big guns, Bart and Johnson. Bernard, nonplussed by the ranting leather-jacketed Ah Ling standing in the courtyard bawling at him, permed head shaking in anger, came into the office in search of Min. "What's he saying? What's he so upset about?"

With Min interpreting and doing her best to smooth things over between them, Bernard apologized readily but was still unclear as to what he was supposed to be apologizing for. Ah Ling grudgingly accepted that face had been restored but he remained annoyed and expressed himself loudly enough for the cyclists outside the factory gate to join in the conversation had they wanted to. "No idea would be so upset," said Bernard later.

But on the appointed day Ah Ling arrived accompanied by his wife and young son. I recognized his wife, Iris, as one of my students at the warehouse. She said she spoke good English because she had previously worked at the reception desk at the Panyu Hotel and was used to dealing with foreigners. She had a senior position in the warehouse office and had her eye on Rupert's job, complaining he couldn't do it properly because he was from Hong Kong and didn't have the right local connections.

In the bus I sat next to Matthew and after spending most of the journey in silence he leant towards me with a fixed frown of concentration.

"Gems. You like gems, no?"

"Gems?" I replied.

"Gemstones. You like, no? I like gemstones. My hobby is collecting gemstones. Tell me where can I buy gemstones here?"

Sitting in the back of the bus watching the dry, empty landscape pass by as we travelled the way to Lianhuashan, the last thing on my mind was precious or semi-precious stones and I was slow to understand what he meant. I was initially surprised that he had singled me out as a man with an interest or expertise in gems; Min was not awash with diamonds or any other jewellery for that matter apart from one pair of earrings. When she was growing up female students were expected to dress in a plain and simple manner without adornment. These strictures didn't just apply to students. After Min graduated she taught English at her university and was once asked by an older professor not to wear a particular dress as it was too "distracting". For her class, he said.

Min had her ears pierced as an adult in England and the first time we returned to China, minutes after arriving home she was taken away to another room. When she re-emerged her earrings were gone and her hair tied up in a ponytail (demure was the in look; loose hair was also viewed with disapproval). I liked that pair of earrings, having bought them for Min myself, and recalled that they were of onyx. Yes, I did like gemstones but didn't know where to buy them in Panyu. Matthew turned away and lapsed into silence.

The road curved upwards steeply as we neared our destination and the bus jerked to a sudden halt in the middle of the road. Ah Ling turned in his seat and announced that everyone would have to get out and walk the rest of the way as his bus couldn't drive up the hill with such a heavy load. "Eh, what? Why?" asked Bernard. It was a fair question. The vehicle had been coping adequately and as a regular passenger (three times a week to teach English at the warehouse) I had experienced Ah Ling thrashing it through far worse conditions than this. It wasn't gold treatment from Ah Ling and I wondered if he was still unhappy with Bernard. Short of asking him, and that didn't seem a good idea, there was no way of knowing.

As he accelerated away we walked up the hill at a more leisurely pace, eventually moving off the road and climbing a steep path into a large flat area, partially paved and enclosed by a wall of rock. This was topped with medium-sized trees and shrubs and looked natural except for occasional sections where rectangular blocks of stone had been removed. I assumed that much of the paved area we were standing on had once been solid rock, hammered and chiselled away as the centuries rolled by.

In one place a solitary chunk of stone protruding from the ground had been carved into a large fist the width and height of a man; as to why or when our local colleagues didn't know. For a tourist spot it was pleasantly empty. The only people we saw were two gardeners raking up leaves from bone-dry brown grass. They stirred up clouds of dust that revolved and swirled in the weak sunlight.

Young palm trees with fresh green leaves were unaffected by the dry conditions, and a row of bushes with red berries stood out against the grey rock background. We walked up a path through sparse woods. The grass was brown and dusty, nearby pools were half empty. Emerging from the trees we passed stalls selling drinks and tourist goods.

Matthew stopped to appraise some rings decorated with pieces of jade, semi-precious stones and bright plastic. He scooped up a handful and tried them on one by one. Evidently designed for smaller hands, one ring refused to come off, squashed behind the joint of his middle finger as if stuck there since birth. He pulled, his cheeks puffed out with the effort, the rest of his body pitted against the ring and his finger. "What gem is this?" he asked irrelevantly, stopping for a breather.

"Have to buy that now," said Bernard with a smile, but as he looked away the ring suddenly came loose.

Matthew's elbow whipped round like the blade of a propeller, narrowly missing the back of Bernard's head.

I wandered over to a sorry-looking brown bear in a cage. It was a miserable addition to the spot. A small boy ambled across and put his hands on the bars. His mother was slow to realize the danger but then pulled him back with a shriek. Nearby a group of labourers in blue jackets looked on idly, occasionally turning to swing their sledgehammers at rocks on the ground, smashing them into smaller pieces to line the base of an empty pool.

The ubiquitous blue clothing of Chinese people in the 20th century didn't originate with the current regime but had its roots in earlier history, something I had discovered in my reading about the first official British delegation to China led by Lord McCartney in 1792. It was a failure in terms of opening up trade between the two countries and having China recognize Britain as an equal, but one good thing to come of it was the sketches and watercolour paintings by William Alexander, the young artist appointed as Draftsman to the Embassy. He painted places and objects of interest: weapons, junks, sampans, shipping and waterways, bridges, pagodas, towers and city walls, but also produced many detailed groups of Qing Dynasty people and figures including Qian Long the Emperor himself. He painted Mandarins, fishermen, soldiers, peasants, watermen and even a prostitute undergoing examination prior to likely corporal punishment. The figures bring the Qing Dynasty to life, and like the labourers smashing rock for the nearby pool, many are dressed in blue.

Walking onwards we followed the path as it climbed and meandered through a dense landscape of cliffs and columns given form by continuous chipping away over hundreds of years. The quarrying had stopped before the supply of rock was exhausted and in places natural forms contrasted with the straight edges and cube-like shapes left behind by unfinished excavations. On one inaccessible ledge five or six small slabs remained, cut free but never put to use. At the foot of the cliffs a young couple punted a bamboo boat across a pool and stopped to look up at characters in the rock above. On one the character for "happiness" or "good fortune" *fu* had been carved a hundred times.

There was no information as to when work stopped at the quarry but at some stage a decision had been made to preserve it as a scenic spot. Rocks were marked on the map with names such as "Lion Rock", "Eight Immortals Peak", "Swallow Cliff", "Lotus Rock", "Bed of the Immortals" and "Guanyin Peak", the latter the Chinese term for the Bodhisattva of Compassion. A bit of imagination was needed to comprehend the naming of some of these and we walked past Lotus Rock without noticing it. The origins of other names were more obvious. Near the entrance we had passed the "Southern Heavenly Gate", a rectangular doorway cut through a wall of rock, easily big enough for two of Ah Ling's minibuses to pass through, and the "Sword Gate", a diagonal guillotine of stone suspended above the path. At one point the way became a narrow staircase of several dozen steps cutting upwards through solid rock. Tall moss-covered walls hemmed us in on either side.

The path took us on a winding climb to the highest point among the rock formations. The view was spectacular and from here we could see the full extent of the quarrying. Stony outcroppings that remained showed the original level of the land before the quarrying had started. The empty space surrounding solitary columns had once been thousands of tons of rock, sliced and hacked away over the centuries. Below us, the path wound between rocks and motionless pools. A sheer cliff face dropped alarmingly to green water far below. It shot down like a knife blade and sucked the gaze after it.

Trees grew like bonsai out of fissures in boulders, their roots spilling in tangled lattices towards the ground. We walked past unfamiliar shrubs with big rubbery leaves and a tree with flat pods hanging from the branches. "They use those to wash clothes," said Min. She had spent her early childhood in Renhua County where she lived during the political movement known as the "Great Cultural Revolution". Situated at the northern edge of Guangdong Province, Renhua was poor, rural and mountainous. In later life the smell of pine needles always took Min back to that time. One of her jobs was to collect the needles and burn them, bringing the ash into school for use as fertilizer. Another task for children was to carry buckets of human excrement for the rice paddies, an ancient practice in China. The single character *tiao* means "to carry on the shoulder with a pole".

Min's memories of her childhood in Renhua are few. She had one toy during that period, a doll. "You could pull its arms and head off", she said when I asked her to describe it. She once told me about a pet dog that used to greet her when she returned from school. It was taken away from her and killed during one of the many campaigns of the time.

Living conditions in Shanghai were still basic for many in the late eighties and early nineties but life was good compared to the years of pain endured in the previous decades. One phrase I heard more than once from the older generation was *xian ku hou tian*, literally "first bitter afterwards sweet". For some in Min's family those years had been bitter indeed involving brutality, torture and death.

As well as the rocks at Lianhuashan there was a restored nine-storey pagoda. It was originally built in 1612 and overlooked a castle fortification constructed in the Qing Dynasty (1644-1912). The Lianhua castle was apparently used by the Chinese official Lin Zexu in the Opium War to garrison his troops and to serve as a line of defence against the invading British forces. Lin Zexu, famous in the history books for seizing opium from British traders and destroying it, a factor leading to the outbreak of war, is now regarded by the Chinese as a national hero. At the time he was blamed for his handling of events and exiled to Xinjiang.

We climbed back into the bus and as Ah Ling reversed out of the car park I watched a group of men at a firing range competing with compressed air guns. Two hands were required to control the large tripod-mounted weapons and with loud bangs they shot tennis balls at metal cut out animals. The prize, Western cigarettes.

19 Warp and weft

The factory was proving slow to recover after the Spring Festival break and was noticeably quieter than when we arrived. Steve remained optimistic and said that it was always like this after the Chinese New Year holiday; large orders would come in soon. But days became weeks and the orders failed to materialize. Instead we heard that due to a global shortage of new business the factories in the Philippines and Sri Lanka had been operating a three day week for some time. Then there was an announcement that the Panyu factory would follow suit and soon be working four days instead of six. This applied to the shop floor only and as office staff we were likely to be under-occupied in the coming weeks.

It should have been the ideal time for Bernard to implement his quality system but he and Lenny were working to different agendas and generally ignored each other. Without the active support of Lenny, Bernard was building on sand. He tried to effect changes by giving direct instructions to the workers but this would have been uphill work even without having to relay everything through an interpreter. The issue of who would interpret for Bernard had in any case become a stumbling block in the way of progress. Bernard and Anne had a fiery disagreement over garment quality and relations with Charlotte were often strained due to personality clashes between the two. Neither Anne nor Charlotte was employed as Bernard's interpreter (or anyone else's interpreter for that matter) and they felt that help was given as a favour, to be withdrawn at will should a recipient prove himself unworthy. Bernard, on the other hand, thought that help should be forthcoming as a matter of course; "all on the same team" after all.

The other problem faced by Bernard was that workers gave priority to any requirement Lenny might have over the needs of his new quality system. Two great camps had emerged within the company, effectively split along the linguistic lines of Hong Kong Cantonese speakers and native English speakers. Both groups pursued different priorities. The only thing they seemed to have in common was an inability to communicate with the other side.

In recent months the balance of power had tipped in favour of Lenny and his faction due to Steve's lengthy absences abroad. The scales had also been set moving in that direction by the earlier loss of Clare, an English work study manager who left the factory shortly before we arrived in Panyu. Her departure created a power vacuum and seriously weakened the position of the English pro-work study faction. At least, this was the only explanation I could think of for the sudden appointment of a new work study manager to a factory without work in an economic climate of world recession. It was after the start of the four day week that Bernard and Steve returned one weekend from Hong Kong with a newcomer to the factory. "Dave," announced Bernard. "New work study manager."

Dave wore a suit, carried a leather briefcase and gazed round the office with a hyper-alert new boy look as he was introduced to his future colleagues. He was in his mid-twenties and came from a garment industry work study job in England. Later he told me he had never been abroad before. The furthest he had been away from home was seven miles.

To celebrate Dave's arrival Steve suggested an evening meal at one of the large hotels in Guangzhou. When living in Panyu he had visited the hotel at least once a week to use the sports facilities there and to eat Western food. The journey was fast in the company Volvo, Rod's preferred method of transport when coming to China. We had been to Guangzhou so many times that I barely noticed details of the journey, but the hotel was something new. It was opulent in the extreme, grand and glittering with a wide imposing staircase of ornate dark wood leading up from the lobby. The new wing of the Panyu Hotel seemed humble in comparison.

"Well, hello there!" said Bernard to the waitress at the restaurant entrance. She turned immediately to lead us to our table, Bernard subjecting her dress to close professional scrutiny. It was a *qipao* or *cheongsam* of blue-green silk that shimmered as she walked, stretching and relaxing across her lower back and the curves of her body. The sides of the dress were slit from ankle to hip revealing a generous but fleeting flash of ochre leg as she walked, falling back modestly when she stood still to take our order.

The *qipao* (literally "riding robe") had come a long way from its origins as a Manchu outer garment previously worn by men and women alike. Qing Dynasty photos show Manchu women wearing an item of clothing resembling a beautifully embroidered but shapeless dressing gown, fully concealing rather than making any attempt to show or flatter a woman's figure. This changed in 1920's Shanghai as the *qipao* developed into a tight-fitting dress often decorated with printed patterns on a single colour background, the only resemblance to the original robe being the collar and fastening folded across the chest. The main addition to this 1990's version seemed to be the elongation of the slit up the side, previously extending only from ankle to knee.

A *qipao* would have been a difficult garment for the company factory to attempt. The next day Bernard discovered quality issues in a garment of considerably less complexity, women's underpants, and he stood at the front of the office handling a pair and studying them closely. Finally some genuine lingerie, but Bernard was critical.

"Look, the fabric's rucked," he said, holding out the underpants for the benefit of Dave and some of the work study engineers. "Must stretch correctly across a lady's bottom," he added with a grin, grasping the underpants firmly in two fists and turning them over to pull taut the material between his hands, demonstrating how creases should form on the underwear when in situ. "Has to be just right for Madame, you know. No seriously, it's the way the thread goes. The warp and the weft have to go the right way. Got it wrong here. Know how to remember the difference between the two? The weft goes from east to weft."

"Ber Lud," interrupted Charlotte. "Ber Lud. Why you stand dere like dat? Why don't you shit?" Bernard looked startled for a second, gave a snort and let out a roar of laughter. "Why don't I what?" he said and burst out laughing again, joined by Dave, his body crumpled in hysterics. "Think you mean 'why don't I sit?'" The two collapsed with laughter once more but eventually Bernard remembered why he had come back into the office.

"Time to do some work. Interpreting. Need your help, Charlotte."

"I don't like you, Ber Lud. You laugh at Charlotte's English."

"Bit of fun, come on now. Back to work."

"No. I not do your work."

"Come on. Serious now. Joke's over."

"No. I not do your work, Ber Lud. You load of crap Ber Lud!

"Not funny now."

Something in the phrase "you load of crap Ber Lud!" resonated with Charlotte and she repeated it over and over in a sing-song voice as if she would never stop. Bernard threw his hands in the air and came over to our table. "Can't do any more work without an interpreter," he said and sat down.

Late that afternoon Bernard was still lamenting his lack of interpreter and Min volunteered to help out.

She was familiar with his quality system having already translated documents needed for its implementation. "Fantastic," he said. "Been having a problem with the examiners. Infuriating. Whenever I pick up a garment and say it has quality problems, shouldn't have been passed, they say they haven't examined it yet, just about to. What rubbish, pulling the wool."

I asked what he was going to do about it.

"Already done it," he replied. "Told them to get two separate racks, one for examined garments and one for unexamined garments, has to be on one rack or the other, no in-between. Now they can't pretend they haven't examined a garment when they bloody well have done. They'd send any rubbish out the factory. Not anymore. Need to check on them though."

Min went with Bernard to the third floor where they were still working on an old order and the examiners were inspecting garments for quality, laying them flat against white boards to help pick out any errors. Bernard stepped over to the racks and searched through the garments that they had already passed. He stopped with an oath and threw up his hands.

"Don't believe it. Look at this. Stitching's coming out and the rabric's fucked, I mean the fabric's rucked. Again! Why has this been passed? Incredible." He thrust the garment in the face of the examiner and said, "uh? uh?" in a loud voice. She looked back impassively. "Ask her why she's passed this garment?"

Min repeated Bernard's question to the examiner in Cantonese and translated her response back into English. "She says she hasn't passed this garment. She hasn't looked at it yet."

"Oh, no, no, no," said Bernard slowly. "This is the rack for examined garments, is it not?"

Min spoke to the examiner again, who nodded her head in agreement. "Yes. She says this is the rack for examined garments."

"If it is on the rack for examined garments it must, ergo, have been examined. Yet she just said she has not examined it. How so?"

Min translated Bernard's apparently incontrovertible conclusion and question for the examiner, but she, far from being discomforted by his raised voice and adversarial style of questioning was the embodiment of the four-character phrase *li zhi qi zhuang* "with justice on one's side, one is bold and assured". She stood tall and gestured earnestly at the racks.

"Well, what's she saying?"

"She says of course this is the rack for examined garments, but she's put some unexamined garments here temporarily because she's run out of space on the other rack. She said you've just been looking at garments she hasn't yet examined even though they are on the rack for examined garments."

"No. Won't do, don't believe it, just don't believe it," said Bernard. He glared at the examiner and finally said, "doesn't anyone in this factory care about their work? Why does she think there are two racks? Went through this last time. Whole point of having separate racks is to keep examined and unexamined garments apart. Tell her that. Tell her I want two separate racks and want them now. Said that last time. Want it done and want it done now."

"She said you were going to arrange for more

racks."

"Where's the line supervisor? Have a word with her," said Bernard already turning and heading in the direction of the supervisor's office. But when they arrived the room was empty. "Should be here," he said, frowning in irritation, "no point having a line supervisors' office without line supervisors in it."

Bernard stood undecided, turned on his heel and went back up the stairs, stopping to inspect some garments on the way. He moved from one floor to another, speculating as to where the line supervisors could be, occasionally distracted by quality problems or other issues. "These button machines wouldn't be allowed in England. No eye guard. Needle misses the hole, strikes the button, could break and splinter into the operator's eye. Same with the band saw. Operators don't use gloves. Unbelievable." Several turns round the factory and finally "ah", he said, as a cluster of supervisors came into view, back on the original floor where the examination had just taken place.

The line supervisor, Ah Mui, was of neat and tidy appearance. She wore trainers, jeans, a t-shirt and, like many of the women in the factory, her long hair was pulled together at the back in a ponytail. "Hey there! Hey there!" said Bernard, attracting her attention by coming up behind her and tugging her hair like a bell pull. Ah Mui turned round, surprised but smiling, and Bernard said to Min, "please ask her where she has just been."

Ah Mui replied that she had been going round the factory looking for needles.

"Ask her why she doesn't have any spare needles."

"The store keeper keeps the needles but he has run

out."

"Need a constant supply of needles. No good if they run out and can't get more. Have to go and talk to the store keeper." Bernard turned and marched off but stopped before he had gone far, distracted by the appearance of a garment a nearby operator was working on. The stitching had run, damaging the fabric.

"Look at that! Needle should be changed. Ask her why she hasn't changed it."

"The operator said it's because there are no spares."

"Ridiculous," said Bernard.

The store was at the far end of the cutting room on the top floor of the factory. An elderly sleepy man, the storekeeper, raised his head and blinked at Min and Bernard from behind a small window. The storekeeper was of the same school of thought as the cleaners who didn't wish to clean. "Not my job to get the needles," he said, volunteering no further information but letting his head sink back onto his chest.

"Whose job is it to get the needles then?"

The storekeeper looked up again, surprised that Min and Bernard were still there.

"Biffo."

"Who or what is Biffo?" asked Bernard.

To produce top quality garments blunt needles must be replaced with alacrity and the tools of production kept in tip-top condition; for the blacksmith the anvil, for the artist the paintbrush, for the work study engineer the stopwatch but for the dressmaker, that complex assembly of metal and moving parts, the sewing machine. How important the sewing machine, the fundamental tool of production in a garment factory! How important the mechanics who service the machines and keep them running! How very important the head mechanic, illuminating the way for his men, shining like a light, working tirelessly and unstintingly in pursuit of mechanical excellence with his love of cogs, whirring parts and delicate machinery! And how, most important of all, was Biffo ever selected for that role?

Biffo, affable head mechanic from Hong Kong, didn't strain himself in pursuit of the company mission. Rod's mantra of "speed, speed, and more speed" was not what he was all about. For Biffo it was more a question of "chill, chill and chill some more". If a sewing machine was causing problems such as leaving skid marks of grease all over the underwear, Biffo would be called. He would respond with the alacrity of a man lying in the sun on some remote tropical island deciding whether it was too much effort to turn over and reach for another beer from the cooler. Usually it was too much effort but if by some form of divine intervention Biffo actually arrived in the vicinity of a faulty sewing machine, occasionally with a screwdriver but more likely a cigarette, he would bluster good naturedly and go away again without doing anything, except if feeling particularly energetic maybe light up another cigarette.

His mechanics followed his relaxed approach to the company mission and most afternoons could be seen squatting on top of some lockers in a sociable cluster blowing smoke rings into the air.

Admirable though these qualities were as a modern interpretation of the great Chinese philosopher Laozi, there was a compatibility issue with Bernard's current mind-set; the latter one of wanting to get things done and to get them done now.

"There you are Biffo," said Bernard after a long hunt around the factory and its environs. "Can get to the bottom of this at last."

Biffo had spent his whole life in Hong Kong but like a large number of its inhabitants, despite British colonial rule, spoke almost no English. "Could you ask him how often he supplies needles to the factory?" Bernard asked Min. Before she had finished translating, Biffo interrupted her and chuckling to himself, smiled hugely and said "Lee doh. Lee doh".

"What's he saying?" said Bernard. "How often?"

"Lee doh. Lee doh," repeated Biffo.

"I don't know," said Min. "'Lee doh' means 'here' in Cantonese."

"Why's he saying 'here, here'? What does he mean?" said Bernard frowning. He raised his voice, loud at the best of times. In a foghorn slow boom he asked Biffo, "how often do you supply needles to the factory?"

"Lee doh. Lee doh," came the reply.

"What!? All I want is an answer to the question."

"Oh, I know what he's saying," said Min. "He's speaking English, not Cantonese. He's saying, 'needle, needle'"

Biffo roared with laughter. Bernard paused, struggling.

"Ask him if he's in charge of supplying the needles." Before Min had finished translating Biffo interrupted again.

"Yes. Lee doh. Lee doh. I am Biffo. How do do? My name Biffo. I am mechanic. Your name Ber Lud.

How do do, Ber Lud?"

"Uh? What the..? Bloody hell! Don't believe this." Bernard raised his voice louder still and threw his hands in the air. "What about the bloody needles?"

Biffo looked round for somewhere to put his cigarette, rolled up his sleeves as if for dramatic effect and reached into his pocket.

"Getting somewhere at last," said Bernard, craning forward. Biffo pulled out a small device that looked like a calculator. He punched the keys and pushed it in Bernard's face. A squashed mechanical voice said, "needle, needle" and Biffo repeated, "lee doh, lee doh", chuckling all the while. Bernard threw up his hands again, management audit long forgotten, and made his way slowly back to the office.

20 Steve told me to sit around and do nothing like

Dave, the new work study manager, came to China armed with a copy of the alternative comic Viz. He said that a friend at home would be sending subsequent issues out to him. With its graphic sexual content I was amazed he had succeeded in getting it past Wang and his men. Many Chinese people still had a fond concept of the "English Gentleman", a stereotype I had been happy to foster, yet here was the new ambassador for England lending his copy of Viz to all and sundry in the second floor office. The Filipino work study engineers leafed through it in troubled silence as Dave accused them of having no sense of humour. He himself was incoherent at the antics of "Johnny Fart Pants" and "Fat Slags", the latter literally forcing their favours on a man in a public toilet.

Dave was fortunate in that as work study manager he had a defined job to do. He fit neatly into the company structure and reported directly to Steve. Somehow Dave was not required to undergo the rite of passage known as the company university.

I asked him how he had heard about the job and he replied, "it's not *what* you know, it's *who* you know." (Later these words of wisdom explained Biffo's appointment as I discovered that he owed his position to nepotism.) Dave said that he had been offered the job by Steve who remembered him as a former colleague when working in the garment industry back in England.

Demonstrating a cooler head and better grasp of negotiating skills than I when offered a job by the company, Dave had said he would only work in Panyu if they "made it worth his while". For Dave this meant doubling his pay.

Every morning Dave left the hotel carrying his briefcase and on arrival at the factory sat down at the back of the second floor office. From this vantage point he could overlook his new team of work study engineers. The briefcase was empty except for the copy of Viz and a picture of his girlfriend that he took out every morning and stood on his desk. At the end of the day he put the picture back in his case and returned with it to the Panyu Hotel. Mornings and afternoons Dave looked busy, marching speedily round the factory with his sleeves rolled up, whistling briskly.

Until this point Min and I had been in the limbo position of employees without a proper boss. This hadn't originally concerned us as Michael's course (lengthy though it turned out to be) was billed as part of the ongoing management training programme. But as the course approached its end we suspected that neither Rod, Bart or Chris had given any further thought to what else such a programme might involve. Instead there seemed to be a tacit understanding, never actually communicated directly to Min or me, that from now on we would be working for Dave as work study engineers. My experience watching people assemble beehive frames, clean light fittings, deal cards and flash different coloured lights at me had been a rare and unexpected addition to my education but it was time to put it behind me. I had nothing against my stopwatch wielding colleagues but the position of work study engineer was not the job Min or I had come to China to do. When an opportunity next presented itself, we would have to speak to Rod, the owner of the company and the man responsible for our employment.

Steve stayed long enough in Panyu to get Dave settled in but after that returned abroad. Following his departure Dave said, "Steve told me to sit around and do nothing like, for the first two weeks, but just find out how everything works and watch what goes on." Perhaps Dave took Steve's advice more literally than had been intended but the factory was quiet and showed no signs of becoming busy again. The sporadic activity that continued after Spring Festival had almost dried up completely and there was little work to do, or even to watch. There were disturbing rumours about cash flow problems for the company.

As the novelty of the situation wore off Dave became homesick and unhappy. Friday afternoons were a difficult time for him and pulling up a chair he would sit slumped with his chin on my desk and tell me about "the lads" back home. What he really missed was finishing work at midday on a Friday, playing football in the afternoon and going to the pub for a drink in the evening.

Dave's homesickness grew worse as the weeks passed, he had trouble sleeping at night, and as a further blow someone stole his copy of Viz from the Panyu Hotel. Had a cleaner taken it or was it now sitting in a vault of the local Public Security Bureau? The lack of activity in the factory didn't help Dave's mood. One of the reasons he had left England was because he was under-employed in his old job. He said it was twice as bad in the Panyu factory as he had to be at work for double the hours. Often when feeling down he questioned how long he would be able to endure his new circumstances. But there was light at the end of the tunnel for Dave. Long hours spent chatting with the Filipino women gradually brought him back to a more optimistic frame of mind.

Emerging from his homesickness, Dave began to exert himself, exercising that most simple of management techniques perfected by managers the world over; whenever Steve asked Dave to do something, Dave passed the instructions on to one of us. Dave didn't speak any Chinese and so, like Bernard, was limited in what work he could actually do in a factory in China. He told me that he wasn't very good at languages but had done French at school and knew that "wazzo" meant bird.

As well as chatting to the Filipino women, Dave set to educating Charlotte in the subtleties of the English language. "Bollocks!" and "I go for gypsy's" became two of her favourite phrases. Another time she asked me what the English word "snash" meant. I asked her what the context was.

"Context is 'I go for snash.'"

"Shouldn't teach her that sort of thing," said Bernard.

"Huh," replied Charlotte, "you bollocks, Ber Lud."

"Enough now. Not funny anymore."

"Bollocks, bollocks Ber Lud."

Dave, young and resilient, had bounced back fast, but for Bernard frustrations were mounting. He wasn't helped by Lenny and Biffo who continued to follow a course of passivity or non-intervention. Bernard was the Yang to Lenny's Yin and yet to become a disciple of Laozi. Instead he pursued the Art of Rod or the *Rodzi*. His preferred method of operation was increasingly to wander around the factory issuing orders, greeting people with the phrase, "want it done and want it done now". He was still experiencing communication problems but for this at least, he had come up with a solution. "Someone should teach me Chinese," he said and went off to telephone Bart to get authorization for lessons.

I was thinking about the Chinese language as well. With Charlotte's help my Cantonese was getting better but I was still having problems with tones. By a quirk of linguistic evolution the word in Cantonese for "yes" if said in the wrong tone has an obscene meaning (equivalent to the most offensive word in the English language), something I only discovered when my students kept dissolving into laughter whenever I replied in the affirmative.

Another awkward mistake arose in a local restaurant when I asked the waitress for more tea "*cha*". She looked concerned, disappeared and came back a few minutes later with the manager, who asked what the problem was. Evidently I had got my Mandarin tones wrong, pronouncing *cha* with a falling tone rather than a rising tone, and giving it the alternative meaning "poor" or "lacking" as in the phrase "the service is poor".

Sometimes tones can cause confusion for Chinese people. On one occasion the company minibus had been cleaned and some of the seats were covered in water. Anne was about to sit down but Min warned her that the seat was wet. The Mandarin word for wet is *shi* but the same sound with a different tone can also mean "yes". Anne thought Min was agreeing with something she had said and sat down in the pool of water.

Learning Mandarin it had been a case of rote learning tones together with characters but it occurred to me that I might not have to do the same with Cantonese. There seemed to be a relationship between the tone of a word in that language and the tone of the same word in Mandarin.

I looked for patterns between the tones in the words I knew in both languages and found that a word with a level tone in Mandarin would almost always have a high level tone in Cantonese. I discovered other relationships such as how a word with a rising tone in Mandarin would generally change to a falling tone when pronounced in Cantonese. I was able to work out approximate rules so that if I knew a Mandarin word I could make a reasonably accurate guess about its tone in Cantonese. Knowing what a tone should be in theory and actually managing to pronounce it correctly in practice was not the same thing at all, but it was still a useful piece of extra knowledge in my attempts to learn the language.

I heard angry noises from Bernard. "Unbelievable! Bart won't approve my Chinese lessons. Just what I needed."

21 Treated like a dog

The long period of quiet appeared to be over. There was a buzz of excitement as a large new order was announced and the morning trickle of workers swelled to a flood. Noise and activity once again clattered across the shop floor. Dave rolled up his sleeves and rearranged the tables in the office so that all work study engineers sat in one block. It was an improvement for us as we finally had our own desks instead of the communal conference table at the back of the room.

New orders usually started with a sample garment being made in Hong Kong. Once approved by the customer the sample was given a red tag and sent across to China, together with the specifications for its manufacture and a selection of the different colours and fabrics required. In Panyu a preliminary meeting was held between the production managers, quality department, line supervisors and senior work study engineers to decide how best to reproduce the red tag sample using the resources of the factory. The line supervisors would then make the garment using the methods discussed and send their copy of the original back to Hong Kong for approval. Once given the go-ahead there would be a final pre-production meeting back at the factory at which all parties would agree on the method and the different operations used to make the garment.

Next it was the work study engineer's task to decide on the best arrangement for the different sewing machines on the shop floor. Known as "line balancing" this involved dividing the machines appropriately between the different sewing operations to avoid bottlenecks in production. A quick and easy operation might just have one machine assigned to it but a slow one several. I was on the third floor with Annette, an experienced work study engineer from the Philippines, and as part of the line balancing for the new garment we concluded that a computerised sewing machine should replace an ordinary machine on one of the lines. Above us on the fourth floor six of these machines stood gathering dust.

The difficulties I was to encounter in trying to move a single sewing machine from one floor to another gave me an insight into Bernard's daily frustrations. The easiest thing would have been to move the machine myself, but according to an internal factory regulation the only people permitted to move equipment were Biffo's mechanics. On this occasion two of them had been instructed to move the machine but they were nowhere in sight. I waited for quite a while and then set off in search of them.

By the time I found the first mechanic I was

probably looking a little hassled. He, on the other hand, had a relaxed, contented look on his face as he squatted on some lockers and watched the world go by. Like the other members of Biffo's team, he was untroubled by the sudden urgency of the new order at the factory. I asked him what was happening about the machine and pointed out that it was supposed to have been moved to our floor some time ago. He looked at me, eyes slowly focusing, and replied that he was perfectly willing to move the machine. I expected him to get up, but he stayed where he was, squatting and smoking, as if the fact of him being "willing" to move the sewing machine was good enough, job done, and the actual physical part of the task irrelevant. Trying not to sound like Bernard ("want it done and want it done now") I nevertheless suggested that "now" would be as good a time as any to move the machine.

"Like I just said, I'm willing to move the machine, but the other mechanic, he isn't willing. Go and ask him."

It took me quite a while to find the second mechanic. When I finally tracked him down I asked what his objection was to moving the machine.

"No problem at all. I'm willing to move it. It's the other mechanic. He's not willing."

So I went back to the first mechanic but he said this was nonsense, he was "willing" and would help anytime. Though impatient with the overuse of the word "willing" (in Chinese *yuanyi*) from two of the most unhelpful people I had ever met, I determined to bring them together to find out who really was willing and who wasn't, otherwise I could spend all day going backwards and forwards between them, each denying what the other had just said. I re-located the second mechanic (he had managed to disappear in the interim) and escorted him back to the first mechanic.

"You are both willing to move the machine. Please move the machine," I said. "Now."

"No, I'm too busy now," replied the first mechanic. "I'm willing but..."

"What?" I interrupted, adding an angry expletive in Mandarin. "You said you were willing just a minute ago."

"Yes, I am willing," he replied in a reasonable tone. "But it's the line supervisor who doesn't want it moved. She's not willing."

I took a deep breath. "Okay. Where's the line supervisor?"

By the time I found the line supervisor and dealt with the objections she put forward (among other things she said the mechanics were "unwilling" to move the machine) the second mechanic had disappeared. Later I found him again and we finally moved the machine, the physical act of which took a couple of minutes compared to the hours spent getting to the bottom of who really was or wasn't willing. I saw how hard it must have been for Bernard, or in fact for anyone who wasn't in a position of authority, to effect any change or even do anything at all in the factory.

Production could start now that the various sewing machines were correctly positioned in their lines. It was the job of the junior work study engineer to time-study the workers in their first attempts at making the new garment, allowing them extra time during the initial learning period when they would inevitably be slower.

But another source of conflict then arose from the application of a US work study system that did away with the stopwatch altogether and applied predetermined codes to every possible hand movement an operator could make. Each code had a time in seconds assigned to it that had already been worked out, but in ideal conditions using fully trained operators with modern machines. The times were too tight for the workers in the company factory and regular disputes occurred between the line supervisors and the Filipino senior work study engineers. These disagreements were almost impossible to resolve as there was no common language between the parties.

Further problems were caused by another surprise visit from Rod and entourage, members of the latter dispersing rapidly on arrival and issuing commands to anyone and everyone around the factory. As if there weren't difficulties enough already, the Hong Kong Director of Quality, a mysterious figure we had never seen before, decided on the spot that machine operators should be wearing gloves. This was a challenge no one was ready for (he might as well have told the operators to work with one hand tied behind their backs) and caused panic on the shop floor as all the time values would have to be recalculated.

I went back to the office for some peace and quiet but on the way bumped into an excited Charlotte who asked me, "what means sitting in own nest?" It seemed that Dave's rearrangement of the desks had led to an angry dispute with Michael. There was some friction between the two of them anyway, perhaps due to the natural competitiveness of two experts in the same field, like two brilliant but bitter intellectuals or two mighty lions fighting over a pride. On top of this they had problems with mutual comprehension. Michael found Dave's vernacular English difficult to understand, and unlike Charlotte had no wish to widen his vocabulary. Dave, for his part, had yet to put in the long hours talking to Michael that he had spent familiarizing himself with the accented English spoken by the Filipino women. He usually referred to Michael as "that Michael" or "that creeping Jesus Michael", the latter presumably a reference to his silent way of walking round the factory.

Michael, former factory expert on work study techniques, had found himself gradually displaced by Dave who grew in confidence day by day, quickly developing an easy superiority and readiness to command as befitted his position. Michael's star was in any case on the wane. The factory was well-supplied with university alumni but there was no new intake and the doors of the classroom were closed. "You know," Michael had recently confided, "Bart is telling me I will be having 60 students. I will be travelling all over the world. Now I am having none."

With Michael's teaching duties on hold and his position as factory work study fount of wisdom supplanted, he was under-employed, lonely and sensitive to slights. I tried to cheer him up with an account of our attempts to obtain a company flat but he looked sadder still. He said he shared a flat with Lenny and some other Hong Kong Chinese. They never spoke any language but Cantonese and ignored him as if he were not there.

For a man teetering on the edge, concerned about

his status within the company and battling feelings of isolation, Dave's arrangement of the desks had not been ideal. All the desks faced the front of the office in a nice tidy block apart from Michael's, ostracized to a far corner of the room where it stood facing the wall, alone.

"Treated like a dog, treated like a dog," he complained to Steve, telephoning him in Hong Kong.

Dave was annoyed at being told by Steve that he would have to rearrange the desks again, and as reported by Charlotte, "Dave said Michael make trouble for himself, he just sitting in his own nest."

*

The start of the new order was a good opportunity for Bernard to revisit a fundamental issue concerning the quality of fabric delivered to the factory. There was little point making machine operators wear gloves if fabric had already been damaged in transit or at the point of delivery. Early on Bernard had attempted to change the method whereby new fabric was brought to the factory: after a beeping and hooting of horns and a leisurely opening of the factory gate, one or two lorries would manoeuvre into the courtyard. The driver, shouting a greeting at the statue-like gardener, would jump down from the cab, open the back of the lorry, climb up and without ceremony toss the bales of fabric out of the vehicle, oblivious as to where they might land. This was bad enough but the bales were often ignored for hours, left in the courtyard gathering dirt and dust until removed later. One of Bernard's early quality improvements was the requirement that bales of fabric were handed down from the lorry and immediately taken to the factory storage area.

By chance Bernard witnessed the first delivery of fabric for the new order and was not happy to see his previous instructions, which he viewed as mandatory, being treated as recommendations only, to be applied at the discretion of the workers as, when or if they felt like it. The suspicion had dawned on him that without Lenny's involvement people were paying no attention to what he said, so he developed the strategy of trying to pin down the workers with Lenny present and have Lenny reaffirm his quality requirements. But this wasn't working either. Something in the dynamic of the conversations between Lenny and the workers alerted Bernard, and the suspicion grew in his mind that Lenny wasn't doing everything he could to fight his corner in matters of quality.

The meeting concerning fabric delivery showed that Bernard's concerns were not entirely groundless. Lenny translated Bernard's question accurately but the men gave an unexpected reply so he added in Cantonese, "look, if anyone ever asks you, you always say no, okay?" Lenny then said to Bernard in English, "they just said no."

With that settled Bernard was able to move on to the final phase of his quality system, the appointment of a new quality manager. "Call a meeting of the line supervisors, one of them will want the job," he said. Min suggested that the line supervisors would be unlikely to volunteer at a public meeting as it would appear too immodest. "Come on, call the meeting," replied Bernard.

After the meeting, at which the line supervisors professed themselves inadequate and without the necessary skills, Bernard threw up his hands. "Don't believe it. What can I do? System won't work without a quality manager."

Min suggested going round the factory and asking them individually whether they were interested in the new position.

"Not just pretty, you're clever too," said Bernard.

The younger women wouldn't even consider the new position but the oldest line supervisor with the most experience indicated that she might be persuaded. Her name was Ah Je and she had worked in the factory for many years before it was bought by the company. Though tempted by the job she was worried about how much support she would get once Bernard left Panyu. After some negotiation and further persuasion from Bernard (who had to "thrice visit the thatched cottage") Ah Je finally agreed but on condition that she had a desk in the office, a pay rise and that Min gave her any help she might need. Having translated Bernard's documents and acted as interpreter at various meetings, Min had a good understanding of the quality system. Ah Je also wanted me to teach her English. "Great! Settled then," said Bernard.

I taught Ah Je in the only unoccupied space in the factory grounds, Michael's classroom, and he gave me the key reluctantly. The weather had turned wet and we splashed down the path through the factory garden. The lawn was submerged in several inches of water, the pond swollen and the sky dark as if awash with black ink. Peels of thunder rumbled across the sky with nearer crashes that sounded like the rock-blasting opposite the Lianhuashan warehouse. Shortly after, the storm was directly overhead and the rain hammered and streamed down the tiles on the classroom roof, cascading in sheets past the cracked windows.

Ah Je was about forty, compact of body and with a low fringe cut just above her eyes. Above the noise of the storm the first thing she asked me was whether England was near Hong Kong. I said it wasn't and she asked, "then why are so many English people there?"

Ah Je had a good ear for English sounds and could soon repeat simple sentences but she had little previous experience of the language. I used Cantonese to explain things and she in turn spoke slowly so that I could understand her Panyu accent. She made fast progress but it would take a long time before she knew enough English to make any practical difference to her work.

*

A few days later Min and I were invited to attend a management lunch with Bart Ryder and a group of young managers from Hong Kong (we were introduced by Bart as graduates of Michael's course). Dennis, an accountant from the company's New York office, was also present. He was in Panyu to see how expenditure might be tightened up in view of looming financial concerns for the company.

But Bart was upbeat during the meal and conducted it like a seminar asking the Hong Kong managers questions such as, "why do we want to own our own factories?" and "why does the company have *guailos* in China?"

Polite laughter followed Bart's use of the word *guailo* (I was all for his attempt to reclaim this prejudicial mode of address for non-Chinese people) but there was a long pause before anyone could think of a good reason for having so many foreigners in the factory. Someone mumbled something about "technical skills".

"Sure," said Bart. "We have *guailos* in the factory who will pass on their skills to local people."

Dennis was listening carefully.

22 When the city gate catches fire the fish in the moat suffer

Bart had introduced Dennis as the chap to come up with solutions to reduce expenses and he set to with a will, hacking right and left, immediately despatching several of our Filipino colleagues back home. Annette, whom I was working with on the third floor was stunned at the news and sat crying at her desk. Back in the Philippines her husband had bought a new house and now there would be insufficient money for the mortgage.

Pausing only to wipe the honest sweat from his brow, Dennis finished with Dave's work study department and moved on to further labours. In the blink of an eye the many were pared to the few and Dave was left with a department lean to the point of emaciation. "It is happening like this sometimes," consoled Michael.

There was now an urgent shortage of work study engineers in the factory but a solution was at hand.

Michael spent the morning typing at the office computer and printed off a single sheet of paper. He took this up carefully, read it through with satisfaction and carried it across the courtyard to attach to the factory gate.

"Now I am having more students," he said and told me he had been tasked with recruiting local Chinese people to train as work study engineers. Michael was seeking recent graduates from PRC universities with a high standard of written and spoken English who also happened to be Panyu residents. His notice, hanging from the factory gate, ended with the following paragraph.

"Selected applicants will be given a thorough training programme on work study functions. An attractive salary with a handsome package of fringe benefits is ready for each correct person."

Certainly from the company's point of view the salary was attractive, attractively low compared to what they had been paying our Filipino colleagues. But what could he mean by "handsome package of fringe benefits"? The main benefit the company could offer a PRC national was somewhere to live but by recruiting locally they hoped to avoid this extra expense. Accommodation was no longer part of the contract. Dennis found this to be an elegant solution for saving expenses so he applied it retroactively to our mainland Chinese colleagues. John was told he was no longer entitled to accommodation and must leave his flat.

Charlotte lived with her parents and wasn't affected by the decision about accommodation, but Dennis had a solution for everyone. In future Charlotte would be paid in RMB instead of Hong Kong dollars. John remained silent about his change of circumstances but Charlotte quizzed everyone firstly on whether they thought it was fair and then as to whether it was legal.

"Isn't that a breach of contract?" she asked, her English ringing clearly round the office, for once her strong Cantonese accent absent.

"Have them in court," said Bernard. He himself had experienced delays in trying to get expenses reimbursed.

While we commiserated with our colleagues, the doors opened and one of the old cleaners pushed into the room, towing a black plastic sack along the floor behind her. It was the first time I had seen her in the office. Normally she confined herself to the corridors outside, sweeping the floor with a face that became blank and mask-like as I approached. With a countenance similarly devoid of expression or emotion she went around the room reaching into the sack, taking out and placing on each person's desk a packet of toilet paper. Christmas had come early to those of us remaining in Panyu. But then I understood; this must be the handsome package of fringe benefits Michael was offering on the company's behalf and we had been allowed into the scheme early (though placing toilet rolls on the desk was, I recalled, a clear violation of the provisions of the company employment manual).

"There's an e-mail for you from Hong Kong," said Dave. Sitting down at the computer I highlighted the brief message from Bart. "I only just learned you guys were staying in the new wing of the Panyu Hotel. Could you please relocate to the Miramar until the company accommodation is ready in order to reduce expenses."

A day later Bart woke up to the fact that Dave was also staying at the Panyu Hotel and told him to move to the Miramar too. We hadn't heard good things about the Miramar from our Sri Lankan colleagues and once more Dave was unhappy and talked about returning to England.

Although the name brought to mind distant sunny climes or a Mediterranean resort, the Hotel Miramar was just a few minutes' drive away on the other side of Shiqiao. It took a full day to pack our things and sort out payment for the Panyu Hotel but then suddenly we were turning out of the forecourt for the last time.

We were swept along in a sea of motorcyclists and small vans through an area of Shiqiao we hadn't visited often. On a pedestrian walkway above a crossroads, socio-political messages in the form of simple painted signs competed unsuccessfully with eye-catching bright neon advertisements. One of the former said *kongzhi renkou shuliang, tigao renkou suzhi* ("control the size of the population, increase the quality of the population").

We had driven past the Miramar itself hundreds of time in the back of Ah Ling's bus and were familiar with the outside of the building. It was a faded dirty yellow with an imposing gateway in the shape of a gallows. We drove through, unloaded our cases and piled up our belongings in a small dusty car park. Unlike the Panyu Hotel there was no green lawn with sprinklers sparkling, palm trees or extensive forecourt with elaborate archways of bright orange tiles.

But a spacious air-conditioned lobby lurked behind tinted glass doors decorated with the Chinese characters for Miramar or *Meileihua* as it was known in Mandarin. The service at reception was irritable bordering on hostile but I was pleasantly distracted by a large vase nearby on which were depicted all 108 heroes from the novel *Shuihuzhuan*, variously translated as "The Water Margin", "All Men Are Brothers" or "Heroes of the Marsh", and about which I had done a dissertation while at university. A number of people in England of a certain age group have heard of this story due to a Japanese television adaptation shown in Britain in the 1970s. The TV series quite likely contributed to my early interest in things Chinese.

Dating from around the 14th century the Water Margin is considered one of the four great classics of Chinese literature, along with "Journey to the West" (also known as "Monkey"), "Romance of the Three Kingdoms" and "Dream of the Red Chamber". Viewers of the TV series would probably be surprised by the extreme nature of some episodes in the original book, featuring fighting and mayhem, drugging and poisoning, drunken debauchery, sexual intrigue, adultery, arson, casual slaughter, cannibalism, and worse. Non-stop action, lively dialogue, and simple, stark descriptions keep the story moving at a brisk pace. Set against the mayhem are humorous episodes, set-piece ruses and stratagems, and also serious themes of idealism, loyalty, bravery, moral behaviour, duty, and above all, brotherhood; as an earlier Chinese phrase from the "Analects of Confucius" puts it, "within the four seas, all are brothers" (*si hai zhi nei jie xiongdi ye*).

Characters from the Water Margin are household names in China, as familiar and much-loved to the

Chinese as Robin Hood or Friar Tuck to the English. I picked out a few figures on the vase and then, aware the others were waiting, followed them out of the lobby.

The path led to a pleasant if small enclosed garden with palm trees and a pond with croaking frogs, but the rest of the hotel had an atmospheric shabbiness and air of neglect that gave the impression of having seen better days. Beyond the garden was a snooker room and a launderette where staff were washing clothes. It was at the top of some concrete stairs. The peeling walls on either side were slimy with emerald mould. We walked past a darkened room in which stood broken pieces of furniture, cluttered desks and a table covered in newspapers on which someone had been daubing Chinese characters with black paint. A fading banner was slung from wall to wall. In the snooker room an attendant looked at us with a dull expression and didn't respond to my greeting.

Our room was on the fifth floor, Dave's on the sixth. At the main reception we were told to ask the service desk attendant on each floor for our room key. A young woman in a blue uniform sat reading a novel and she looked up irritably, greeting us with the words, "you can't have the key now."

She put down her book with a sigh and led the way along a dimly lit corridor. Dust and dirt in fluffy tangled piles had accumulated close to the walls, safely out of range of passing feet. "You might find it dirty," Annette had said. She had been well qualified to speak on the subject, having lived in the Miramar for eight months before moving into a company flat.

Our bedroom smelled like a hamster cage in need

of its weekly clean and I slid open the windows and pushed my head outside. Something was wrong with the air conditioning and a disturbing crackling noise came from the void above the damaged ceiling tiles in the bathroom as if we were hosts to a nest of cockroaches. The tiled floor looked as if it hadn't been cleaned since the day it was put down and the carpet was greasy and covered in cigarette burns. I sat on the bed, rolled down into a trough, and lay there staring at the ceiling.

Sometime later there was a knock at the door and we were joined by Dave and Pete, one of the Filipino work study engineers to escape Dennis's cull. The fridge was stocked with beer and we drank it in ironic celebration of our change of fortunes. It seemed an appropriate moment to drink the enormous bottle of Champagne we had bought at Bernard's instigation months before. I telephoned the Panyu Hotel to ask him to join us but, "no, no, not up to it" he said, "go ahead without me". An attack of flu had singled him out and prevented his attending at the factory over the last few days.

Dave, Pete and Min held mugs and glasses ready in anticipation of the bubbling liquid. I braced myself as I removed the cork but there was a distinct lack of pressure as it came out and nothing happened. "Pop!" said Dave. The champagne had a strange smell and though it might once have been bubbly and full of energy, now it neither fizzed nor sparkled. It was completely flat. Min turned on the stereo and Dave took photos of us standing with the empty bottle, clinking our mugs together.

The Hotel Miramar was a place of contrasts. The

Western restaurant was clean, comfortable, served a good toasted cheese sandwich and we left the meal feeling more optimistic about our future stay. But then returning to our rooms we discovered that guests weren't permitted to keep key cards on their persons. Every time we returned to our room we would have to ask the attendant at the service desk to let us in. No great hardship for us but an awful imposition on her. She glared and sucked in her breath angrily as if I'd asked her to run to Beijing and back, snatched the key card down from a hook and muttered as she rose to her feet. What if we were to request something larger, like a clean towel, what terrible frustrated wrath would that bring down?

She unlocked the door noisily and we stood in the entranceway waiting for the lights to go on but there was no merry hum or buzz of electric power. "What have you done with it?" she snapped, holding up the key and pointing at the chain. I had no idea what she meant, but she continued to rave about us having lost a piece of plastic. "Where is it? What did you do with it?" she repeated. With an explosive sigh of frustration she turned on her heel and stamped off down the corridor.

A minute later she came back and pulled a plastic comb out of her pocket which she rasped into the key slot. Protesting pinging noises accompanied the passage of the comb as its teeth bent, broke off and dropped to the floor. The lights flickered momentarily and then we were in darkness again. She sighed loudly, disappeared and came back with another comb which she forced impatiently in on top of the first one, hammering it down with her fist. The lights came on and went off again. "Let me do it," said Min, intervening. Finally we had light and crunched in over the broken comb teeth littering the floor.

As I sat there thinking that it might be time to have another go at Bart about the company accommodation after all, the telephone rang. It was late and we weren't expecting a call.

"Wei? Wei?" I said.

A young woman's voice at the other end asked in Mandarin whether I had eaten yet. As a student I had learned various different ways of greeting people in Chinese; *wei* for telephone conversations, *ni hao* or *ni hao ma* for general use, *zao ah* for mornings and also the rather less obvious *chifanle meiyou* ("have you eaten yet?"). I soon stopped using the latter phrase in greeting as the response was usually a look of surprise. This was the first time I had ever heard someone use the expression and the caller's voice was pleasant and engaging. If this was a courtesy call from Miramar management it more than made up for the surly attendant outside.

"Yes, thank you. I have eaten," I said. "How about you? Have you eaten yet?"

"Yes, I've eaten. Where do you come from?"

"I'm from England," I replied and asked what part of China she was from.

"Who's that?" asked Min.

"I'm from Shanghai," said the woman.

"Hotel management," I replied to Min, "originally from Shanghai."

"Is there a woman with you?" asked the caller, the voice losing some of its warmth.

I realized I wasn't talking to hotel management

when her next question concerned whether I was "looking for a friend". I said I wasn't and she asked if I might know of anyone else in need of female companionship. I didn't mention our colleagues but the following morning Dave said he had been telephoned by a caller late in the evening. As she didn't speak English the conversation didn't develop far. Pete, already a guest of the Miramar for many months, had changed rooms to evade a determined admirer who rang him at all hours of the night.

We received more phone calls from women offering companionship than we did from room service, a bizarre contrast to the formality of having to produce our marriage certificate before being allowed to share a room in the hotel.

As time went by some of the staff became more friendly and we were given our own square of plastic to ensure a supply of electricity while we were in the room. The irritable attendant rotated shifts with another woman who was as pleasant and sunny as the first was bad tempered. The new attendant sat studying English from a textbook and was always looking for opportunities to try it out. When I spoke to her and changed from Mandarin to Cantonese she jumped out of her seat and clapped her hands.

Living in the Hotel Miramar was a disconcerting up-and-down experience, generally more down than up. Dave had his own frustrations and didn't like the idea of a prolonged stay. People partied in his room when he wasn't there, changing television channels and playing his cassette tapes. On one occasion one of the partygoers hit the record button on his stereo by mistake and erased some of his music.

I telephoned Bart again and asked what was happening about our accommodation.

"We're working on it," Bart replied. Then he said, "we're building a house for you guys."

"Building a house?" I repeated, stunned.

"Yeah, you'll love it. It'll be awesome. It'll be ready in a couple of weeks."

Bart wasn't joking but had been speaking literally, as confirmed later by Joan Wong. Apparently it would be cheaper to build a house rather than rent a flat for a few hundred RMB a month. Joan was also of the opinion that our new residence would be ready in two weeks but in the meantime we went to have a look.

The company house and the neighbouring buildings in its locality were tucked away in an exclusive corner of Shiqiao resembling a Chinese Beverly Hills. Expensive new cars shone in the sunlight behind tall iron gates. Looking through we glimpsed paved courtyard gardens with leafy shrubs and tinkling water fountains. The houses were packed tightly together and to make up for lack of horizontal space climbed upwards like small tower blocks, each several stories high. I had never before seen private buildings of such size and grandeur in either Shanghai or Beijing.

"Yes! It's got a barbie," said Dave, pointing to a built-in barbecue and seats, as we emerged onto the roof of the company house. We had started at the bottom and worked our way up room by spacious room. "This is gonna be great. Get the beers out, I'll work on my tan, it'll be great in the summer."

The house was structurally finished but there was still several weeks' of decorating and finishing off to do, not to mention sorting out electricity and running water. The total absence of builders or workmen didn't inspire confidence but it wasn't a wasted trip as we'd had a chance to look round another corner of Shiqiao. We continued to be surprised by the prosperity in Panyu. As far away as Shenzhen and Hong Kong, Shiqiao was famous for a market area known as *Din Hei Gaai* (Electrical Goods Street). Several hundred individual shops and booths selling stereos, cameras, televisions and CD players were packed into a small pedestrianized area. Stall owners played video games on wide screen televisions or treated shoppers to karaoke set demonstrations.

New goods were delivered throughout the day and in some shops the stereos were stacked from floor to ceiling and spilled out into the street. Glass counters were loaded with different makes of Walkman and calculator but the owners themselves did all their calculations by abacus. *Din Hei Gaai* had apparently been raided by the police many times and one local person said the goods were smuggled in from Japan.

Back near the Miramar we soon became familiar with the local streets and alleys. Behind the hotel ran the Shiqiao river and along the road were shops selling brightly coloured Chinese cups, mugs, bowls and vases. A local stationery store sold any number of different-sized abacuses. Upstairs they had a sports department with weight training equipment, exercise bikes, fishing rods, air rifles and their spare parts.

Shiqiao was small and intimate, and local people around the streets began to recognize us. On one occasion Min rang to book a taxi and the person at the other end of the phone said he knew who we were, he had seen us around the Miramar. We had our photos developed in a shop run by a local family. Playing in the street outside, a small child always stared at me. His mother picked him up and said, "*giu ah suk*" ("call him uncle").

Charlotte told us there was a gym nearby and one night we set off in a light drizzle in search of it. We passed a building site where labourers with hair plastered to their foreheads slid about in kung fu shoes and wellington boots. Further along the street the empty carcases of a row of old houses stood before the foundations of a new tower block. Workers balanced on the crumbling walls and dislodged bricks with sledgehammers. We followed a road where loudspeakers broadcast advertisements at the empty street and finally arrived at the gym. Three women sat by a coffee table beside the door.

"Are you open?" I asked in Chinese.

"Wah! You speak excellent Mandarin," one of them said as she let us in.

"No, I don't. It's really very poor."

"Wah! And you're modest, just like a Chinese person."

A sign in large red characters above a mirror at the far end of the gym greeted us with the phrase "Health is Wealth". Pictures of Arnold Schwarzenegger and Sylvester Stallone graced the walls and a selection of Jane Fonda and other Western aerobic videos stood in a row of bookshelves. There was a growing awareness of body image and health in China with fit, tanned people advertising products on television. Charlotte and other young women we knew went to aerobics classes regularly but had no interest in traditional

Chinese methods for keeping healthy like *taijiquan* or *qigong*.

The gym was usually busy in the evenings with a mixed clientele ranging from the serious bodybuilder to those taking a more relaxed, experimental approach. Many people just visited the gym to use the sauna upstairs, an intimate arrangement demonstrated to us proudly by one of the women on our first visit. The owners were surprised to have foreigners in their gym and I was pointed out as the *lek jai* ("smart boy") who could speak Chinese. Sometimes we went with Steve who was a serious weight trainer, short and stocky. On the occasions he didn't come one of the women always asked me, "Fei Lo le?", which means "where's fatty then?" or "where's the fat guy?".

The temperature rose throughout Panyu and the air turned muggy, heavy and thick. In the gym the mirrors steamed over, the walls became damp and the floor slippery. The gym had no air conditioning and the doors at either end were thrown open in a vain attempt to encourage a draught. Despite the conditions I enjoyed the atmosphere and the evening walk from the hotel to the gym and back again. The streets were always crowded with late night strollers and shoppers, and people sitting on the pavement outside their stalls, cutting and preparing vegetables for the evening meal. The women at the entrance were always friendly and on one occasion when I arrived on my own offered me food and a plate of biscuits.

23 The gruel is meagre and the monks are many

The new order that briefly gave life to the factory ended as suddenly as it had started. No announcement was made. We were just aware of the shop floors rapidly emptying till vacant seats and silent machines replaced noise and activity. Operators paid on a piece rate basis could no longer earn enough to survive and were leaving in search of other work. We saw them arriving in the morning, talking in groups around the clocking-in machine and then shuffling out of the factory, arms draped over one another's shoulders. The factory was punctured, its lifeblood streaming away.

We also heard rumours that staff in the Hong Kong office were being struck down and made redundant without warning. And that was not all. Dennis the foot soldier, despatcher of numerous colleagues on the battlefield, was himself taken out of the game by an arrow from above; in short he got the shaft and was laid off too now that his work was done. It reminded me of Chapter 13 of the Art of War and the description of the five types of spy to be employed. With the brevity typical of classical Chinese the word for spy *jian* is qualified in each case by a single other character, such as *fan jian* a "turned spy" or double agent, *sheng jian* a "spy who lives". Spy type number four is qualified with the character *si* meaning "death" and is often translated as "expendable spy". Dennis had been expended and any one of us could be next. What employee was not expendable?

"Place is a disgrace," said Bernard after his short term contract was not renewed for a second time. Time was running out for his quality system but he had loosened up concerning its implementation now that Ah Je had assumed the role of quality manager. "What's going to happen to me?" Ah Je frequently asked Min as Bernard showed himself to be increasingly disengaged from the humdrum concerns of factory life, adopting the Taoist principle of *wuwei*, non-action or doing nothing.

Eventually it was a strong sense of social injustice, aroused to militancy by the incident of the executive canteen, that plucked Bernard from his forays into Taoism. Following another dull morning of suffocating heat and fraying tempers, together with the rest of the office staff we collected our bowls as usual from the back of the office, descended the steps and went to queue for food in the hybrid opera house canteen. Having followed this routine for months I was well accustomed to the local water and earth and so familiar with the environment and eating arrangements that I barely noticed them. But today something was different, quite apart from Bernard's unusual behavior. He had stopped in his tracks like a statue and stood blocking the way.

"What's going on? Who's that for," he asked in his deep, rich voice, pointing a finger at a long table covered in a white table cloth. It stood at the far end of the audience seating area where we usually ate our lunch.

"No idea mate," shrugged Dave.

"Maybe the factory have important visitor," suggested Charlotte as we moved past Bernard to sit in our normal places.

The table beyond, resplendent with bright white cloth, sparkling glasses, chopsticks, delicate China bowls and dishes, shimmered like a mirage on the opposite side of the room. Looking towards this vision from our humble food-splattered corner, we seemed transported to a Chinese tale of the supernatural where drowsing after a meal, the character finds he has slipped from the mortal to the fairy world, a realm of beautiful fox spirits, half-dressed and alluring.

Lenny came in loosening his tie. He sat down at the table, took a sip of tea and belched loudly.

"What the...?" gasped Bernard.

A few minutes later Ah Ban came skipping down the steps. He walked past us as if we were indeed ghosts or beings who had slipped into some realm impenetrable to human eye, and greeted Lenny with gusto. Over the next few minutes, in ones and twos, employees from Hong Kong, none of whom usually frequented the canteen or were regular supporters of the efforts of the canteen staff, took their seats at the table.

A procession of cooks emerged from the kitchen with plates and dishes and served Lenny and the others. Wonderful aromas wafted across the room, rich, savoury, sweet and tempting. Had my first eating experience in the canteen resembled the tableau before us, no doubt I would have accustomed to the water and earth a whole lot faster than had been the case. I would have been as enthusiastic as our Hong Kong colleagues who praised the cooks with cries of "*ho sik, ho sik*" ("tastes good, tastes good") amid the laughter, good cheer, and warmth of their shared meal.

But it wasn't the fairy realm of Liao Zhai we were inhabiting. It was more like a scene from a drama of the Warring States Period or the Romance of the Three Kingdoms. On one side was the Hong Kong faction, large and powerful, occupying the best ground. Below them was a loose grouping of the lesser factions comprising England, the Philippines, Sri Lanka and the People's Republic of China.

"Why are they having special food? This place! I don't believe it," boomed Bernard, throwing up his hands in his gesture of old. "I've had it with this place."

"That's taking the piss like," added Dave.

No one else commented though Anne said something to Charlotte in an undertone. An expression like a weary grin or grimace passed suddenly across her face and was gone.

No explanation was given as to why a special menu was to be prepared for our Hong Kong colleagues. The lunch hour continued in this way for several days, the mutterings and rumblings from Bernard growing louder all the time.

Later it emerged that it was all part of the company's attempt to clamp down on expenses. I had noticed before that around midday Lenny, Ah Ban and our other Hong Kong colleagues would jump into a taxi and head towards Shiqiao. It was their practice to have lunch at the Panyu Hotel every day, claiming the food and taxi trip as expenses for later reimbursement. With the company facing financial problems they could no longer reclaim these costs and now had to eat in the factory with everyone else. This was problematic for Lenny and his companions as they hadn't previously put in the necessary hours training their palettes for the culinary delights of the opera house canteen.

Faced with the prospect of having to put in overtime at that establishment, Lenny cast aside his Taoist principles of non-action and raised a stink with Joan Wong back in Hong Kong. A piece of electronic mail explained that as our Hong Kong Chinese colleagues were now eating in the factory, a "decent canteen" must be set up for them as soon as possible.

Eventually Bernard could stomach the inequality no longer. He took up arms in the form of the office telephone. His complaints may have had an effect because a few days later staff in the second floor office (excluding the local payroll clerks) were told to go to lunch half an hour later at the new time of 1.00 p.m. At the canteen we were given the special menu too and discovered that Lenny and Ah Ban were well justified in the high praise they had given it. "*Ho ho sik*", "the food is excellent", said Charlotte happily.

But the next day on entering the former opera house we were greeted by a hand-written sign that said: "Hong Kong and Overseas Staff Eating Area". An arrow below the words pointed up onto the stage. We followed it to a small room-like space enclosed and hidden by walls of cardboard boxes, the type usually used to ship garments out of the factory. Sitting down we were served with the new food but noticing it was quieter than usual I was suddenly aware of the absence of Charlotte and Anne. As local Chinese people they had been excluded by the sign. Ah Ban and Anne were both production managers with the same responsibilities, but were expected to eat different food in separate areas because one was from Hong Kong and the other from China.

"You're right," said Bernard in reply to my observations, chopsticks poised. "This segregation would cause a revolution in England. Couldn't get away with it. What's that, sweet and sour pork?"

"Too right, mate," said Dave.

The next day Min and I ignored the new eating area and sat downstairs with Anne and Charlotte.

Then a rumour circulated that expatriate staff were going to have to eat all their meals in the factory. "Breakfast, lunch and dinner in the factory!" said Dave. "No way. They can't be serious!"

The rumour was later confirmed in an e-mail from the Hong Kong office. "For overseas employees three delicious hot meals will be provided every day. No other meal allowances will therefore be provided. Employees are of course free to cook food within their own quarters."

That sounded reasonable but cooking in our own quarters would be problematic as we were still in the Miramar. The staff there had objected when I tried to

277

open the window. I couldn't begin to imagine the outcry if we tried to cook in the room.

The three meal a day regime was implemented soon after and, like characters in some Victorian mill, we found ourselves working a twelve-hour day at the factory. We were bussed in for breakfast in the morning and back to the hotel after the evening meal. Ah Ling the driver had a long day ferrying everyone around but he was usually cheerful, reserving any negativity for cyclists who strayed in front of his minibus. The cooks tried hard to produce food everyone liked but after a short period they had exhausted their repertoire and people began to grumble that the evening meal was leftovers from lunch.

"Maybe we'll get some toast," Dave had said on the first day of breakfast. This was wildly optimistic. Fish and chips would have been more likely.

The factory breakfast did make a change from hotel food but I never developed a taste for *juk*, an easy dish for anyone to make; take a bowl of rice, pour water on top of it, mix it up and serve in a bowl. For Min it was comfort food and she loved it, calling it "porridge", but for me the dictionary term "gruel" summed it up better. The four-character phrase "the gruel is meagre and the monks are many" seemed an apt description of the circumstances.

Soon the food was no longer an issue for Bernard as his contract had finally come to an end, this time not to be renewed. More pressing was his concern that the company might not be able to pay him for the work he had done. "Bunch of cowboys," he said.

*

We were travelling to Hong Kong for the weekend, and as Office Head Wang still refused to let us leave China via Lianhuashan, we took the same roundabout route as before to the Shenzhen border. After a frustrating day of slow bus and train rides we finally arrived and joined separate queues, one for foreigners and the other for mainland Chinese.

I was soon across the border and waiting for Min in a no man's land between China and Hong Kong, a long aerial corridor with thick glass windows overlooking a watery ditch below. Coarse grassy reeds and vegetation grew in the water, and steep banks on either side climbed to high barbed wire fences. Illegal immigrants from China or "IIs" ("eye eyes") as they were referred to in Hong Kong were often portrayed in lurid tones by the media and viewed by some residents as a danger to hikers in less populated areas. Steve, who lived in a remote district surrounded by woodland, told us of a fleeting encounter with one of these people. Driving back home one night he came across a young woman, running, disorientated and speaking Mandarin. She disappeared into the night and he never saw her again.

The crowd coming from the Chinese side of the border had thinned to a trickle but there was no sign of Min. I retraced my steps and found her at the head of a queue of angry people. She was arguing with an even angrier guard in a green uniform. He was shaking his head and saying, "*bu xing, bu xing*" ("no good, no good").

Our experiences dealing with difficult officials and

bureaucrats in relation to visas, both in England and in China, had been fantastic assertiveness training for both of us. The guard was angry, Min was angry but determined too, and like the examiner back in the factory "with justice on her side she was bold and assured".

In response to my enquiry about the cause of the delay, Min gave the guard a withering look that would have given pause to any man not grown reckless with anger and adrenalin. She said *he* was demanding a green card and without one would not let her leave China.

"I crossed by this border without a green card just a few months ago," she said to the guard, trying a new argument. "Look at the stamp in my passport."

"Well that was last time," said the guard. "And this is this time." He repeated the phrase several times for effect, accompanying it with a decisive chopping gesture. He finished by turning his back on Min. "Wei! Hurry up," shouted someone from further down the line.

The guard turned back again and frowned to see Min still standing there. She held up the booklet of rules and regulations we had been given by the Guangzhou Public Security Bureau and pointed to the relevant section.

"Hurry up," came another shout from the queue, "I've got a train to catch."

The guard looked at the booklet for a moment but refused to take hold of it. The queue was growing in size and there were impatient noises and murmurs from people worried about missing their train. They hissed loudly and looked at their watches with exaggerated pantomime gestures. The guard looked hassled, hesitated as if he couldn't decide what to do, seemed about to let Min go, but suddenly flared up again.

"That book of rules and regulations is no longer valid," he said and made a dismissive gesture with his hand.

"Yes they are valid," replied Min. "If you had looked at the date of issue you would have seen that they are valid for another year."

The sarcastic tone caused the guard to open his eyes wide with indignation. He paused as if about to say something, but suddenly could take no more. He turned quickly on his heel and retreated into a nearby office, slamming the door behind him, to noisy shouts of disbelief from the queue behind Min.

After a long wait he emerged with a calmer expression and handed Min's passport over to a colleague. "Here, deal with that would you?" he said.

"Where's your green card?" asked the second guard after flicking through Min's Chinese passport and looking at the ILR stamp without comprehension. Once more Min showed him the rule book and the translation of her British permanent residence visa we had made in Guangzhou.

"That's not valid. Where's your green card?"

The first guard's break time in the back office had done him good and he was all for allowing Min out of China. In fact he couldn't seem to get rid of her quickly enough, urging his colleague to stamp the passport and be done with it. But the second guard was fresh and lively (for the time being), couldn't read the English and wouldn't accept that the stamp indicated permanent residence. It had to be a green card. The argument went round again.

"Do you have an English dictionary with you perhaps?" asked Min. Remarking so bluntly on lack of English skills caused both men to freeze on the spot, glaring. Finally, without saying anything further to Min the second guard summoned a third guard and told him to deal with the passport. Fortunately the new arrival looked younger and more junior than the other two, and under the influence of their combined urging and promptings, eventually stamped the passport.

The original guard handed back Min's passport and looked up for the next person. But Min was still standing there.

"Could you clarify the regulations for me," said Min. "For next time."

"The regulations are none of your business!" shouted the first guard, face reddening again.

"If you don't tell me the rules, how will I know whether I can come through next time or not?"

"Look!" the guard shouted as he retreated once more to his office, slamming the door behind him. "This time is this time, and next time is next time."

The subsequent delay with Hong Kong immigration who, as on the last occasion, demanded to see a plane ticket and kept us waiting for half an hour, seemed minor in comparison. It was dark when we finally emerged and rain was falling heavily. Red, pink and blue neon reflected against the slick and shiny streets.

The rain was still coming down in heavy drops when we set out the next morning. Half way to the office the sky turned black and the heavens opened unleashing rain by the bucket load. It had poured throughout the night and the drains were so full that with this extra pressure of new water they turned into small fountains, flooding the streets. Pedestrians held their shoes in their hands and with their trousers rolled up above their knees ventured through deep stretches of water. Streets became small lakes and the rain came down harder than ever.

In the office we bumped into Rod. "How are you getting on?" he asked. Rod was in a hurry but we had been meaning to talk to him for some time. As the owner of the company he seemed to be the only person who could get anything done. It was time for us to bid farewell to stopwatches and time studies and move on to the rest of the management training programme. Min said that she didn't see herself doing work study as a career.

"Work study? Why are you doing work study?" asked Rod, apparently baffled. "That's a total waste of time for you."

"Yes," he continued, looking thoughtful. "You're from the wrong background to do work study. You're not a working class girl. What work do you want to do?"

"A position in management," said Min. Rod didn't respond. As the silence lengthened Min added, "I had thought of working in the merchandizing department."

"I don't see you doing that," said Rod. "You're not greedy enough". Seeing Min's expression he added, "you don't want a Rolex do you?"

"A what?" replied Min.

"See what I mean? No, that's not for you."

"I'm interested in accounting," Min added.

"Yes, that's more like it" said Rod enthusiastically. "I can see you as an accountant." He took out a pencil and wrote the words "bean counter" in a small note book. "I'll look into that. It's easily arranged if that's what you want to do. Brilliant. We can train you in both the Western and Chinese systems of accounting. We'll start by having you work in an accounting firm here in Hong Kong for a year or two." Rod frowned and added, "of course, it'll cost a bit but that's something for us to worry about". Then he brightened. "Why don't you come to Hong Kong next week and have a chat with someone in the accounts department here?" Min said there was the problem of the visa and Rod looked surprised. "What visa?" he asked.

Rod seemed to have no memory of our interview with him in England. It was as if he had been knocked down by a London bus on the way out and his memory wiped clean. He was fiddling with his pen and shifting in his seat so we didn't describe the latest developments trying to obtain a Hong Kong multi-entry visa for Min. We had made another application, this time to the British Embassy in Beijing as the nearest authority in charge of Hong Kong visas for PRC nationals. The only form of payment the Embassy would accept was FEC, in cash, delivered by hand, a little awkward for us in our Panyu location 1,000 miles away. They refused every other form of currency including RMB, Hong Kong dollars and even Sterling. Eventually Min was able to contact an old Shanghai school friend working in Beijing who delivered the money in person.

Rod looked at me and said, "you shouldn't be doing

work study either. But I think you'd be good in human resources. Yes, we'll train you up as a personnel manager. And Min will make a great accountant. It's pointless you two being in work study, a complete waste of time."

Personnel manager of an international garment company! That had a ring to it. It was a change from the original job but I liked the idea. Min looked happy at the idea of having some formal training as an accountant.

"I'll catch up with you later," said Rod in a hurry to leave, and the spark of optimism I had felt faded as I contemplated his retreating figure. The only time he hadn't been in a hurry was at the job interview in London, and as I remembered that occasion I saw why we had accepted the jobs so readily. With his persuasive optimism Rod was a master salesman but now I had the advantage of previous experience and despite wanting to believe him thought it highly unlikely he would deliver. In the words of the English four-character phrase, "once bitten, twice shy".

We went to see Joan Wong to pick up the microwave oven we had won at the company Christmas party all those months ago. But she had given it away to someone else, or it had been taken without her knowledge. She didn't seem to know or care which, and in its place was a ramshackle device for warming food. On the way out Joan commented that we had completed our probation period and were now permanent staff.

24 Shrinking the dragon to an inch in length

Back in Panyu I had been contacted by some elderly friends of my Granddad, Ronnie and Peggy, who were staying in Hong Kong and wanted to visit us and see some of the local sights. The encyclopaedia I had bought in Shanghai said Panyu was famous for two things, the rock quarry at Lianhuashan and the *Yuyinshanfang*, a Qing Dynasty house and garden situated in a village called Nancun to the north of Shiqiao.

The Yuyinshanfang was apparently one of four famous Qing Dynasty houses and gardens within the whole of Guangdong Province, and here it was practically on the doorstep, referred to on our map as a *ming sheng gu ji* (place of historic interest and scenic beauty).

Against my advice Ronnie and Peggy were staying at the Miramar too and first thing in the morning the four of us took a taxi to the bus station. While Min was buying the tickets and I stood chatting to Ronnie and Peggy, a man asked me if we wanted to go anywhere, indicating his motorbike as transport. I told him that we intended to travel by bus but he persisted, repeatedly saying his motorbike was, contrary to appearances, a taxi and he could take us anywhere we wanted. The only way to get four people (five including Min) on that bike would have been by forming a human pyramid. None of us were stunt riders and two of our party were nearly 80 years of age so I rejected his offer, more than once, as he wouldn't take no for an answer.

"What did he say?" asked Ronnie. Following my explanation he looked thoughtful and rummaged around in his pockets. He was wearing the kind of shapeless clothes favoured by middle-aged to elderly English ramblers. Numerous zip pockets boasted extreme utility at the expense of other attributes normally associated with garments such as shape and cut. As some of the zip pockets were apparently located on duplicate inner layers it took Ronnie some time to find the item he was after. The man with the motorbike still scented the possibility of commerce and every few seconds he repeated "*ni qu nali?*" (where are you going?). He drew closer as he saw Ronnie patting himself down, misconstruing the gesture as looking for a wallet.

"Ah, got it," Ronnie said finally, a wry smile on his face as he pulled out a small camera and added the words, "I want a photograph of a taxi."

The appearance of the camera had the desired effect and the man jumped smartly off his bike to avoid being included in the shot. But Ronnie didn't lower his camera. "No, no," he said and with a stern look and firm gesture indicated that the man should return to his motorbike.

"No don't you move," continued Ronnie as the man, looking hassled, took his bike by the handlebars and tried to wheel it backwards out of the camera angle. Ronnie panned round determinedly, following the man struggling with his bike where it had become blocked in by a taxi of the four-wheeled variety.

The man tried pushing the motorbike forwards. A small adjustment of Ronnie's camera allowed him to keep it in frame. Backwards, forwards and back again the man pushed his bike but escape was hopeless and eventually Ronnie triumphed. He stowed his camera with a look of satisfaction, the sort of look a man gives when he gets what he wants after a pleasurable struggle that can only have one outcome.

"They really do seem to have some fear of photographs. Why is that?" asked Peggy. My answer, that I thought the man was probably operating illegally, was only half way out my mouth but trailed into incoherence as my eyes came into unwilling focus on the penis of a youth standing directly behind Peggy and leaning back against the wall of the bus station. We had seen some unkempt people in Panyu, mainly members of the local begging fraternity, but this was a departure into new territory. The youth had long matted hair, a jacket with no shirt beneath it and a pair of zipless and buttonless trousers out of which dangled his (unwashed) member as if it was the most normal thing in the world. He was chatting away to a small circle of friends, relaxed and uninhibited, carrying this new style better than I wear a tie.

Peggy was looking at me, puzzled by my

inattention. Had I imagined it? My eyes flicked back casually to the youth. No, I hadn't. The apparition remained. I unconsciously checked my flies, earning a frown from Min who happened to emerge from the bus station at that moment. Should I explain the situation? I could have wrapped it up in an interesting discussion of the graphic elements of obscene Chinese characters. But then I saw Ronnie putting away his camera, an air of victory still lingering about his person. I imagined the scene, Ronnie a look of cool determination, "I want a photo of a beggar's penis".

So I directed Peggy and Ronnie to the bus, shielding them from he of the gaping flies and shortly after we bumped noisily out of the station with a whining and crunching of gears. Leaving Shiqiao behind us the road deteriorated rapidly and in places dwindled to a country track.

Half an hour later we were standing beside a wide dusty road with no signs or other indications that we were close to one of the Four Famous Gardens of Guangdong Province, or any garden at all for that matter. We seemed to have subjected Peggy and Ronnie to a tough, potholed route in which passengers were tossed around inside the bus on a journey more rodeo than method of transport, to a journey's end of precisely nowhere.

Along one side of the road were small stalls and minor shops, and on the other a murky pool of refuse and water. The expanse of floating rubbish and debris stretched away to a far muddy bank that climbed to a bleak grey factory building. People sat watching the world go by and there was the usual crowd of men loitering on motorbikes offering transport services.

After we had been misdirected once and set off in totally the wrong direction, a man in his sixties pointed us the right way. He was very helpful but seedy in the extreme with a pinstripe Western-style suit, greasy, grimy, polished and covered in so much layered dirt that it was impossible to make out the original colour.

Following the old man's directions we turned off the main road onto a narrow but busy alleyway. The consumer goods we had seen for sale in Shiqiao were available here too and business was brisk. A procession of small children walked past us, barefoot, all staring with curiosity.

After walking for about 15 minutes we arrived at the gates of the Yuyinshanfang and paid the nominal entrance fee. There appeared to be no other visitors and we stepped into a narrow corridor flanked by solid brick walls, so high you had to crane your neck to follow the bamboo growing up the sides to the very top. Green leaves framed against the blue sky were a glimpse of rich saturated colour compared to the grey dusty streets we had left behind us outside.

A leaflet handed out at the door said that the Yuyinshanfang house and garden were completed in 1860 by a Qing Dynasty official called Wu Bin in honour of his ancestors. The name of the garden *yuyin* has the literal meaning "extensive shade" but also a secondary meaning of "bounty bestowed by prior generations on one's descendants", appropriate in this case as Wu Bin built the house on land left by his forbears. The *shanfang* part of the name, as well as meaning "mountain house" also referred to the location Nancun which in former days was known as Nanshan (South Mountain).

Wu Bin had been a successful man, passing imperial examinations at provincial level and earning himself a position as an official in the imperial Ministry of Punishment. Later his eldest and second sons also passed the exams and locally this was celebrated in the pithy phrase "one household, three successful provincial level exam candidates" (pithy in Chinese that is, comprising only five characters *"yi men san ju ren"*).

In imperial China, to discourage corruption and local favouritism, officials were sent to take up office in distant provinces. Wu Bin built the Yuyinshanfang as a retirement house for himself and his family after returning to Panyu following his years of working away from home.

This was the first garden I had visited in China without sharing the experience with hundreds of other people. One or two families strolled around and some gardeners squatted among the plant beds chatting as they pulled out weeds. Silence descended as we stepped into an atmosphere of tranquillity and seclusion, the high walls blocking both sounds and sight of the outside world. The contrast with the streets beyond was marked. It was a green oasis of trees, plants, shaded pools, tiled floors and covered walkways, separated by just a few feet of brick wall from the dirt, dust and noise of the streets beyond.

According to the leaflet the total area of the garden was 1,598 square meters and it was famed for the way it compressed into such a small space buildings decorated with carvings and paintings, verandas, pavilions, balconies, bridges, rockeries and ponds. To do so the designers employed the twin techniques of "hiding and not revealing" and "shrinking the dragon to an inch in length".

One of the best known gardens in China is the fictional "Grand Prospect Garden" described by Cao Xueqin in his novel "Dream of the Red Chamber", written in the Qing Dynasty around 1760. The author details the planning and rapid construction of the garden in preparation for a visit from the imperial concubine. In one scene principal characters tour the garden shortly after its completion to add the final touch by naming the various locations.

Names were seen as an important part of the overall design of the garden and aimed to enhance enjoyment of the scene through subtle literary or poetical allusion. The same technique was used in the Yuyinshanfang with Chinese characters decorating pillars, names on large rectangular boards adorning the principal buildings and paired sets of writing beside the doorways. The latter are called antithetical couplets or more simply *lian* in Chinese. A pair on either side of the entranceway set the theme of the garden.

"Remainder land three bows red rain ample, shady sky one corner green clouds deep" (*yu di san gong hong yu zu, yin tian yi jiao lü yun shen*).

The meaning doesn't immediately leap out at the reader, that the garden though small is yet rich with bright blossom and green shade. The words "remainder" (*yu*) and "shady" (*yin*) are a pun on the garden's name Yuyinshanfang, indicating that the couplets are a comment on the garden as a whole. Educated people in former times would have understood "three bows" referred to the modest length of the garden. One bow was apparently 100 paces or the length of an arrow's flight. The Yuyinshanfang at only 300 paces was considered small in area but this contrasts with the "ample red rain", referring to flame vines and other bright flowers in bloom all year round. The phrase "green clouds deep" refers to the dense shade from leaves, greenery and vegetation.

The central structural element of the garden was the Lotus Pool, around which were constructed the principal buildings such as Deep Willow Hall, the main reception area or reading room, and directly opposite a smaller study referred to as the Villa Facing the Pool. The latter, a room for Wu Bin's calligraphy practice, was another wordplay as the character *chi* means both pool and ink stone.

The rooms and garden were linked by shaded walkways creating an effect where garden and buildings merged into one so the garden became part of the house. Sometimes it seemed as if the garden was inside the house or was the house inside the garden?

Bonsai and pot plants softened the angles of hedges and low walls, and jagged ornamental rocks contrasted with the straight lines of the buildings. Rocks are a basic feature of Chinese gardens, often positioned to reflect in water, or placed as a structural element to create hills and grottoes. The occasional pine tree gave further structure to the garden but in some places there were gaps and areas in need of rebuilding or repair.

We followed a shaded walkway round the pond to the octagonal Exquisite Waterside Pavilion. The prime spot for appreciating the garden, it was spacious inside with a high ceiling, walls and windows patterned with intricate dark lattice work of circles and squares. The design was such that each window opened onto different views of the garden with names such as "Wintersweet in Full Bloom" or "Orange Osmanthus Greets the Rising Sun".

Beneath the windows were ancient chairs for reclining, small tables and other pieces of Qing Dynasty furniture of a dark wood that matched the tone and colour of the lattice work. It was where Wu Bin would have relaxed, drunk wine and composed poems with his friends as the scent of lotus flowers drifted across from the pond. In the hot Panyu summer the pavilion would have been a cool and welcome retreat.

"I want a photo of a Chinese woman in a chair," said Ronnie, seeing Min testing one of the reclining seats.

Another part of the garden was taken up with a large ancestral family temple. A bronze Buddha looked down on us, wreathed in thick incense floating from coils suspended from above. Visitors could buy a coil that would last for almost three weeks.

*

The impression of the Yuyinshanfang and its ambience of calm lingered in my mind for several days. After seeing Ronnie and Peggy off and returning to work we discovered echoes of a similarly leisurely lifestyle at the factory. The day we returned Dave came into the office and shouted, "come and look at this."

He led me to the third floor and turning into a

narrow opening pointed to a staircase. "I only just discovered it," he said and sprinted up two steps at a time. Following him I emerged onto the factory roof, eyes dazzled and closing involuntarily against bright sunlight.

The roof and a low wall which circled it at waist height were a brilliant white and forcefully reflected the rays of the sun into the eyes of anyone rash enough to be standing there in the already sweltering heat. After my eyes stopped watering I stepped to the edge and enjoyed a bird's eye view of the surrounding countryside, shaded pools bordered by trees, shambling buildings, densely crowded rooftops and dusty grey roads. Distant specks resolved into cyclists as they approached and passed below us, pedalling away in slow-motion towards Shiqiao, shrinking back into dots and blurring in the sunny haze.

The sun beat down on the builders and their construction opposite the factory. Shouts and the sounds of hammering floated upwards. When we first arrived it was little more than foundations but now it was nearly complete. Panyu was thriving and had a raw energy that seemed unable to penetrate the gates of the company factory.

"We'll have to bring some chairs up here," said Dave, taking off his shirt and stretching in the sun, turning his face to the heavens and shifting to a more comfortable position. "I've got to start working on my tan."

He wore cut-off shorts, trainers and a pair of designer sunglasses bought on his last trip to Hong Kong. His shorts were decorated with a drawing of a flexed biceps I had done for him that morning. He had rolled up his sleeve and posed for me in the second floor office, watched by perplexed local staff. Soaking up the sun on the roof he was in his element, and told me his plans for summer barbecues at the company house.

Dave had a new haircut from a salon opposite the Miramar. It was a small establishment with fairy lights in the windows, battered furniture and three young women wearing jeans and t-shirts who were surprised to see us and said they weren't used to cutting "foreign" hair. They didn't look very enthusiastic about our patronage. Dave for his part had some misgivings about the décor and well-used interior, taking it all in with a quick glance. "Go on Pete," he said. "You go first. I want to see how it turns out before I have mine done." Pete grinned and stepped forward. Shortly after, distracted or flustered by the hearty shouts of encouragement from Dave, the hairdresser snipped a small piece from one of Pete's ears.

"Aiyah! Sorry ah! Sorry ah!" she shrieked as blood flowed down Pete's cheek.

"Hoooo, haaaa, haaa, haa, ha, ha, ha, mmmf, mmmf," came great bursts of laughter from Dave as he slipped out of control from his chair to the floor.

"Sorry ah! Sorry ah!" the hairdresser repeated endlessly, mortified with embarrassment yet barely able to make herself heard over Dave's shrieks. "This has never happened to me before," she added in Cantonese and I translated for the benefit of Pete. He replied that it had never happened to him before either. The wound wasn't deep but there was an alarming amount of blood. Pete took it well considering there was no sterilising equipment in the salon, just a cold tap and dirty cloth which the scissors were wiped on from time to time.

"Where is it? Where's your ear Pete?" asked Dave, as if searching around the floor for something. As he collapsed again into hysterical laughter I sat down for my turn and was given a hair wash by one of the other two women. It took at least twenty minutes and was very thorough. No water was used. Instead she kept pouring, kneading and massaging more shampoo into my scalp until she'd used half a bottle.

By the time I was passed along to the woman who cut hair she had largely recovered her confidence and I saw that she had wiped Pete's remaining blood from the scissors. I wanted a very short haircut but she had other ideas. It became a battle of wills in which I was only able to prevail because she was distracted by the site of Pete at which she would burst out, "sorry ah! Sorry ah" again and again. At one point a youth came in with the latest Panyu style, long hair with a bouncing, curling perm. He saw me talking to the hairdresser and asked her with polite interest whether I could speak Chinese. She replied tetchily, "Huh! No, he can't. All he can say is 'too long, too long!'"

Dave ended up with a reasonable haircut, a shorter version of his previous style. Pete, in addition to a throbbing ear, came out with a comical quiff that made him look like Elvis. I eventually settled for a haircut that wasn't quite short enough for me but was way too short for the hairdresser. "This is a fashionable place," she said "and not for the kind of haircut you want." I saw her point in a way. If long bouncing perms are all the rage you don't want a customer emerging from your salon, blinking round in the bright sunlight with a style suited to a British skinhead or Chinese convict, depending on your cultural background. But I thought it preferable to the bleeding Elvis style sported by Pete.

Along with the hot weather and rising temperatures Dave's doubts about his work had fully evaporated and he began to enjoy ex-pat life in Panyu. He took a photo of himself surrounded by the remaining Filipino women and sent it back home to the lads with the caption, "it's a tough job but someone's got to do it."

He shrugged off his homesickness and soon after stopped writing to his girlfriend. Eventually the photo disappeared from his desk and he informed me after a weekend in Hong Kong that he and Mali, one of the Filipino women, were "an item". Or to use the Chinese phrase the two of them were like "like paint sticking to glue".

With its whitewashed walls and lack of shade the roof was becoming unbearably hot and the skin of Dave turning extraordinarily pink. Dave couldn't be criticized for a lack of planning in not bringing any sunscreen lotion. The factory roof was a hidden gem I suspected Rod himself was unaware of, though come to think of it his face was often red.

I suggested that we go back to the office for a break from the heat. We walked past the cutting room where the five or six workers were all asleep, sprawling across the tables in the sticky warmth. The mechanics were sitting on top of their lockers, drowsy eyes half open, cigarettes held limply between their fingers, burning but un-smoked. Beside the monkey cage the gardener stood immobile as he watered the grass.

The office was cooler but no one was working. I reached for my Walkman and tuned in to a Guangzhou radio station. Local radio was providing a window into local culture and at night I often drifted off to sleep with Cantonese echoing inside my head. Though the factory was quiet, radio shows painted a different picture of the area, reflecting bustle, wealth and energetic commercial forces. Chat shows were interspersed with frenetic disco music and advertisements for every product you could think of including shampoo, soap, sheets, motorbikes, stereos, wireless karaoke sets, mineral water, contact lenses, make-up, clothes, protective equipment for labourers and even paper shredders. Some of the advertisements were in the form of Cantonese dialogues.

"Ah Wong, have a look at this shirt! D'you like it? I had to send someone to Hong Kong to get it for me. You just can't buy shirts like this locally."

"What d'you mean? Yesterday I went to the Bai Li Department Store in Guangzhou. They've got them there on the fourth floor. Guess what? They've also got suits, leather shoes, watches, jewellery and other products too."

"Wah! Is that really true?

"You bet it is! Go and look for yourself if you don't believe me."

But by far the majority of advertisements on the radio were for Chinese medicine and local restaurants. There were medicines to cure stomach ulcers caused by stressful lifestyles, for enlivening the blood circulation and nourishing the spirit, for improving the functioning of the liver and even for curing acne. Some of the medicines appeared to be very powerful.

"Wei! What's wrong with you?" (*strong chiding voice*)

"I keep coming out in a cold sweat and I've got a terrible fever. My mouth feels bitter and dry. I'm restless all the time and feel like vomitting." (*agonised voice*)

"Well, what are you waiting for? Hurry up and drink some medicine from the Zhang Wang Medicine Factory. It doesn't matter whether you've got a cold, hepatitis, gastritis or problems with your gall bladder. It's good for all of them."

"But does it really work?" (*agonised voice becomes stronger*)

"You bet it does. The prescription has been used for the last two thousand years."

A local radio programme advertised Chinese, Thai and Mongolian restaurants around Guangzhou. The speciality of one of them was *zhutongfan*, a rice dish served in a bamboo tube. With their rice, customers could have partridge, eel or "field chicken", the latter meaning frog in Chinese.

Sometimes medicinal benefits and eating out merged into one product.

"Hey, Ah Lam, why don't we go to the Zhang Family Snake Restaurant tonight? Those guys have been working with the local snake technical research centre to produce some really special snake dishes for the summer."

"Really?"

"Yes. You probably didn't know this but in summer you need more nourishment because of the hot weather. Experts say the best way of getting it is by eating snake. The research centre has produced more than 45 different varieties of snake dish. They also have snake wine and snake drinks which are an excellent form of nourishment when the weather's hot and cool foods should be eaten."

"Wah! Excellent! We must go and see what it's like."

"Of course we must! Absolutely. Come on! The snake there is incredibly cheap, and when you've finished your meal, guess what?"

"What?"

"Free takeaway snake! Yep, you heard me correct. Every customer will be presented with some free takeaway snake."

25 Roll up the sleeping mat and fry some squid

Following another quiet week in the factory, remarkable only for the progress Dave made with his sun tan, we e-mailed Bart to find out if a decision had been made following our recent discussion with Rod in Hong Kong. Bart didn't reply immediately and when he did, it wasn't to outline my new duties as a personnel manager or Min's training programme as a company accountant. Instead we received the following cryptic message. "I will be in the factory Monday and will meet with you two."

Monday was muggy and humid and I stood at the first floor balcony watching an impromptu toss the caber competition from the back of a truck. There were shouts and hoots of laughter as the rolls of fabric were launched into the air, spinning and twisting in lazy parabolas before slamming into the dusty ground of the factory courtyard.

Bernard and his quality system might as well never have existed, an illusion shimmering briefly from one factory floor to another. I thought of the Zhuangzi tale about the man who wakes up from a dream in which he is a butterfly and wonders if he is now a butterfly dreaming he is a man. I imagined Bernard waking up back in England, looking over to his wife and saying, "had the most extraordinary dream, dreamt I was a quality consultant, place called Panyu."

"Ahem."

I was disturbed by a discreet cough behind me and saw Johnson approaching. He had heard I was teaching at the Panyu warehouse and wanted to know if I would give English lessons to his staff in the third floor office. I had barely spoken to Johnson after our first meeting in the dusty courtyard at Lianhuashan months ago, but his friendly presence had made a lasting impression. I said I would be happy to teach his staff provided Bart had no objections, and Johnson padded off.

The temperature had risen throughout the morning and I went back into the office to cool down. On hot days like this, Dave, the Filipinos and the rest of us would take turns to stand in front of the air conditioning unit, arms held up and away from the body, legs bent, the powerful jet of cool air blowing through our clothes and carrying away body heat. But sometimes even that seemed too much effort. A heavy lethargy had settled over the factory. Through the window we saw the occasional person walking past the office, feet dragging, seemingly about to falter, crumble and not get up again. Everyone in the two offices had given up the pretence of work, including Michael who was furtively writing letters home in the corner. Without a single student he had nothing to do.

He had even given up searching for Albert.

The general lethargy was pierced by a screaming of sirens and the metallic sound of official Mandarin broadcast at high volume through loudspeakers. A murmur passed through the office, and the staff, both locals and foreigners alike, crowded out of the door towards the balcony. The few workers remaining left their sewing machines and went through the factory gates to join a large group of people standing silently around a grey propaganda wagon, source of the noise and shrieking speakers.

Shortly afterwards three blue trucks rolled slowly into view and halted directly opposite the factory. At the back of each vehicle stood shaven, handcuffed prisoners. They had white placards hanging round their necks. Black characters painted in large letters listed their crimes as rape and robbery. The men remained expressionless as the stream of strident speech from the loudspeakers continued without pause. After 20 minutes the procession departed, the noise fading into the distance. Later that day I saw on the news that they were all executed.

*

Bart Ryder found Min and me having lunch with Charlotte in the audience pit of the old opera house. He, Rod and several others had arrived from Hong Kong to carry out another factory inspection.

"You aren't eating in the executive canteen?" he asked, referring to the small area on the stage concealed from where we sat by cardboard boxes, the latter a miniature Great Wall separating Hong Kong Chinese and foreigners from local Chinese workers.

Bart wasn't really expecting a reply and I mused as to how far he would be able to take the definition of "executive canteen" without feeling that words and reality had parted company. Could, for example, one single cardboard box constitute an executive canteen? If so, would the addition of another cardboard box turn it into an executive canteen with lounge?

Bart pulled out a chair and sat down with the eagerness of a man attending the dentist to have all his teeth removed. I asked what he thought about Rod's plan for me to work in personnel and for Min to do accounting. I was aware of Charlotte attempting to engage Bart in conversation and was glad she was there to lighten the atmosphere.

"Charlotte, would you mind leaving us for a while?" said Bart. She looked at him, stood up quickly and left.

"Now why are you two doing work study?" asked Bart.

A very good question. As I thought about Bart's involvement in that decision and his earlier enthusiasm for the course he began a rambling narrative about how badly the company was doing, how the factories were at a standstill in Sri Lanka, how they had expanded too fast and how they had lost profits. "We made a real botch job with you guys," he said. This was startling frankness from Bart. Thick and fast in an ever-increasing torrent he continued to describe the disasters, woes and tribulations besetting the company. Bart's destination was clear, no matter the route a circuitous one with many detours and pauses for breath. He seemed unable to get the final words out, but after looping round his journey's end in ever-decreasing circles, he finished abruptly by saying, "which means you can no longer work for us".

Well that was that, our brief career in the garment industry at a decisive end; finally to be let into Bart's confidence only to be let go by the company minutes later. Bart sat there looking sad and I put out my hand for him to shake, which he did. Min did the same.

I remembered a story Min's aunt had told me, almost prophetically, of the method by which the boss in old China would indicate that employees had to leave. It was based on the phrase *juan pugai* "roll up the sleeping mat", a euphemism for leaving employment, whether voluntarily or otherwise. At the celebratory meal at the end of a season of labouring, the boss would walk round the table and place a type of wrapped roll into the bowl of the man who had to move on. All understood that this item of food symbolized the roll of bedding, and that if it was dropped into your bowl it was time for you to leave.

As it happened we were sitting in a canteen and it would have been a lot easier for Bart if he could have just dropped a spring roll onto our plates. I'm sure he would have preferred it that way. We were also sitting in an old opera house. I looked round at the familiar whitewashed walls, the stone floor and the stage. It struck me as ironic that here in a place constructed for acting and make-believe, Bart had finally removed the company mask. I thought back to the interview with Rod and Chris and imagined them on the stage reprising their roles from our London interview. But we never saw either of them again and for Min and I the performance was over. Well almost.

"Let me know if you want any help with visas," said Bart beginning to perk up and make his way back to the part of general manager. I sensed that by the time he left the gloom of the opera house he would be completely back in character and the moment for favours would be lost. So I asked him for the rest of the day off to think about what we were going to do next. Bart said "sure". Min asked if the company would pay for our flight back to England. "Sure," said Bart again. Then Min asked for references and for the company to fund a short stay in Hong Kong for us to sort out our bank account and a few other loose ends. "Er, sure," said Bart a final time.

"Ah there you are, Bart! I found you at last," came a loud voice booming across the canteen. It was Johnson, goodwill radiating from his face and person. "You know our staff in the third floor office need an English teacher. They asked me to find them someone and I remembered Alex is teaching at the Panyu warehouse. I asked him and he said he would help out. I hope there's no problem with that." He saw Bart's expression and paused, "is there a problem?"

Bart led Johnson out of the canteen and Min and I got up and left the factory.

*

I had mixed feelings as I stepped into Ah Ling's minibus to go to the warehouse for the last time. The weather had taken a turn for the better, the humidity replaced by a pleasant warm breeze. The muddy grey land was changing. Fresh green rice seedlings grew in the paddy fields. The water glistened and sparkled in the sun as we drove past. I saw peasants wearing blue shorts, white T-shirts and wide straw-brimmed hats. They were bent over in the rice fields, knee-deep in mud and water. It was the image that had formed in my mind when Clara spoke of Panyu being a scenic place back in London, and I felt regret that I wouldn't see Panyu change season into full summer.

It came as a surprise to Rupert and the rest of the warehouse staff to learn that there would be no more English classes. I spoke to everyone there in Cantonese now and they didn't believe me at first when I told them I'd "had my squid fried" (the Cantonese equivalent for rolling up the sleeping mat). In the final lesson Li Sanmei pronounced a flawless "th" sound. It came out polished and perfect as from a 1950's BBC news reader. We were all stunned and sat there in silence. Later I left them a tape recording of the phonetic alphabet. They took us out for a meal and at the end gave me a present, a round glass container for putting things in. "Just like a warehouse," said Iris. "So you remember us."

A couple of days before we were due to leave there were two deliveries to the factory, both from the company's Hong Kong office. The first was Min's new Hong Kong visa we had applied for in Beijing; it wasn't the multi entry visa we were hoping for.

The second was a parcel for me. Someone had remembered my birthday. As I opened it a company "with compliments" slip dropped out and floated down onto the desk. Inside was a pen with the company's name written on the side. "Ha, ha. Just what you always wanted," said Dave.

We packed our things. Shanghai beckoned and the summer stretched ahead of us.

Afterword

In a way Panyu County no longer exists. It has been swallowed up by Guangzhou, lost the designation "county" and become a suburb of that vast city. I have never been back to Panyu but from frequent trips to Shanghai and the occasional visit to Beijing I am sure I wouldn't recognize it if I did, such has been the pace of change and urban development in China. From Chinese websites I see that the Yuyinshanfang has been greatly expanded, as has Lianhuashan, the latter a major tourist spot with apparently the largest statue of the Bodhisattva of Compassion anywhere in the world.

The factory was bought by a competitor a couple of years after we left and has been sold on several times since then, the main players departing over the course of time. To finish with an extract from a poem that opens the mighty 120 chapter Chinese novel "Romance of the Three Kingdoms":

Rolling onwards the waters of the Yangzi fade in the East,
Waves and spray wash away the heroes.
Right and wrong, victory and defeat, in an instant are nothing.
The green hills remain, how many times the setting sun is red.

Gun gun chang jiang dong shi shui
Lang hua tao jin ying xiong
Shi fei cheng bai zhuan tou kong
Qing shan yi jiu zai, ji du xi yang hong

18733996R00179

Printed in Poland
by Amazon Fulfillment
Poland Sp. z o.o., Wrocław